WARFARE IN HISTORY

Military Society and the Court of Chivalry in the Age of the Hundred Years War

WARFARE IN HISTORY

ISSN 1358-779X

Series editors
Matthew Bennett, Royal Military Academy, Sandhurst, UK
Anne Curry, University of Southampton, UK
Stephen Morillo, Wabash College, Crawfordsville, USA

This series aims to provide a wide-ranging and scholarly approach to military history, offering both individual studies of topics or wars, and volumes giving a selection of contemporary and later accounts of particular battles; its scope ranges from the early medieval to the early modern period.

New proposals for the series are welcomed; they should be sent to the publisher at the address below.

Boydell & Brewer Limited, PO Box 9, Woodbridge, Suffolk IP12 3DF

Previously published volumes in this series are listed at the back of this volume

Military Society and the Court of Chivalry in the Age of the Hundred Years War

Philip J. Caudrey

THE BOYDELL PRESS

© Philip J. Caudrey 2019

All Rights Reserved. Except as permitted under current legislation no part of this work may be photocopied, stored in a retrieval system, published, performed in public, adapted, broadcast, transmitted, recorded or reproduced in any form or by any means, without the prior permission of the copyright owner

The right of Philip J. Caudrey to be identified as the author of this work has been asserted in accordance with sections 77 and 78 of the Copyright, Designs and Patents Act 1988

First published 2019
The Boydell Press, Woodbridge
Paperback edition 2022

ISBN 978-1-78327-377-5 (hardback)
ISBN 978-1-78327-695-0 (paperback)

The Boydell Press is an imprint of Boydell & Brewer Ltd
PO Box 9, Woodbridge, Suffolk IP12 3DF, UK
and of Boydell & Brewer Inc.
668 Mt Hope Avenue, Rochester, NY 14620–2731, USA
website: www.boydellandbrewer.com

A catalogue record for this book is available
from the British Library

The publisher has no responsibility for the continued existence or accuracy of URLs for external or third-party internet websites referred to in this book, and does not guarantee that any content on such websites is, or will remain, accurate or appropriate

In Memory of Dr Bruce Rosen (1938–2017) –
Colleague, Mentor and Friend

Contents

Acknowledgements ix

Abbreviations xi

Introduction 1

1 Military Service 23

2 Lordship 63

3 Region, Locality and Community 96

4 Soldiers, Civilians and Chivalric Memory 132

Conclusion 180

Appendix 1: Deponents' Collective Military Records According to their Own Testimony 189

Appendix 2: Lancastrian Retainers: Scrope & Hastings Defendants 190

Appendix 3: Plaintiffs' and Defendants' Biographies 194

Bibliography 199

Index 213

Acknowledgements

I first encountered the surviving records of the Court of Chivalry as a doctoral candidate from the University of Tasmania, Australia, writing a thesis on 'War and Society in Medieval Norfolk', and engaged in a harried three-month research trip to the UK during the English summer of 2006. Of all the manuscripts I examined across numerous London and regional archives, it was the *Scrope v. Grosvenor*, *Lovel v. Morley* and *Grey v. Hastings* armorial cases that most seriously piqued my interest, leaving me determined to explore their potential beyond the narrow parameters of a doctoral thesis. It is to my supervisor, Michael Bennett, that I owe the most significant debt of gratitude, for having shaped my understanding of medieval history and for having introduced me to the records of the Court of Chivalry.

I am equally indebted to Anne Curry, with whom I first discussed the idea of writing this book, at the Agincourt anniversary conference held in Norwich in July 2015. Little did I realise that Anne's initial encouragement, and insights on the topic, would prove just the beginning of her significant contribution to the finished product. As my reader, she has provided incalculable assistance in improving the overall quality of the work and its final shape is, to a considerable degree, the result of her perceptive criticisms and suggestions.

I would be remiss if I did not also thank my colleagues at the University of Tasmania, Elizabeth Freeman and Rod Thomson, for their assistance and support. Rod, in particular, was instrumental in advising me to send my manuscript to Boydell & Brewer and granted me the benefit of his long years of experience as an academic author as I set about the task of writing my first book. I would also like to express my gratitude to Philip Morgan, who very generously supplied me with an unpublished version of his most recent article on Sir Robert Grosvenor, which at the time of our communication was still more than eighteen months away from publication.

This book would not have been possible without the patient assistance of the numerous staff at The National Archives, the British Library and various other regional records offices, where I spent considerable time. An especial thanks to the staff at the College of Arms, London, who provided me with working space and an opportunity to spend several weeks intensively examining the *Grey v. Hastings* transcripts. I would also like to thank Caroline Palmer of Boydell & Brewer, who has provided clear and concise guidance every step along the road towards publication, as I navigate this process for the first time.

I would like to thank my family, first and foremost my parents, who have endured, with unmatched stoicism, my countless hours of musings on Court of Chivalry matters over innumerable telephone conversations and the occasional visit home. Lastly, I wish to acknowledge the significant debt of gratitude I owe to the late Bruce Rosen who was my mentor at Jane Franklin Hall Residential College, my colleague in the School of History & Classics at the University of Tasmania, and a friend to whom I could turn for advice and who lent me the benefit of his wisdom and experience on countless occasions over the past three years as I gradually brought together the various strands of this study.

Abbreviations

ADSM	Archives départementales de la Seine Maritime, Rouen
AN	Archives Nationales, Paris
Bell et al., *The Soldier*	A. R. Bell, A. Curry, A. King and D. Simpkin, *The Soldier in Later Medieval England* (Oxford, 2013).
BIHR	*Bulletin of the Institute of Historical Research*
BL	The British Library
BNF	Bibliothèque Nationale, Paris
BPReg	*Register of Edward, the Black Prince*, ed. M. C. B. Dawes, 4 vols. (London, 1929–33).
CAD	*Calendar of Ancient Deeds*
Cal. Scots. Docs.	*Calendar of Documents Relating to Scotland*
CCR	*Calendar of Close Rolls*
CFR	*Calendar of Fine Rolls*
CIPM	*Calendar of Inquisitions Post Mortem*
CP	G. E. Cockayne, *The Complete Peerage of England, Scotland, Ireland, Great Britain and the United Kingdom*, ed. H. V. Gibbs et al., 13 vols. (London, 1910–59).
CPR	*Calendar of Patent Rolls*
CS	Camden Society
EHR	*English Historical Review*
Foedera	*Foedera, Conventiones etc.*, ed. T. Rymer, 20 vols. (London, 1704–35).
HMC	Historic Manuscripts Commission
HPC, 1386–1421	*The History of Parliament. The House of Commons, 1386–1421*, ed. J. S. Roskell, L. Clark and C. Rawcliffe, 4 vols. (Gloucester, 1992).
JCAS	*Journal of the Chester Archaeological Society*
JGReg I	*John of Gaunt's Register 1372–1376*, ed. S. Armitage-Smith (London, CS, 3rd Series, xx–xxi, 1911).
JGReg II	*John of Gaunt's Register 1379–1383*, ed. E. C. Lodge and R. Somerville, 2 vols. (London, CS, 3rd Series, lvi–lvii, 1937).
LCHS	*Transactions of the Historic Society of Lancashire and Cheshire*

MS. Fr.	Manuscrits français
NAF	Nouvelles acquisitions françaises
NRO	Norfolk Record Office
ODNB	*Oxford Dictionary of National Biography: From the Earliest Times to the Year 2000*, ed. H. C. G. Matthews and B. H. Harrison, 61 vols. (Oxford, 2004).
Parl. Writs.	*Parliamentary Writs*, ed. F. Palgrave, 2 vols. (London, 1827–34).
PCM	London, College of Arms, *Processus in Curia Marescalli*, 2 vols. (Grey v. Hastings).
PL, ed. Davis	*Paston Letters and Papers of the Fifteenth Century*, ed. N. Davis, 2 vols. (Oxford, 1971–6).
POPC	*Proceedings and Ordinances of the Privy Council of England, 1385–1542*, ed. Sir N. H. Nicolas, 7 vols., (London, 1834–7).
Reg. Chichele	*The Register of Henry Chichele, archbishop of Canterbury, 1414–1443*, ed. E. F. Jacob, 4 vols.
Reg. Sudbury	*Registrum Simonis de Sudbiria, diocesis Londoniensis, 1362–1375*, ed. R. C. Fowler, 2 vols. (Oxford, Canterbury and York Society, 1927–38).
RS	Rolls Series
Scrope Cartulary	B. Vale, 'The Scropes of Bolton and Masham, c. 1300–c. 1450: A Study of a Northern Noble Family with a Calendar of the Scrope of Bolton Cartulary' (D. Phil, York, 1987), Volume 2.
Scrope v. Grosvenor	*The Controversy between Sir Richard Scrope and Sir Robert Grosvenor in the Court of Chivalry c.1385–1390*, ed. Sir N. H. Nicolas, 2 vols. (London, 1832).
The Soldier Experience	*The Soldier Experience in the Fourteenth Century*, ed. A. R. Bell and A. Curry with A. Chapman, A. King and D. Simpkin (Woodbridge, 2011).
SRO	Suffolk Record Office
TNA	Kew, The National Archives
TRHS	*Transactions of the Royal Historical Society*
Vale, 'The Scropes'	B. Vale, 'The Scropes of Bolton and Masham, c. 1300–c. 1450: A Study of a Northern Noble Family with a Calendar of the Scrope of Bolton Cartulary' (D. Phil, York, 1987), Volume 1.

The place of publication is London unless otherwise stated. All manuscript references are to documents in Kew, TNA unless otherwise stated.

Introduction

In 1832, the antiquary Sir Harris Nicolas published two, of what he hoped would be three, volumes on 'The Controversy between Sir Richard Scrope and Sir Robert Grosvenor': an armorial case heard before the Court of Chivalry between 1385 and 1390.[1] In justifying his publication of this long-forgotten medieval dispute, Nicolas enthused that he was

> farther cheered by the gratifying reflection that these volumes will rescue many of the heroes from oblivion whose prowess at Cressy [sic], Poietiers [sic], Najara [sic], and various other celebrated battles, renders the history of the reign of Edward the Third the brightest page in the annals of British chivalry, and laid the foundation of the military renown of this country.[2]

Unwittingly perhaps, Nicolas' patriotic focus upon English martial prowess came to set the agenda for almost all future discussions of *Scrope v. Grosvenor*, and, indeed, additionally came to shape subsequent historical analysis of two other surviving armorial cases heard before the Court of Chivalry: *Lovel v. Morley* (1386–7) and *Grey v. Hastings* (1407–10).[3] All three disputes have attracted considerable interest from modern historians, who have utilised them, in far more nuanced fashion, as tools for exploring the military, social and cultural history of the fourteenth-century English gentry.[4] This book seeks to add a further chapter to this rich historiography. Before outlining the overarching themes of the present study, however, a word must be said about the cases themselves, and, more generally, about how the Court of Chivalry arose, how it functioned, what types of cases it heard, the extent to which its records have survived, and why *Scrope v. Grosvenor*, *Lovel v. Morley* and *Grey v. Hastings* have come to enjoy such a prominent position within the existing scholarship on the Court.

---

[1] *Scrope v. Grosvenor*.
[2] *Scrope v. Grosvenor*, I, p. 14.
[3] TNA, C 47/6/2 (Scrope); TNA, C 47/6/3 (Grosvenor); TNA, C 47/6/1 (Morley); TNA, PRO30/26/69 (Lovel); London, College of Arms, *Processus in Curia Marescalli*, 2 vols. (Grey and Hastings).
[4] See pp. 16–18.

Three Armorial Cases

On 20 August 1385, the Yorkshire baron, Richard, Lord Scrope came before the Court of Chivalry and alleged that on Richard II's recent Scottish expedition, Sir Robert Grosvenor of Cheshire had borne Scrope's arms, *azure a bend or*, contrary to right, for which injury Scrope prayed remedy of the judges.[5] Grosvenor, for his part, denied Scrope's accusation, claimed ancestral right to the arms in question, and added for good measure that had he been aware of Scrope possession of the arms, he would have been the one to lay the challenge before the Court.[6] The case, having first been heard at Newcastle on the way back from Scotland, was soon adjourned to Westminster, where it would take five long years to resolve with total legal costs exceeding 4,000 marks.[7] Both plaintiff and defendant claimed that their families had long maintained the disputed arms, and each, as the judges demanded, acquired testimony from a host of witnesses who could recall occasions when they or their ancestors had borne the arms in war and tournament, or had displayed them in various locations throughout the realm, especially in churches and manor houses in their home counties.[8] Witnesses were interviewed by appointed commissioners between June 1386 and January 1387.[9] Most of the depositions were taken at York (for Scrope) and Chester (for Grosvenor), although Scrope also acquired witnesses from neighbouring northern shires, the Midlands, the West Country and East Anglia, whilst a vast contingent of the Lancastrian army – soon to depart for Spain – gave evidence on his behalf at Plymouth.[10]

In hindsight, it could be argued that Scrope was never going to lose the case. He was a distinguished baron, a soldier of the highest chivalric renown, heir to one of the foremost northern families of the day, and perhaps most importantly, he had his lord, John of Gaunt, Duke of

---

[5] J. G. Nichols, 'The Scrope and Grosvenor Controversy', *Herald and Genealogist*, I (1863), p. 386.
[6] Nichols, 'Scrope and Grosvenor', pp. 387–8.
[7] Nichols, 'Scrope and Grosvenor', pp. 386–7; Vale, 'The Scropes', p. 97.
[8] *Scrope v. Grosvenor*.
[9] Both parties nominated sets of regional commissioners, who were to interview their witnesses and gather any relevant written material pertinent to their cause. P. Morgan, 'Sir Robert Grosvenor and the Scrope-Grosvenor Controversy', in *Courts of Chivalry and Admiralty in Late Medieval Europe*, ed. A. Musson and N. Ramsay (Woodbridge, 2018), p. 80.
[10] *Scrope v. Grosvenor*, I, pp. 49–223.

Lancaster (third son of Edward III), in his corner, who not only spoke for him personally, but undeniably mobilised members of his affinity to testify in his defence.[11] As such, by the time Scrope had mined his own wide-ranging connections and tapped into the power-base of the Lancastrian affinity, he had in excess of 250 witnesses at his disposal, many of whom were figures of regional or national standing. Grosvenor, by contrast, relied almost exclusively upon his local ties in Cheshire, Lancashire and North Wales, whence he garnered more than 200 witnesses,[12] although a significant number admitted to being his kinsmen by blood or marriage, or members of his affinity, and relatively few were men of serious account beyond their native shire.[13]

In light of this very obvious disadvantage, it is perhaps unsurprising that Grosvenor became increasingly intransigent as the case unfolded. He frequently refused to attend the proceedings and in 1389 launched an appeal in which he claimed that Scrope had manipulated the commission in his favour. Yet, when a new commission was established to hear Grosvenor's appeal, he again failed to attend, prompting Scrope to accuse him of stalling tactics. Grosvenor's exertions ultimately did him little good and in May 1390 the Court found in Scrope's favour, awarding him the arms together with costs and damages of 500 marks. Yet, just to add an extra layer of drama to an already dramatic dispute, Grosvenor refused to pay, eventually resulting in a stand-off at a meeting of Parliament in November 1391, when Scrope found Grosvenor in the parliament chamber and asked King Richard to prevent him from leaving until he had paid the costs and damages. A week later, in what was veritably a theatrical conclusion, Grosvenor publicly absolved Scrope of the underhanded tactics of which he had earlier accused him, claiming that his legal council had persuaded him

---

[11] Vale, 'The Scropes', pp. 95–105. On Scrope's relationship with Gaunt, see A. Goodman, *John of Gaunt: The Exercise of Princely Power in Fourteenth-Century Europe* (London, 1992), pp. 288–90.

[12] Morgan has recently argued that the Grosvenor family was rather less obscure than has traditionally been acknowledged. Morgan, 'Sir Robert Grosvenor', pp. 75–94.

[13] Testimony does not survive for everyone who was interviewed. In Sir Harris Nicolas' published edition, there are 247 depositions for Scrope and 151 for Grosvenor. Of Grosvenor's 151 surviving witnesses, 27 admitted to being his kinsmen and 33 are known to have been members of his affinity. *Scrope v. Grosvenor*; R. Stewart-Brown, 'The Scrope and Grosvenor Controversy, 1385–1391', *LCHS*, 89 (1938 for 1937), pp. 1–22; Nichols, 'Scrope and Grosvenor', pp. 391–5; Vale, 'The Scropes', p. 100.

to make the charge. He then begged that he could not afford to pay the damages, in response to which Scrope, feeling his honour now redeemed, forgave Grosvenor the debt.[14]

The year after *Scrope v. Grosvenor* began, the Court of Chivalry adjudicated a second case arising from the Scottish expedition of 1385, this one revolving around the competing claims of John, Lord Lovel of Oxfordshire and Wiltshire, and Thomas, Lord Morley of Norfolk, to Morley's arms, *argent a lion rampant sable crowned and armed or*.[15] Lovel, the plaintiff, claimed the arms by descent from the Lords Burnell through his grandmother and may additionally have had his eye upon the sizeable Burnell-Haudlo inheritance, to which he would have enjoyed a good claim in separate legal proceedings had he won his case before the Court of Chivalry.[16] Morley, in response, claimed ancestral right to the arms, with the result that his deponents – like Scrope's and Grosvenor's – comprised a body of militarily experienced gentry, who could attest to occasions when he, or his ancestors, had borne the disputed arms on campaign, together with non-military witnesses, who primarily focused upon written and iconographic evidence of the Morley family's possession and display of the arms in their native East Anglia.[17] As happened in *Scrope v. Grosvenor*, the Court once again roamed extensively across regional centres and the surrounding countryside, where batches of witnesses were interviewed. The 62 surviving depositions on behalf of Lord Lovel were mostly taken in Oxfordshire, Wiltshire and Dorset, whilst Lord Morley's surviving witnesses, who were much more numerous than Lovel's, comprising 160 individuals, gave their evidence primarily in the eastern counties, at various manors, religious houses and parish churches, though the two main locations where they spoke were

---

[14] *CPR, 1388–92*, p. 258; Vale, 'The Scropes', p. 104; Nichols, 'Scrope and Grosvenor', pp. 395–400.

[15] C 47/6/1; PRO30/26/69.

[16] *CIPM*, XV, nos. 719–29; A. Ayton, 'Knights, Esquires and Military Service: The Evidence of the Armorial Cases before the Court of Chivalry', in *The Medieval Military Revolution: State, Society and Military Change in Medieval and Early Modern Europe*, ed. A. Ayton and J. L. Price (London, 1998), p. 84.

[17] P. J. Caudrey, 'War, Chivalry and Regional Society: East Anglia's Warrior Gentry Before the Court of Chivalry', in *Fourteenth Century England VIII*, ed. J. S. Hamilton (Woodbridge, 2014), p. 120.

Norwich and London.¹⁸ *Lovel v. Morley* proved far less of a drawn-out affair than *Scrope v. Grosvenor*. After a little over a year, the case was awarded in Lord Morley's favour, an outcome Lovel appeared to accept, for the two men later served together on Richard II's Irish expedition in 1399 with Morley bearing the arms.¹⁹

A generation later, in 1407, a third well-documented armorial dispute, *Grey v. Hastings*, came before the Court of Chivalry.²⁰ Its origins were markedly different from *Scrope v. Grosvenor* and *Lovel v. Morley*, for, unlike these earlier cases, neither protagonist – Reginald, Lord Grey of Ruthin (Denbighshire), and Sir Edward Hastings of Elsing (Norfolk) – claimed longstanding possession of the disputed arms, *or a manche gules*. Both agreed that these belonged to their mutual kin, the recently extinct Hastings earls of Pembroke. The issue at stake was rather whether Grey or Hastings was the true inheritor of the Pembroke arms and thus by implication the potential heir to a significant portion of the Pembroke estates, and possibly even to the earldom of Pembroke itself.²¹ The case is easily the most complicated of the three and requires some explanation. It ultimately arose from the death of the childless, sixteen-year-old John Hastings, Earl of Pembroke, in a jousting accident in 1389.²² Eleven years later, on Henry IV's Scottish campaign of 1400, both Grey and Hastings mustered bearing the arms of the late Pembroke earl. Grey challenged Hastings' right and the dispute ended up before the Court of Chivalry, although not for another seven years, because Hastings was still a minor at the time of the original challenge.²³ Both men claimed that they were the rightful heir to the arms of the last Pembroke earl. Grey's claim rested upon the fact that his grandmother, Elizabeth, was the aunt of

---

¹⁸ Ayton, 'Knights, Esquires and Military Service', pp. 85–6; Caudrey, 'War, Chivalry and Regional Society', p. 123.
¹⁹ *CPR, 1396-9*, pp. 525, 538, 545.
²⁰ *PCM*.
²¹ R. I. Jack, 'Entail and Descent: The Hastings Inheritance, 1370 to 1436', *BIHR*, 38 (1965), pp. 1–19.
²² Thomas Walsingham, *Historia Anglicana*, ed. H. T. Riley (RS, 28.1, 1863–4), II, p. 195; *CPR, 1388-92*, p. 469.
²³ M. H. Keen, 'English Military Experience and the Court of Chivalry: The Case of Grey v. Hastings', in *Nobles, Knights and Men-At-Arms in the Middle Ages*, ed. M. H. Keen (London, 1996), p. 172. Originally published in: P. Contamine, C. Giry-Deloison, and M. Keen (eds.), *Guerre et société en France, en Angleterre et en Bourgogne, XIVe-XVe siècle* (Lille, 1991), pp. 123–42.

Laurence, the first Hastings earl of Pembroke. Hastings, meanwhile, although a cadet whose branch of the family stemmed from a second marriage, could claim descent in the direct male line back to the first earl of Pembroke's grandfather, who was his own great-great-grandfather. Grey thus had a superior claim through the family's senior branch in the female line, Hastings a weaker claim through a junior branch, but in the direct male line.[24]

Matters were further complicated by the fact that the Greys had not always enjoyed good relations with their Pembroke cousins,[25] whereas Sir Edward Hastings' father, Sir Hugh Hastings III, was clearly well liked by the last earl's mother and aunt, the Countesses of Pembroke and Norfolk, who, Sir Edward claimed, had begged his father to bear the Pembroke arms in full during the 1380s when the last earl was still a child.[26] These complexities were reflected in each protagonist's choice of deponents, for Hastings – like Scrope, Grosvenor and Morley before him – provided a long train of witnesses who could attest to occasions when his ancestors had campaigned bearing the Pembroke arms with a difference, or when his father had borne the Pembroke arms in full on the Spanish expedition of 1386.[27] Grey, by contrast – having already defeated claims to the Pembroke inheritance from his Strathbogie and Talbot cousins, and having bought off his other cousin and potential rival, Thomas Beauchamp, son of the Earl of Warwick – focused his attention upon the crucial matters of lineage at play, for he undoubtedly enjoyed a better claim to the Pembroke arms than the cadet Hastings of Elsing.[28] Hastings, in turn, accused Grey of stealing muniments crucial to his defence and later in the dispute challenged him to judicial combat over the arms, although this aggressive strategy

---

[24] Jack, 'Entail and Descent', pp. 2, 5.

[25] John Hastings, Earl of Pembroke (d. 1375), had attempted to disinherit Reginald, Lord Grey in the early 1370s, after Grey had heard the rumour that Pembroke had died abroad and promptly started hunting on his lands as if by right. Such was Pembroke's hostility toward his Grey cousins that upon hearing from captivity that his countess, Anne, was finally pregnant, he became distraught, fearing that should the child die without an heir, the Greys would eventually acquire the Pembroke inheritance. Jack, 'Entail and Descent', pp. 6–9.

[26] M. H. Keen, *Origins of the English Gentleman: Heraldry, Chivalry and Gentility in Medieval England, c.1300–c.1500* (Gloucester, 2002), p. 57.

[27] Keen, 'Grey v. Hastings', pp. 178–82; Caudrey, 'War, Chivalry and Regional Society', pp. 125–6, 135.

[28] Jack, 'Entail and Descent', pp. 10–11.

was met with a studiously straight bat and nothing ever came of it.[29] The case dragged on for three years amidst much bitter wrangling until the Court eventually found in Grey's favour and Hastings ended up in much the same predicament as Sir Robert Grosvenor, albeit without the benefit of Lord Scrope's magnanimity.[30] Still smarting from defeat, Hastings stubbornly continued upholding his claim even as his family's fortunes tumbled. He almost immediately launched an appeal against the Court's verdict, but the decision was still pending in 1416, in which year Grey successfully had him incarcerated in the Marshalsea prison as a debtor. There Sir Edward lingered in increasingly poor health for the next twenty years, dying an aggrieved and broken man, fifteen months after his eventual release, in 1438.[31]

The Court of Chivalry

Two questions naturally arise from the above accounts of *Scrope v. Grosvenor*, *Lovel v. Morley* and *Grey v. Hastings*: firstly, why were these contests over coats-of-arms worth such sweat and tears; and secondly, why was the Court of Chivalry considered the appropriate venue for their adjudication? The answer to the first of these questions is in some ways the more straightforward. When Richard, Lord Scrope observed before the Court that 'the highest and most sovereign things a knight ought to guard in defence of his estate are his troth and his arms',[32] he was eloquently encapsulating the fundamental role heraldic identity played in the lives of the late medieval English gentry. The origins of heraldry were undeniably military. With the noble and knightly warrior encased in armour, it was the personal device on his shield, surcoat, pennon or banner that allowed friend and foe alike to recognise him on the field of battle and enabled spectators to pick

---

[29] C. G. Young, *An Account of the Controversy between Reginald Lord Grey of Ruthyn and Sir Edward Hastings in the Court of Chivalry* (London, 1841), pp. 9, 24.
[30] Hastings was ordered to pay costs of £987 10s. 10¾d. Grey publicly swore that in addition to this sum he intended to extract from Hastings a further 1000 marks. *PCM*, I, p. 642.
[31] A letter of Hastings', written from prison in 1421, complained that his body and limbs 'aperted and I brought in til langweryn sickenesse that I am nevir like to be heill'. Young, *Grey v. Hastings*, p. xiii; Jack, 'Entail and Descent', pp. 15–18.
[32] *PCM*, II, p. 131.

him out from the throng in the meleé of a tournament.[33] Identified in this fashion, a knight who performed valiant deeds 'did honour' to his arms, whilst dishonourable conduct, such as acts of cowardice or the breaking of oaths, could result in a knight's arms being publicly reversed, or turned upside down, as a symbol of his shame.[34] More than this, however, arms were not merely a personal device, but provided a visual record of the wearer's familial and social ties. In the words of Jones, 'As designs were passed down from one generation to the next they came to embody the heritage and lineage of the family.'[35] When bearing his arms in war or tournament, then, a knight not only placed his own reputation on the line, but simultaneously sought to uphold the good name of his ancestors, the previous bearers of the self-same arms, by adding his own chapter to his family's potentially rich catalogue of military achievement.[36] By the time *Scrope v. Grosvenor* and *Lovel v. Morley* came before the Court of Chivalry in the mid 1380s, armigerous society was expanding beyond the nobility and knightly class to encompass many of those middling and lesser gentry who followed them to war.[37]

In such a highly-charged atmosphere, in which armorial bearings were supposed to be unique to the individual, it is entirely unsurprising that heraldic controversies should have arisen on a regular basis and required adjudication. The first known case of two English knights bearing the same arms on campaign dates from 1300, during Edward I's siege of Caerlaverock Castle in Scotland, when two members of the

---

[33] Keen, *Origins of the English Gentleman*, p. 11; D. Crouch, *The Image of Aristocracy in Britain 1000–1300* (London, 1992), pp. 220–2; A. Ailes, 'The Knight, Heraldry and Armour: The Role of Recognition and the Origins of Heraldry', in *Medieval Knighthood IV*, ed. C. Harper-Bill and R. Harvey (Woodbridge, 1992), pp. 1–21. Jones cautions against the assumption that heraldic devices, in the heat of battle or tournament, would have been of much use as personal identifiers. R. W. Jones, *Bloodied Banners: Martial Display on the Medieval Battlefield* (Woodbridge, 2010), pp. 11–15.

[34] Keen, *Origins of the English Gentleman*, pp. 32, 51; Jones, *Bloodied Banners*, pp. 20–1. For an infamous example of the fall-out from a claim of dishonourable conduct, see H. E. L. Collins, 'Sir John Fastolf, John Lord Talbot and the Dispute over Patay: Ambition and Chivalry in the Fifteenth Century', in *War and Society in Medieval and Early Modern Britain*, ed. D. Dunn (Liverpool, 2000), pp. 114–40.

[35] Jones, *Bloodied Banners*, p. 20.

[36] Jones, *Bloodied Banners*, pp. 20–1.

[37] Keen, *Origins of the English Gentleman*, pp. 71–86; Bell et al., *The Soldier*, pp. 104–14.

besieging host, Brian Fitz Alan and Hugh Pointz, appeared in the arms, *barry or and gules*.[38] This case, if it was ever submitted to judgment, may well have been heard by the Constable and Marshal of England – the hereditary Earls of Hereford and Norfolk – who had enjoyed a disciplinary/judicial role in English armies for at least a century prior to the commencement of the Hundred Years War.[39] The earliest concrete evidence of the Court of Chivalry's existence, however, derives from Edward III's triumphant Normandy expedition in 1346–7. Some time after the battle of Crécy (1346), we know that the Oxfordshire baron, Nicholas, Lord Burnell challenged the armorial right of his Norfolk counterpart, Robert, Lord Morley and demanded that his case be heard before the Court of Chivalry, where it duly was heard, during the ensuing siege of Calais (1347). The registers for this dispute have not survived, and we know about the case only because when Morley's grandson, Thomas, found himself before the same Court forty years later in *Lovel v. Morley*, his grandfather's earlier victory over Burnell proved pivotal to his defence, and he consequently drummed up a host of elderly witnesses who could recall the favourable verdict of 1347.[40] Most tellingly, one of these witnesses, John Molham, aged 70, testified that on the Crécy-Calais campaign he had been in the service of William Bohun, earl of Hereford (the Constable of England), and had held the office of clerk to the Court of Chivalry for the *Burnell v. Morley* hearing.[41] There was nothing in Molham's deposition to suggest that the Court was a particularly new construct, or that there

---

[38] *The Roll of Caerlaverock*, ed. and trans. T. Wright (London, 1864), pp. 15–16. It is not clear whether there were ever judicial proceedings, or how the matter was resolved. Keen, *Origins of the English Gentleman*, p. 170.

[39] M. H. Keen, 'The Jurisdiction and Origins of the Constable's Court', in *Nobles, Knights and Men-At-Arms*, ed. M. H. Keen (London, 1996), pp. 135–48. First published in: *War and Government in the Middle Ages*, ed. J. B. Gillingham and J. C. Holt (Woodbridge, 1984), pp. 159–69. Keen's analysis of the medieval origins of the Court of Chivalry corrected several errors from the only book on the Court, which concentrated primarily upon its early modern history. G. D. Squibb, *The High Court of Chivalry* (Oxford, 1959). A new and more detailed forthcoming study will doubtless further illuminate the process. A. Musson and N. Ramsay, *Law and Arms: The Medieval English Court of Chivalry* (forthcoming).

[40] E.g., C 47/6/1, nos. 10, 96, 102. The outcome of *Burnell v. Morley* was also crucial to the case of the plaintiff, John, Lord Lovel. E.g., PRO30/26/69, nos. 167, 169, 175, 176, 186, 204, 227. On the deponents' contrasting memories of the case, see pp. 172–4.

[41] *PCM*, II, p. 98.

was anything unusual about members of the English host bringing their grievances before its judges.[42] Indeed, Edward III's appointment of a special commission during the siege to hear 'all manner of disputes over arms and helm crests' may well have reflected standard operating procedure on a drawn-out campaign, granting licence to such complaints.[43] The appointment of this commission, combined with the survival of the judgment in a second case adjudicated before the Court of Chivalry during the siege, between John Warbleton and Thibaud Russell, strongly hint that several disputes may well have arisen simultaneously within King Edward's 26,000-strong army.[44] This appears very likely, for an extended siege with a large force offered ample opportunity for gentry from far-flung parts of the realm – in the manner of Brian Fitz Alan and Hugh Pointz before them – to encounter others coincidentally bearing the same arms.[45]

The Court of Chivalry, then, appears to have been reasonably well established by 1347. Its origins, however, had their genesis in the legal framework available to the English Crown in the later Middle Ages. The Court arose in large measure because the writ of English common

---

[42] Keen, 'The Jurisdiction and Origins of the Constable's Court', pp. 145–6.

[43] Squibb, *The High Court of Chivalry*, p. 14.

[44] It certainly appears, through Edward's appointment of commissioners to oversee such complaints, that he was seeking to stamp his royal authority over the proceedings. Keen, *Origins of the English Gentleman*, p. 40; R. Barber, 'Heralds and the Court of Chivalry: From Collective Memory to Formal Institutions', in *Courts of Chivalry and Admiralty in Late Medieval Europe*, ed. A. Musson and N. Ramsay (Woodbridge, 2018), p. 23. On the approximate size of the Calais army, see Bell et al., *The Soldier*, p. 140.

[45] Scattered evidence hints at how common such encounters might have been. Both *Scrope v. Grosvenor* and *Lovel v. Morley*, for example, had their origins on Richard II's Scottish campaign of 1385. Nichols, 'The Scrope and Grosvenor Controversy', p. 386; Ayton, 'Knights, Esquires and Military Service', p. 84. A throwaway line by one of Morley's witnesses implied that the defendant's late brother, Sir John Morley, had similarly had his armorial right challenged when serving in the Black Prince's army in Spain in 1367. C 47/6/1, no. 32. And, although a dispute over identical badges rather than heraldic arms, Froissart recounts in his chronicle a rather glamorous altercation between Sir John Chandos and the French knight, John de Clermont. As they were viewing each other's battle lines, they met and discovered that they were wearing the same badge. Clermont claimed the device was rightfully his, the two exchanged heated words, and promised to settle their differences on the battlefield. Clermont was killed in battle the following day. Jean Froissart, *Oeuvres de Froissart publieés avec les variants des divers manuscrits par M. le Baron Kervyn de Lettenhove*, 25 vols. (Brussels, 1867–77), V, pp. 417-19.

law ran no further than the borders of the realm, with the result that English soldiers who developed grievances against one another whilst overseas required a separate judicial body to adjudicate their complaints.[46] Although *ad hoc* commissions, overseen by the Constable and Marshal of England, or their proxies, had sufficed in earlier generations, the unparalleled numbers of English soldiers serving abroad from the 1340s onwards required the adoption of a stricter legal process for judging such matters.[47] The Court of Chivalry was part of the solution, and it is surely no coincidence that references to the authority of the Constable and Marshal, who were its presiding judges, hereafter become much more plentiful than they had been before.[48]

The types of cases the Court of Chivalry's judges came to oversee – disputes over ransoms and indentures, judicial duels, treason trials, and armorial controversies – make plain that its purpose was to deal with specifically military-chivalric complaints.[49] Yet, the precise limits of its jurisdiction were not necessarily clear-cut. In theory, as one particular proctor – speaking before the Court in the early 1390s – eloquently phrased it, the Court's jurisdiction 'was and is formally dissevered from the laws, statutes and customs of the realm, so that it must not involve itself with matters of common law', adding emphatically that its purpose was to deal with matters 'having their commencement and cause in deeds of chivalry and arms'.[50] Unfortunately, such cases

[46] Keen, *Origins of the English Gentleman*, p. 27.
[47] Keen, 'The Jurisdiction and Origins of the Constable's Court', pp. 142–6; On the militarisation of English society during the 1330s and 1340s, see A. Ayton, 'Edward III and the English Aristocracy at the Beginning of the Hundred Years War', in *Armies, Chivalry and Warfare in Medieval Britain and France. Proceedings of the 1995 Harlaxton Symposium*, ed. M. Strickland (Stamford, 1998), pp. 173–206. The Crown's ongoing efforts to maintain greater army discipline are revealed in the adoption of 'ordinances of war' as a code of conduct for individual campaigns. M. H. Keen, 'Richard II's Ordinances of War of 1385', in *Rulers and Ruled in Late Medieval England: Essays Presented to Gerald Harriss*, ed. R. E. Archer and S. K. Walker (London, 1995), pp. 33–48; A. Curry, 'The Military Ordinances of Henry V: Texts and Contexts', in *War, Government and Aristocracy in the British Isles, c. 1150–1500: Essays in Honour of Michael Prestwich*, ed. C. Given-Wilson, A. Kettle and L. Scales (Woodbridge, 2008), pp. 214–49.
[48] Keen, 'The Jurisdiction and Origins of the Constable's Court', p. 146.
[49] Keen, 'The Jurisdiction and Origins of the Constable's Court', p. 135. For a more detailed assessment of each type of case, see Keen, *Origins of the English Gentleman*, pp. 27–42.
[50] A. Rogers, 'Hoton v. Shakell: A Ransom Case in the Court of Chivalry, 1390–5', *Nottingham Medieval Studies*, 7 (1963), p. 62.

often shaded into legal areas that *were* covered by English common law. To cite a prime example of how an element of confusion could arise, disputes over armorial rights, as we have seen, were often linked to issues of inheritance and property law. In *Grey v. Hastings*, for instance, the judges focused exclusively upon which party had the better right to the Pembroke arms: any disagreement over inheritance of the Pembroke earls' titles or estates would have needed to have been pursued in separate legal proceedings elsewhere.[51] That the Court of Chivalry's judges at times overreached themselves is underscored by a complaint, laid by the Parliamentary Commons in 1389, that the Constable and Marshal were interfering in matters of common law, 'to the great prejudice of the King and his crown and to the grievance of his people'.[52] This in turn led to the first formal definition of the Court's jurisdiction, via a royal statute in 1390, which unequivocally defined its remit as limited to 'contracts touching deeds of arms and of war out of the realm, and also of things that touch arms and war within the realm which cannot be determined nor discussed by common law'.[53]

The Court's narrow concern with military-chivalric matters, most of which arose 'out of the realm', directly impacted its character and function in other ways too. Dealing strictly with complaints to which English common law did not pertain, the Court came to employ the civil law procedures that held sway in Continental Europe,[54] whilst its judges, adjudicating military-chivalric grievances, sought to apply to their judgments the 'law of arms' – that ill-defined body of military customs to which chivalric society theoretically sought to adhere[55] – in an age in which European legal scholars, especially in Italy and France, were seeking, in the words of Keen, 'to bring their legal expertise to bear…to give…the 'law of arms' a respectable and coherent legal

---

[51] The same would have applied to Lord Lovel's pursuit of the Burnell-Haudlo inheritance, had he won his case against Lord Morley before the Court of Chivalry. Caudrey, 'War, Chivalry and Regional Society', p. 120.
[52] *Rotuli Parliamentorum*, ed. J. Strachey et al., 7 vols. (1767–1832), III, pp. 65, 265.
[53] *Statutes of the Realm*, ed. A. Luders, T. E. Tomlins, et al., 11 vols. (1810–28), Statute 13 Richard II, cap. 2.
[54] A. Musson and N. Ramsay, 'Introduction', in *Courts of Chivalry and Admiralty in Late Medieval Europe*, ed. A. Musson and N. Ramsay (Woodbridge, 2018), pp. 1–2, 11–13.
[55] Keen, 'The Jurisdiction and Origins of the Constable's Court', p. 147; Keen, *Origins of the English Gentleman*, pp. 28–9.

footing'.⁵⁶ In short, England's Court of Chivalry was merely one national expression of European-wide efforts to regulate warfare and address soldiers' grievances over the course of the fourteenth century,⁵⁷ and it comes as no surprise, given the Court of Chivalry's remit, that the chivalric ethos bubbled aggressively beneath the surface of the Court's proceedings, in an atmosphere in which personal and family honour was at stake.⁵⁸ We possess, for example, written record of protagonists before the Court making grandiose claims about what they would do if judgment went against them;⁵⁹ we find others casting aspersions upon the honour of their opponents;⁶⁰ and it appears that aggrieved parties

---

⁵⁶ Keen, 'The Jurisdiction and Origins of the Constable's Court', p. 147. On the 'law of arms', see M. H. Keen, *The Laws of War in the Late Middle Ages* (London, 1965), pp. 7–22.

⁵⁷ The foundation of the Court of Chivalry was paralleled by the concurrent evolution, during the second half of the fourteenth century, of the Court of the Admiralty, whilst similar tribunals, dealing with military and naval matters, were established all over Continental Europe during this period. On the Court of the Admiralty, see T. K. Heebøll-Holm, 'The Origins and Jurisdiction of the English Court of Admiralty in the Fourteenth Century', in *Courts of Chivalry and Admiralty in Late Medieval Europe*, ed. A. Musson and N. Ramsay (Woodbridge, 2018), pp. 149–70. On European developments, see Musson and Ramsay, 'Introduction', pp. 10–13; L. Hablot, 'French Armorial Disputes and Controls', in *Courts of Chivalry and Admiralty in Late Medieval Europe*, ed. A. Musson and N. Ramsay (Woodbridge, 2018), pp. 29–45; B. Schnerb, 'The Jurisdiction of the Constable and Marshals of France in the Later Middle Ages', in *Courts of Chivalry and Admiralty in Late Medieval Europe*, ed. A. Musson and N. Ramsay (Woodbridge, 2018), pp. 135–47; L. Tanzini, 'The Consulate of the Sea and its Fortunes in Late Medieval Mediterranean Countries', in *Courts of Chivalry and Admiralty in Late Medieval Europe*, ed. A. Musson and N. Ramsay (Woodbridge, 2018), pp. 171–85.

⁵⁸ Underscoring the Court's military-chivalric remit, its depositions were largely taken down in French (the language of chivalry). On the role of French language and culture in the evolution of medieval chivalry, see M. H. Keen, *Chivalry* (London, 1984), pp. 27–34.

⁵⁹ E.g., In *Burnell v. Morley* (1347), Robert, Lord Morley reportedly swore that if the case went against him, 'he would never again be armed against Christians or in the war of his liege lord'. Young, *Grey v. Hastings*, p. iv.

⁶⁰ E.g., Thomas, Lord Morley publicly labelled John Montagu, Earl of Salisbury, a 'false knight' when appealing him of treason before the Court of Chivalry in 1399. 'Morley v. Montagu', in *Camden Miscellany XXXIV*, ed. M. Warner and M. H. Keen (CS., 5th Series, 10, 1997), pp. 155–6, 170, 173, 183.

in all manner of cases were quite prepared to 'determine their quarrel by strength' via judicial combat.[61]

More generally, beyond the Court of Chivalry's distinctive purview and function, what makes it so enticing to the historian, and yet, at the same time, so elusive, is the fact that its original registers have been lost and what we know of its proceedings, depositions and judgments survive only in later, often incomplete, transcripts.[62] In some cases, we know the claims of each party, but possess neither depositions nor result; in others, we have only a judgment;[63] in a few rare instances, enough evidence has survived to enable the historian to reconstruct a relatively detailed portrait of the entire case.[64] The extent of the surviving source materials has thus heavily shaped the existing scholarship on the Court and the greatest attention has naturally been paid to those cases whose transcripts have survived in bulk, with *Scrope v. Grosvenor*, *Lovel v. Morley* and *Grey v. Hastings* – the three armorial controversies with which we began this chapter – standing at the forefront.[65]

[61] E.g., Sir Edward Hastings challenged Lord Grey to a duel in desperation, once it became apparent that Grey would likely win their case. Young, *Grey v. Hastings*, p. 24. Judicial combats, of course, fell within the Court of Chivalry's purview. Keen, *Origins of the English Gentleman*, pp. 32–5. Such challenges were not exclusively about the maintenance of honour. They could also serve as a legal manoeuvre designed to bring the opposing party to the negotiating table. For example, Henry Inglose, when claiming that John Tiptoft had refused to pay the wages due to him and his company during the Agincourt expedition (1415), likely challenged Tiptoft to a duel simply to bring the facts of the case, as he saw them, to light. BL, Cotton MS Titus C1, fo. 191v–192r. On Inglose's motives, see Keen, *Origins of the English Gentleman*, p. 33.

[62] Keen, *Origins of the English Gentleman*, p. 29.

[63] The following cases survive only in fragments: *Salisbury v. Montagu* (*CPR, 1385–9*, p. 67); *Baude v. Singleton* (*CPR, 1391–6*, pp. 332, 576; *CPR, 1396–9*, p. 89); *Scrope v. Kighlee* (*CPR, 1399–1401*, p. 401); *Gerard v. Chamberlayn* (C 47/6/5); *Inglose v. Tiptoft* (BL, MS Cotton, Titus C I, fo. 192).

[64] Several cases involving ransoms, indentures, judicial combats and treason trials, where the surviving evidence is fuller, have been published. *POPC*, VI, pp. 57–9, 129; A. S. Ellis, 'On the Arms of de Aton', *Yorkshire Archaeological Journal*, 12 (1893), pp. 263–6; 'Morley v. Montagu', ed. Warner and Keen; A. Rogers, 'Hoton v. Shakell: A Ransom Case in the Court of Chivalry, 1390–5', *Nottingham Medieval Studies*, 7 (1962), pp. 74–108 and Rogers, 'Hoton v. Shakell' (1963), pp. 53–78; J. G. Bellamy, 'Sir John de Annesley and the Chandos Inheritance', *Nottingham Medieval Studies*, 10 (1966), pp. 94–105; M. C. Jones, 'Roches contre Hawley: la cour anglaise de chevalerie et un cas de piraterie à Brest 1386–1402', *Mémoires de la Société d'Histoire et d'Archéologie de Bretagne*, 64 (1987), pp. 53–64.

[65] See pp. 16–20.

Across all three of these disputes, we possess the questions that were put to each deponent, miscellaneous details about the cases and their proceedings, and, fortuitously, hundreds of depositions.[66] *Scrope v. Grosvenor* and *Lovel v. Morley* survive as near-contemporary copies, drawn up after the two cases went to appeal to the King in Chancery.[67] For *Grey v. Hastings*, we possess only a hand-written seventeenth-century transcript, surviving in the form of two bound volumes, now labelled *Processus in Curia Mariscelli*, and housed in the College of Arms, London.[68] All three collections are to varying degrees incomplete. *Scrope v. Grosvenor* survives amongst the Chancery Miscellania of The National Archives in London in two large rolls, one for each of the parties, totalling over 400 membranes stitched together.[69] Both rolls, however, are missing depositions, especially Grosvenor's, which contains the testimony of only 151 of what we know were more than 200 witnesses.[70] *Lovel v. Morley* likewise exists in two rolls housed in the same location, although it is apparent that each roll survived independently. Lovel's, which contains only 62 depositions, is seriously incomplete, its first deposition beginning at number 157.[71] Morley's is much more fulsome, containing 177 depositions provided by 160 individuals. It has a gap in its proceedings from mid-April to mid-August 1386 and no testimony survives for several of the witnesses named in the Court's itinerary. [72] A tantalising glimpse of what we are missing is provided by the eighteenth-century antiquary, Rev. Francis Blomefield, whose topographical history of Norfolk contains a number of additional depositions not found on

---

[66] *Scrope v. Grosvenor*; C 47/6/1; PRO30/26/69; *PCM*.

[67] Vale, 'The Scropes', pp. 97–8; Ayton, 'Knights, Esquires and Military Service', p. 85.

[68] *PCM* is the most complete of three surviving MSS. The other two contain only extracts. College of Arms, MS Philipot P.e.1; BL, MS Harley 1178. The first of these is said to have derived from a register in the possession of Henry, Earl of Kent (1541–1615), a descendant of the Greys of Ruthin. This may also be where the much fuller transcript, *PCM*, originated. Keen, 'Grey v. Hastings', p. 168.

[69] C 47/6/2; C 47/6/3; Vale, 'The Scropes', p. 98.

[70] Stewart-Brown, 'The Scrope and Grosvenor Controversy', pp. 20–2. The bulk of the Grosvenor material is preserved in C 47/6/3. Additional fragments are to be found in a variety of locations. BL, MS Harley 293, pp. 183–93; BL, MS Lansdowne 85, art. 75; BL, MS Add. 39851, p. 56; Chester, Eaton Hall, Grosvenor Estate Archives, Adds. 1264. On these fragments, see Morgan, 'Sir Robert Grosvenor', pp. 80–1.

[71] PRO30/26/69.

[72] C 47/6/1. On the shortcomings of both rolls, see Ayton, 'Knights, Esquires and Military Service', p. 86.

either roll.⁷³ The transcript for *Grey v. Hastings*, meanwhile, is relatively detailed, running to over 700 pages, although fewer depositions survive from this case than the other two, especially for Grey. We have, in total, testimony from around 100 witnesses for Hastings and 38 for Grey, as well as a summary of the background to the dispute, a list of the questions the witnesses were asked, and an interesting set of hand-written notes on the case, jotted down by the antiquary, Sir Charles Young, in the early 1840s.⁷⁴ The surviving evidence across all three cases is patchy at best. What remains is nonetheless plentiful and well worth exploring.

The Court of Chivalry and the Historian

So, what use have historians made of the surviving records of *Scrope v. Grosvenor*, *Lovel v. Morley* and *Grey v. Hastings*, and what, consequently, is there left to say? The most noteworthy aspect of the testimony is, without a doubt, its revelation of lengthy military careers that seemingly take many witnesses from one famous siege or battle to the next, appended by depositions outlining valorous deeds performed by the protagonists and their kinsmen. Such testimony, highlighting brilliant careers in arms and bringing the Hundred Years War alive as a series of vignettes, naturally proves enticing, if not downright seductive. Certainly, as we saw at the beginning of this chapter, Sir Harris Nicolas was thoroughly seduced when he first came upon *Scrope v. Grosvenor* in the 1830s.⁷⁵ Modern historians have naturally proven rather more circumspect in their conclusions, yet Nicolas was right to point to the value of these heraldic disputes as windows into the military careers of the English gentry and the chivalric culture of the age, and it was in his footsteps that Maurice Keen – the doyen of modern historians of medieval chivalry – trod, when he first stimulated a renewed scholarly interest in the Court of Chivalry in the 1970s and 1980s.⁷⁶

---

⁷³ F. Blomefield, *An Essay Towards a Topographical History of the County of Norfolk*, 11 vols. (London, 1805–10), II, pp. 437–9.
⁷⁴ *PCM*; Young, *Grey v. Hastings*. See also, Caudrey, 'War, Chivalry and Regional Society', p. 123.
⁷⁵ See above, p. 1.
⁷⁶ On the other hand, some historians have been rather more dismissive of the value of these surviving armorial cases. Michael Prestwich, for instance, characterised the evidence as 'often tedious', and suggested that the sharp connection between coats-of-arms and personal honour has been rather overdrawn, pointing out that knights, whilst on campaign, were quite prepared to discard their arms when necessary, or, indeed, to wear someone else's. M. Prestwich, *Armies and Warfare in the Middle Ages: The English Experience* (London, 1996), pp. 54, 113, 223.

In an incisive article, published in 1976, Keen homed in upon some of the more outstanding careers of the Hundred Years War's first phase (1337–1360), recounted in *Scrope v. Grosvenor*, with the aim of illustrating the complexities of military careerism, and the ways in which this related to the vibrant martial culture and consequent military enthusiasm of the age,[77] later expanding upon this theme by assessing the impressive appetite of witnesses across all three cases for the Crusade.[78] Keen next turned his attention towards the later *Grey v. Hastings* case, whose testators largely recalled the Hundred Years War's second phase (1369–1389), and suggested that in comparison with the deeds recounted in *Scrope v. Grosvenor* and *Lovel v. Morley*, the Hastings testimony 'had not...the kind of resonance in recall that the great campaigns of the 1340s and 50s had had'.[79] Finally, elaborating upon his earlier research, Keen went on to tackle all three disputes from a predominantly heraldic perspective, mining the testimony en route to the larger goal of identifying 'the time and detail of the change from the early period of the practical use of heraldry in war and tournament, to the second stage when it became more closely associated with claims to the status of gentleman or nobleman'.[80] In essence, Keen drew perceptively upon the Court of Chivalry material as one of many sources for enabling the historian to assess the closely overlapping subjects of military careerism, chivalric culture and heraldic identity in later medieval England.[81]

If Keen's body of research on the Court cast a noticeably wide net, subsequent scholarship on *Scrope v. Grosvenor*, *Lovel v. Morley* and *Grey v. Hastings*, chiefly by Andrew Ayton and Adrian Bell, has adopted a somewhat narrower, though no less constructive, approach, highlighting the potential of the testimony for identifying gentry

---

[77] M. H. Keen, 'Chivalrous Culture in Fourteenth-Century England', *Historical Studies*, 10 (1976), pp. 1–22.

[78] M. H. Keen, 'Chaucer's Knight, the English Aristocracy and the Crusade', in *Nobles, Knights and Men-At-Arms*, ed. M. H. Keen (London, 1996), pp. 101–19. First published in: *English Court Culture in the Late Middle Ages*, ed. J. Scattergood and J. W. Sherborne (London, 1983), pp. 45–61.

[79] Keen, 'Grey v. Hastings', p. 182.

[80] Keen, *Origins of the English Gentleman*, p. 159.

[81] Keen also published extensively on other aspects of the Court of Chivalry. *Morley v. Montagu*, ed. Warner and Keen; Keen, 'The Jurisdictions and Origins of the Constable's Court', pp. 135–48; M. H. Keen, 'Treason Trials under the Law of Arms', in *Nobles, Knights and Men-At-Arms*, ed. M. H. Keen (London, 1996), pp. 149–66. First published in: *TRHS*, fifth series, 12 (1962), pp. 85–103.

military participants, gauging patterns of military service, and probing the dynamics of military recruitment. Focusing primarily upon *Lovel v. Morley*, Ayton broke down the witnesses' autobiographical information by age, rank, and longevity and frequency of service, particularly emphasising the utility of the testimony for uncovering the depth of military involvement amongst the lesser gentry.[82] Bell, tackling the same types of issues from a rather different perspective, illustrated – in his study of the detailed retinue rolls for the two English naval expeditions of 1387 and 1388 – how the Court of Chivalry's records, in conjunction with other sources, can provide vital additional information when reconstructing the personnel of English armies.[83] More recently, expanding upon their earlier work, both Ayton and Bell have demonstrated how the Court's depositions can be used, together with pay accounts, muster and retinue rolls, letters of protection and grants of pardon, to flesh out the military autobiographies of the witnesses, bringing to light campaigns they saw no need to mention before the Court, and enabling one to verify their participation on many of those they did describe, whilst simultaneously reconstructing some of the networks that helped shape their patterns of military service.[84]

The existing scholarship, then, has largely focused upon the military-chivalric potential (and shortcomings) of the three cases,[85] perhaps appropriately enough, since the Court had unequivocally been designed

---

[82] Ayton, 'Knights, Esquires and Military Service', pp. 91–6.

[83] A. R. Bell, *War and the Soldier in the Fourteenth Century* (Woodbridge, 2004), pp. 140–50. See also, an online, updated version of the relevant section: A. R. Bell, 'Evidence from the Court of Chivalry', www.soldier-lews1.rdg.ac.uk

[84] A. Ayton, 'Military Service and the Dynamics of Recruitment in Fourteenth-Century England', in *The Soldier Experience*, pp. 45–57; A. R. Bell, 'The Soldier, "adde he riden, no man ferre"', in *The Soldier Experience*, pp. 209–18; Bell et al., *The Soldier*, pp. 117–22, 167–70; A. Ayton, 'William de Thweyt, Esquire: Deputy Constable of Corfe Castle in the 1340s', *Somerset and Dorset Notes and Queries*, 32 (1989), pp. 731–8; A. Ayton, 'From Brittany to the Black Sea: Nicholas Sabraham and English Military Experience in the Fourteenth Century', in *Courts of Chivalry and Admiralty in Late Medieval Europe*, ed. A. Musson and N. Ramsay (Woodbridge, 2018), pp. 95–120.

[85] On the shortcomings of the surviving testimony as a military source, see Bell et al., *The Soldier*, pp. 2–3. For other recent studies that have made fleeting use of the Court of Chivalry material, with a focus upon the military careers of those who deposed, see J. Sumption, *Divided Houses: The Hundred Years War III* (London, 2009), pp. 735–7; R. Barber, *Edward III and the Triumph of England: The Battle of Crécy and the Company of the Garter* (London, 2013), pp. 376–81.

in the first place to deal with matters 'having their commencement and cause in deeds of chivalry and arms'.[86] Yet, the chief contention of this study is that the value of these three disputes lies in their breadth, as much as in their depth, of material. There are a variety of issues that have long been central to studies of the late medieval English gentry that the *Scrope v. Grosvenor*, *Lovel v. Morley* and *Grey v. Hastings* testimony touches upon in interesting and unexplored ways, but none of these have received any more than passing attention from historians. Perhaps most obviously, it has long been acknowledged that the influence of the Lancastrian affinity was keenly felt in both Richard, Lord Scrope's and Sir Edward Hastings' witness lists.[87] Yet, this inviting opportunity to investigate the character of magnate–gentry relations from a bottom-up perspective, unbounded by county borders, has never been pursued in any great detail.[88] Indeed, even the wider role of lordship in these disputes, including the role played by the protagonists themselves as 'good lords' to some of their lesser deponents, has received surprisingly little attention.[89] It would be equally helpful to reconstruct the bonds of inter-gentry solidarity that the protagonists in each case enjoyed with their witnesses, and some attempt has been made to do this on a regional basis.[90] Yet, as Sir Harris Nicolas inadvertently revealed – when he engaged in the enormous (and incomplete) task of providing individual biographies for every Scrope and Grosvenor witness – a full prosopographical analysis of the witness lists is quite simply impossible, given the obscurity of a significant proportion of those who deposed.[91] Perhaps due to the potential magnitude of such a task, hardly anything has been written about the political and social

---

[86] See pp. 11–12.
[87] Keen, 'Grey v. Hastings', p. 175; Vale, 'The Scropes', pp. 95–105; Goodman, *John of Gaunt*, pp. 214, 279–80, 288–90; Caudrey, 'War, Chivalry and Regional Society', pp. 127–31.
[88] See pp. 65–82.
[89] Vale, 'The Scropes', pp. 101–3; Ayton, 'Knights, Esquires and Military Service', pp. 94–5; Ayton, 'The Dynamics of Military Recruitment', pp. 48–53; Bell et al., *The Soldier*, pp. 117–22.
[90] M. J. Bennett, *Community, Class and Careerism: Cheshire and Lancashire Society in the Age of Sir Gawain and the Green Knight* (Cambridge, 1983), pp. 12–16, 82–3, 166; P. Morgan, *War and Society in Medieval Cheshire, 1277–1403* (Chetham Society, 3rd Series, 34, Manchester, 1987), pp. 129–32; Vale, 'The Scropes', pp. 101–3; Caudrey, 'War, Chivalry and Regional Society', pp. 119–45; Morgan, 'Sir Robert Grosvenor', pp. 75–94.
[91] *Scrope v. Grosvenor*, II, pp. iii–vi.

bonds that prevailed between the protagonists and their witnesses, and amongst the witnesses themselves.[92]

Even more significantly, historians have largely shied away from treating the role of personal and collective memory before the Court as an issue worth exploring in its own right.[93] Simply put, with such a large body of veterans recalling often decades-old military experiences, the types of questions historians of modern conflicts ask about the way war is remembered and misremembered, and how it is neatly packaged, sanitised, and, on occasion, transformed into an exercise in nostalgia, are entirely pertinent to any analysis of the surviving Court of Chivalry depositions.[94] Yet, the only study to have ostensibly addressed the issue of memory on its own terms (using the Scrope testimony as a sample) focused purely upon what was said before the Court and ignored the pre-existing relationships that bound Scrope to his witnesses, thereby inadvertently disconnecting each deposition from the circumstances in which it was provided and the practical constraints under which each deponent spoke.[95] Given the breadth of these issues, this book adopts a deliberately eclectic approach to the *Scrope v. Grosvenor*, *Lovel v. Morley* and *Grey v. Hastings* material. On the one hand, it explores a range of largely-neglected themes, pertinent to the military, social and cultural history of the late medieval English gentry; on the other, it addresses – through the prism of these three cases – the much larger question of the extent to which soldiering, and the cultural values of chivalry that lay behind it, influenced the lives of those who testified before the Court, as well as the extent to which such attitudes and values remained central to gentry life as the triumphs of the Crécy-Poitiers era receded ever further into the past.

---

[92] See above, n. 89.

[93] Ayton, 'Knights, Esquires and Military Service', pp. 86–90; Caudrey, 'War, Chivalry and Regional Society', pp. 135–9; Morgan, 'Sir Robert Grosvenor', pp. 86–93.

[94] E.g., For a summary of the extensive scholarship surrounding British experiences and memories of the two World Wars, see D. Reynolds, *The Long Shadow: The Great War and the Twentieth Century* (London, 2013). On the role of memory in medieval culture, see M. J. Carruthers, *The Book of Memory: A Study of Memory in Medieval Culture* (Cambridge, 1990); M. T. Clanchy, *From Memory to Written Record: England 1066–1307*, second edition (Oxford, 1993). For a perceptive overview of English chivalric memory, see N. Saul, *Chivalry in Medieval England* (Cambridge, Mass., 2011), pp. 283–304.

[95] J. T. Rosenthal, *Telling Tales: Sources and Narration in Late Medieval England* (Philadelphia, 2003), pp. 63–94.

This book is divided into four chapters. Chapter 1 takes the testimony of Sir Robert Grosvenor's and Sir Edward Hastings' militarily active witnesses – most of whom participated in the second phase of the Hundred Years War – as a case study, investigating their war records, assessing the individual motives and constraints that lured them into a career in arms, and considering their family's ongoing contribution to the war with France. By homing in upon the young warriors of the 1370s and 1380s, and by highlighting continuities of military service into the fifteenth century, rather than looking back to the much-studied 1340s and 1350s, one may assess the role of: (1) generational change, (2) family traditions of military service, and (3) the extent to which the martial inclinations of the gentry cooled between the twilight years of Edward III's reign and the revival of English martial glory under Henry V.

Chapter 2 turns to the character of lordship before the Court, taking as a starting point the contrasting roles played by the Lancastrian affinity as an active military and political institution in *Scrope v. Grosvenor* in the mid 1380s, and as a ghostly fifteenth-century relic of John of Gaunt's authority amongst sections of the East Anglian gentry in *Grey v. Hastings*. From there, we turn to other magnate affinities, whose retainers testified before the Court. In particular, the retinues of Gaunt's brother, Edward, the Black Prince, and the Bohun earls of Northampton and Hereford, will provide an interesting portrait of the bonds created by magnate militarism, whilst the deaths of these great lords remind one of the fragility of the magnate affinity as a political and military structure. Finally, attention will shift to the personal affinities of three of our Court of Chivalry protagonists – Lords Grey and Morley, and Sir Edward Hastings – considering the ways in which they drew lesser men to speak on their behalf: men who were not necessarily their kinsmen, friends or associates, but who undeniably enjoyed vertical ties with them as servants, tenants, household attendants, or other types of miscellaneous followers. Chapter 3 expands upon the above themes, essentially probing the personal connections that bound Scrope and Morley to their witnesses and that drew the latter to speak in the former's defence. In essence, both Chapters 2 and 3 seek to confront the grey area between personal relationships and the wider mobilisation of an entire region on a protagonist's behalf.

Lastly, Chapter 4 moves into less certain terrain: the world of 'chivalric memory'. It comprises a linking chapter between the world of the fourteenth-century Court of Chivalry and the cultural values of its deponents, and the world of England's fifteenth-century gentry, who were derided as the century progressed for their apparent aversion to military service, yet who surely had not undergone a cultural sea-change since the days of *Grey v. Hastings* in the early 1400s. Chapter 4 probes the martial culture of England's fourteenth-century gentry, soldiers and civilians, lay and ecclesiastical, as outlined before the Court of Chivalry, recognising that military service and the chivalric ethos did not always go hand in hand, in the process questioning whether the English gentry, in a cultural sense, underwent the 'cooling of bellicose ardour' attributed to them by Keen.[96] In sum, these three armorial cases before the Court of Chivalry provide a unique opportunity for investigating the role war-making and chivalric culture played in shaping the outlook and governing the daily concerns of England's gentry between the triumphs of Crécy (1346) and Agincourt (1415).

---

[96] Keen, 'Grey v. Hastings', pp. 177–8.

1

Military Service

The surviving testimony in *Scrope v. Grosvenor*, *Lovel v. Morley* and *Grey v. Hastings* provides ample evidence of the militarisation of the English gentry during the final two-thirds of the fourteenth century.[1] Witnesses collectively recalled over 20 individual campaigns, spanning more than eight decades, from the devastating rout of the English army at the battle of Bannockburn in 1314 to Reginald, Lord Grey of Ruthin's Welsh campaigns of the early 1400s.[2] Twenty elderly deponents detailed their service in Scotland during the 1330s, and as many as 46 outlined at least one Scottish expedition on which they had served prior to 1385. Even more impressively, more than 350 witnesses described their participation in the first phase of the Hundred Years War (1337–60). According to their testimony, 98 men served on the Crécy-Calais expedition in 1346–7; 109 on the Rheims campaign in 1359–60; and 92 in Gascony in 1369. Smaller numbers of deponents were present at most of the key battles of the high Edwardian age, including 22 at the battle of Sluys (1340), 32 at the battle of Winchelsea (1350), and nine at the battle of Poitiers (1356), whilst handfuls were also present at the battles of Buironfosse (1339), Morlaix (1342), Auberoche (1345) and Mauron (1352). Additionally, 28 and 22 deponents respectively fought in Spain under Edward, the Black Prince in 1366–7 and John of Gaunt in 1386–8, and at least 135 deponents accompanied Richard II into Scotland in 1385 (a not unexpected figure, since both *Scrope v. Grosvenor* and *Lovel v. Morley* had their genesis on this expedition).

---

[1] *Scrope v. Grosvenor*; C 47/6/2; C 47/6/3; C 47/6/1; PRO30/26/69; *PCM*. It is unlikely we will ever retrieve the testimony of every witness from all three disputes. Scrope's, Grosvenor's, Morley's and Hastings' witness lists appear largely complete (and hence are the principle subject of this study), whereas the bulk of depositions for Lovel and Grey appear to be missing. In total, at least 247 depositions survive for Scrope; 151 for Grosvenor; 177 for Morley; 62 for Lovel; 38 for Grey; and nearly 100 for Hastings. The survival of scattered depositions in other locations only serves to reinforce just how much more testimony may once have existed. E.g., Blomefield, *History of Norfolk*, II, pp. 437–9.

[2] See Appendix 1.

Quite apart from all of this, more than a dozen witnesses – ranging from great knights to obscure esquires – outlined their participation on crusading enterprises, whilst a few others even alluded to their years in garrison service.³ These figures, it should be noted, represent an underestimate. They include only those witnesses who detailed specific expeditions on which they had participated. A significant body of veterans made vague declarations in their depositions of having served in France or elsewhere, without specifying where or when, whilst most, obviously, refrained from mentioning aspects of their military records unrelated to the case at hand.

This body of evidence has enabled historians of military service to draw a number of important, and now well-worn, conclusions: (1) that both England's greater and lesser gentry became accustomed to regularly bearing arms during the reign of Edward III; (2) that whilst some deponents developed a commitment to a single lordly retinue, the vast majority moved freely between a variety of commanders; (3) that esquires and gentlemen were not merely young men awaiting promotion, but were oftentimes career professionals of immense military experience, vital to the effective functioning of English armies as military subcontractors and hardened warriors; (4) that most deponents were teenagers (or at least no older than their twenties) when first armed; and (5) that a significant minority went on to campaign intermittently or near-continuously for upwards of 20 or 30 years, with some still active on the cusp of old age.⁴ In essence, historians have used the Court of Chivalry testimony to draw out the gentry's patterns of military service in terms of the length, breadth and intensity of their careers in arms, as well as the character their service took as defined by where, under whom, and how consistently they bore arms.

So how, then, is one to take this body of evidence and examine it afresh? In much of the existing scholarship on individual cases, quantifying military participation, as we have just seen, has proven an

---

³ On garrison service, see below, pp. 35–6, 58–60.
⁴ Keen, 'Grey v. Hastings', pp. 167–85; Ayton, 'Knights, Esquires and Military Service', pp. 81–104; Keen, *Origins of the English Gentleman*, pp. 25–70; Caudrey, 'War, Chivalry and Regional Society', pp. 119–45; Ayton, 'Military Service and the Dynamics of Recruitment', pp. 45–57; Bell et al., *The Soldier*, pp. 260–70. For an overview of English armies during this period, see A. Ayton, 'English Armies in the Fourteenth Century', in *The Wars of Edward III: Sources and Interpretations*, ed. C. J. Rogers (Woodbridge, 1999), pp. 303–19.

automatic point of entry.⁵ This approach, however, though invaluable in many respects, runs the risk of turning careers into typologies, in which deponents are discussed solely in light of their war records, and the context in which they served is left largely unexplored.⁶ Each militarily active deponent, after all, bore arms for his own personal reasons and often in the face of external pressures – familial, regional, lordly, and as a broad expectation of his social class.⁷ Moreover, historians of the Court have primarily focused upon the degree of continuity of personnel between the halcyon years of the mid fourteenth century and the later campaigns of the 1370s.⁸ Far less has been written about this same issue for the period between the 1370s and the early fifteenth century, despite the fact that many of the families who spoke in these disputes would go on to serve in the Hundred Years War's third and final phase (1415–53).⁹ In a different context, Simon Payling has hinted at the maintenance of family military traditions into the fifteenth century and, as a noticeably militarily active subset

---

⁵ E.g., Keen, 'Grey v. Hastings', pp. 178–82; Ayton, 'Knights, Esquires and Military Service', pp. 86, 88, 91; Caudrey, 'War, Chivalry and Regional Society', pp. 124–6.

⁶ For examples of a more impressionistic approach to the Court of Chivalry material, see Bennett, *Community, Class and Careerism*, pp. 15–16, 82–3, 166; Keen, *Origins of the English Gentleman*, pp. 62–3; Sumption, *The Hundred Years War III*, pp. 735–7; Barber, *Edward III and the Triumph of England*, pp. 376–81; Bell, 'The Soldier, "hadde he riden, no man ferre"', pp. 210–17.

⁷ For an overview of the motives traditionally ascribed to English gentry participants, see J. A. Tuck, 'Why Men Fought in the Hundred Years War', *History Today*, 33 (1983), pp. 35–40; A. Ayton, 'War and the English Gentry under Edward III', *History Today*, 42 (1992), pp. 3–40; A. Ayton, 'The Military Careerist in Fourteenth-Century England', *Journal of Medieval History*, 43 (2017), pp. 4–23.

⁸ Keen, *Origins of the English Gentleman*, pp. 25–70; Bell, *War and the Soldier*, pp. 140–50; Ayton, 'Military Service and the Dynamics of Recruitment', pp. 45–57. This trend has likely arisen because *Scrope v. Grosvenor* is the only one of the three disputes to enjoy publication and it is the period between the 1330s and 1380s that it recalls. *Scrope v. Grosvenor*.

⁹ On the merits of a longer-term approach towards the study of military service, in this instance investigating Welsh soldiering between the reigns of Edward I and Henry V, see A. Chapman, *Welsh Soldiers in the Later Middle Ages 1282–1422* (Woodbridge, 2015).

of the English gentry, it would surely be worth investigating how this applied to those who spoke before the Court of Chivalry.[10]

This chapter, then, addresses the evidence of military service before the Court in a slightly different light. Rather than retracing old ground by quantifying the military careers of deponents *en masse*, or focusing upon those who campaigned in the highly successful Crécy-Poitiers era, this chapter turns instead towards the Hundred Years War's second phase (1369–89) and explores the relationship between the young military gentry of this epoch and those who fought the wars of Henry V a generation later. This will be undertaken in the first instance by reconstructing the war records of Sir Robert Grosvenor's and Sir Edward Hastings' testators (who primarily served in the war's second phase) as a first step towards engaging, over the coming chapters, with Keen's long-held sentiment that we may perceive 'a distinct cooling of bellicose ardour'[11] amongst those testators who recalled the 1370s and 1380s, when compared with their mid-century forebears. The military careers of the high Edwardian age have besides been thoroughly explicated by Keen and Ayton from the Scrope and Morley testimony, which has shown quite clearly that these older deponents served frequently in the king's wars and that a significant minority did so over such a long period of time that they were still in arms as grizzled veterans after 1369.[12] It is in light of this high degree of militarisation that one must assess the subsequent military careerism of the English gentry during the Hundred Years War's second and third phases, thereby situating the military testimony provided before the Court in a broader late medieval setting, rather than a purely fourteenth-century one.

The second part of this chapter turns away from the deponents' war records *per se* to explore the overarching character of the military service they performed, identifying in the process the varying roles war-making came to play in their wider careers. These men may all

---

[10] S. Payling, 'War and Peace: Military and Administrative Service amongst the English Gentry in the Reign of Henry VI', in *Soldiers, Nobles and Gentlemen: Essays in Honour of Maurice Keen*, ed. P. Coss and C. Tyerman (Woodbridge, 2009), pp. 240–58. See also, Bell et al., *The Soldier*, pp. 68–84, 117–29.

[11] Keen, 'Grey v. Hastings', pp. 172–8.

[12] Keen, 'Chivalrous Culture', pp. 15–22; Keen, *Origins of the English Gentleman*, pp. 43–70; Ayton, 'Knights, Esquires and Military Service', pp. 88–95; Ayton, 'Military Service and the Dynamics of Recruitment', pp. 45–57; Ayton, 'The Military Careerist', pp. 5–7.

too easily be lumped together as having served on three, four or five campaigns, or over 10, 20 or 30 years, or in one, two or three different military theatres. Yet, such broad similarities can mask a tremendous diversity of motive, which may best be laid bare by means of individual exemplar. This chapter, in short, seeks to trace – through the prism of the Court of Chivalry testimony – the nuances of the English gentry military experience over the 80-odd years between the 1330s and the 1410s, moving the conversation forward into the fifteenth century and seeing what the careers in arms of Grosvenor's and Hastings' testators in particular can tell us about the character of English military society between the dotage of Edward III and the triumphs of Henry V.

English Military Society, 1369–1415: The Evidence of the Grosvenor and Hastings Testimony

The Grosvenor and Hastings Testimony: Military Service

Sir Robert Grosvenor and Sir Edward Hastings, in their respective Court of Chivalry cases, shared plenty in common. Both were defending their arms against a plaintiff of higher social rank. Both lacked their opponent's resources. And both additionally had a poorer claim to the arms under dispute. Grosvenor relied heavily upon the support of sections of the Cheshire and Lancashire gentry, whilst Hastings sought assistance from the gentry of his native East Anglia. Both men brought together witnesses who could recall occasions when their family had borne the disputed arms in a military setting and in consequence much of the military testimony on their behalf came to focus upon a few very specific campaigns on which they, or their ancestors, had participated.[13] A number of Grosvenor's older deponents recalled his father-in-law's armorial dispute against the Cornish esquire, Thomas Carminowe, on the Rheims expedition in 1359–60. A few men also described Grosvenor's presence at Sandwich for the aborted voyage of 1372, and approximately one-quarter of his militarily active witnesses recalled the Scottish campaign of 1385, on which the dispute with Richard, Lord Scrope had arisen. Most notably, three-quarters of Grosvenor's militarily active deponents outlined in detail his participation on the expedition of 1369, during which he had served in the retinue of Sir James Audley at the sieges of

---

[13] See above, pp. 2, 6.

Brux and La Roche-sur-Yon, the capture of the castle of Belle Perche, the fall of Limoges, and at various other locations in Gascony, Anjou and Poitou.[14] Hastings, meanwhile, a generation later and with only a single expedition under his belt, turned to older men who could recall their campaigning days with his father, Sir Hugh III, in the Lancastrian military retinue in the 1370s and 1380s.[15]

Most of the men who provided this body of evidence for Grosvenor and Hastings had been born between the mid 1340s and mid 1360s and had thus been young (or relatively young) men during the final third of the fourteenth century.[16] Their depositions can additionally be fleshed out by turning to the financial records, muster rolls, and letters of protection for individual expeditions.[17] Collectively, these men comprise an impressively active sample of English soldiers from the northwest and eastern counties, who had almost all been too young to participate in the victories at Crécy (1346) and Poitiers (1356), yet were potentially not so far advanced in age by 1415 that they were unable to return to France as veteran soldiers under Henry V. Even though barely any, as we shall see, made this commitment in person, the continuities between the war's second and third phases may still be measured through an assessment of their families' ongoing contributions to the English war effort.

Both protagonists were supported by virtually the same number of testators with experience fighting in the Hundred Years War's second phase. 38 of Grosvenor's witnesses and 39 of Hastings' respectively recalled at least one specific campaign between 1369 and 1389.[18] Taken separately, and supplementing their testimony with evidence from other military sources, the level of military commitment of these two medium-sized sample groups was indeed impressive. Sir

---

[14] Stewart-Brown, 'The Scrope and Grosvenor Controversy', pp. 16–17. For a narrative account of Audley's military actions in 1369, see Sumption, *The Hundred Years War III*, pp. 29–32.

[15] Keen, 'Grey v. Hastings', pp. 182–3; Caudrey, 'War, Chivalry and Regional Society', pp. 125–6.

[16] Only 34 of Grosvenor's 151 deponents were fifty years of age or older, meaning the rest were born no earlier than 1336. *Scrope v. Grosvenor*. Twenty-three of Hastings' 36 deponents who gave their age were younger than 50 years old, meaning they were born no earlier than the late 1350s. *PCM*.

[17] Unless otherwise stated, all additional military records were accessed at www.medievalsoldier.org

[18] *Scrope v. Grosvenor*; *PCM*.

Edward Hastings, with his reliance upon old Lancastrian soldiers, had amongst his testators six veterans of John of Gaunt's *chevauchée* through northern France in 1373;[19] nine who were present at the siege of St. Malo in 1378;[20] 21 who journeyed to Scotland in 1385;[21] and 22 who joined Gaunt on his Spanish enterprise in 1386.[22] Yet, Hastings' testators were not exclusively Lancastrian military followers and, as we shall see in Chapter 2, by no means all were members of the Lancastrian affinity in peacetime. These gentry were predominantly 'socio-professional' knights and esquires,[23] who campaigned at intervals throughout the 1370s and 1380s, with small numbers of deponents present on all the noteworthy expeditions of the period. Six were in Gascony in 1368–70;[24] two at the disastrous sea-battle off La Rochelle in 1372;[25] two in Brittany in 1374–5;[26] five on Sir John Arundel's

---

[19] Nicholas Braynton; Simon de Burgh; Sir Thomas Erpingham; Robert Lymworth; Robert Poley; Sir Ralph Shelton II. *PCM*, I, pp. 413–21, 495–7, 529; C 76/56, mm. 14, 25; A. Curry, 'Sir Thomas Erpingham', in *Agincourt 1415: Henry V, Sir Thomas Erpingham and the Triumph of the English Archers*, ed. A. Curry (Gloucester: Tempus, 2000), p. 60.

[20] Sir William Berdewell; Robert Fishlake; David Hemenhale; Sir Thomas Hengrave; Thomas, Lord Morley; William Plumstead; John Roger; Sir Ralph Shelton II; Thomas Swynborne *PCM*, I, pp. 390–2, 405–6, 423–4, 429–35, 435–9, 458–64, 478–80, 492; E 101/36/39, m. 9d.

[21] Sir William Berdewell; Sir Robert Berney; John Bryston; Richard Chyrche; Hamo Claxton; Thomas Clifford; Sir Thomas Erpingham; Robert Fishlake; Sir John Geney; Sir Thomas Gerbergh; David Hemenhale; Sir Leonard Kerdiston; John Kirkstead; Robert Lymworth; Sir Robert Morley; Robert Poley; John Reymes; Sir Ralph Shelton II; Thomas Swynborne; Sir John Wilton; Sir John Wiltshire. *PCM*, I, pp. 390–2, 401–4, 405–6, 413–21, 421–2, 423–4, 425, 429–35, 439–42, 444–5, 451–3, 456–7, 458–64, 464–7, 467–9, 474–6, 495–6, 496–7, 497–8, 500, 519–20.

[22] Edmund Barry; Sir William Berdewell; Sir Robert Berney; Thomas Clifford; Simon de Burgh; Sir Thomas Erpingham; Sir Simon Felbrigg; Sir John Geney; Thomas Lucas; Robert Marian; Sir Robert Morley; Constantine Mortimer; John Payn; Robert Poley; John Reymes; John Roger; Sir Ralph Shelton II; John Spekkesworth; Thomas Stanton; Sir John Wilton; Sir John Wiltshire; Sir William Wisham. *PCM*, I, pp. 390–2, 392–5, 395–7, 397–9, 399–401, 401–4, 421–2, 423–4, 425, 427–9, 439–42, 443–4, 444–5, 445–51, 474–6, 486–7, 495–7, 497–8, 500, 502–3, 509–11, 513–14.

[23] For a discussion of this terminology, see pp. 46–7.

[24] Sir Thomas Gerbergh; Sir Thomas Erpingham; Sir Robert Morley; William Plumstead; John Roger; Sir Ralph Shelton II; *PCM*, I, pp. 478–80, 496–7; C 61/82, mm. 7, 8; C 76/52, m. 16; Curry, 'Sir Thomas Erpingham', p. 60.

[25] Thomas, Lord Morley; Sir John Wiltshire. *PCM*, I, pp. 401–4, 435–9.

[26] William Plumstead; John Roger. C 76/57, m. 7; *PCM*, I, pp. 397–9.

calamitous voyage in 1379;[27] 14 on the Earl of Buckingham's Brittany expedition in 1380;[28] and 13 in naval service.[29] Additionally, three deponents participated on the Bishop of Norwich's Flemish Crusade in 1383 and four others crusaded elsewhere.[30]

Grosvenor's testators served with similar intensity, though their war records reveal a rather different host of military experiences. In their case, far less was said about their overall careers in arms. Their testimony, as touched upon, focused upon the Gascony and Scottish campaigns of 1369 and 1385, on which Grosvenor himself had participated. Twenty-seven men recalled the former expedition[31] and at least nine the latter.[32] From other military sources, we may discern

[27] Sir William Berdewell, Robert Fishlake, Thomas Pickworth; William Plumstead; Sir Miles Stapleton. *PCM*, I, pp. 390–2, 404–5, 429–35, 442–3, 478–80.

[28] Sir William Berdewell; Thomas Clifford; Simon de Burgh; Robert Fishlake; Sir Thomas Gerbergh; David Hemenhale; Robert Lymworth; Thomas, Lord Morley; Thomas Pickworth; William Plumstead; Thomas Stanton; Sir Miles Stapleton; Thomas Swynborne; Sir John Wilton. *PCM*, I, pp. 404–5, 405–6, 413–21, 429–35, 435–9, 442–3, 458–64, 478–80, 486–7, 496–7, 497–8, 500; E 101/39/7, no. 1 m. 1; C 76/65, m. 28.

[29] Edmund Barry; John Bere; Sir William Berdewell; Sir William Calthorp; Robert Fishlake; Sir Leonard Kerdiston; Sir Robert Morley; William Plumstead; John Roger; Sir Ralph Shelton II; Thomas Stanton; Sir John Wilton; Sir William Wisham; E 101/32/20, m. 1; E 101/37/10, m. 1; E 101/36/32, m. 4; E 101/40/39, m. 1; E 101/40/33, mm. 1, 2d, 11, 20; E 101/40/34, mm. 5, 26; E 101/41/5, mm. 1, 3d, 6, 7, 13; C 76/72, m. 7; C 76/91, m. 13.

[30] Flanders: Sir William Berdewell; Sir Thomas Gerbergh; Sir Ralph Shelton II. *HPC, 1386–1421*, II, pp. 125–6; C 76/67, mm. 7, 16. The Mediterranean, North Africa or Prussia: Alexander Denton; Sir Thomas Erpingham; Robert Fishlake; John Parker. *PCM*, I, pp. 429–35, 439–42; 453–5; 533. On the Flemish crusade, see J. Magee, 'Sir William Elmham and the Recruitment for Henry Despenser's Crusade of 1383', *Medieval Prosopography*, 20 (1999), pp. 181–90.

[31] Geoffrey Boidell; Sir Richard Bolde; Sir William Brereton; Sir Hugh Browe; William Chisnale; Hugh Coton; Robert Danyell; Thomas Duncalf; Vivian Faxwist; John Frodesham; Thomas Halghton; William Hilton; William Hulme; Sir William Legh; William Legh; Thomas Legh; John Massy; Richard Monlegh; Robert Pilkington; William Praes; William Sodyngton; William Slene; Thomas St Pierre; Robert Toft; William Tranmer; Sir Ralph Vernon; Richard Vernon. *Scrope v. Grosvenor*, I, pp. 256–7, 257–8, 261–2, 262–3, 267–8, 269, 271, 275, 277–8, 282–3, 285–6, 286–7, 287, 288, 291, 295–6, 299, 300–1, 302, 308, 309, 311, 314–15, 316, 319, 320, 322.

[32] Sir John Assheton; Sir Hugh Browe; Arthur Davenport; Thomas Davenport; Owen Glyn Dwr; John Hanmere; Sir John Massy of Puddington; John Maynwaring; Sir Ralph Vernon. *Scrope v. Grosvenor*, I, pp. 254–5, 255, 256–7, 259, 263, 271, 271–2, 274, 275–6.

the presence of small numbers of Grosvenor witnesses on most of the campaigns outlined by Hastings' supporters. Three men were in Gascony in 1370;[33] two on Gaunt's *chevauchée* in 1373;[34] five in Brittany in 1374–5;[35] three at St. Malo in 1378;[36] four in Brittany in 1380;[37] three on the Flemish Crusade in 1383;[38] seven in naval service;[39] one in Ireland and one on Gaunt's Spanish enterprise.[40]

Perceived purely from the standpoint of aggregating levels of military participation, these war records, above all else, reinforce the limits of relying upon the Court of Chivalry testimony in isolation, and underscore the importance of augmenting their testimony, where available, with evidence from other military records.[41] Both sets of witnesses were concerned only with occasions when they had seen the defendant, or his ancestors, bearing the disputed arms on campaign, and whilst Grosvenor's witnesses very obviously limited themselves to the two specific expeditions of the war's second phase on which their defendant had been present, even amongst Hastings' more effusive supporters, who recalled the impressive career in arms of Sir Hugh Hastings III at some length, significant gaps remained. Only four of those who spoke for Hastings mentioned four or more campaigns, and whilst ten recalled three expeditions, these rarely reflected the sum-total of their military experience.[42] Take Sir Ralph Shelton II, for instance. He described three campaigns he had undertaken

---

[33] William Chisnale; John Frodesham; John Leycestre. C 61/83, m. 7; C 61/83, m. 2; C 76/53, m. 9.

[34] Richard Massy; Robert Pilkington C 76/56, mm. 18, 26.

[35] Sir William Brereton; Sir Hugh Browe; Robert Danyell; Sir William Legh; William Legh. C 76/56, m. 13; C 76/57, m. 10; C 76/57, m. 10; E 101/35/6, m. 2.

[36] Sir John Assheton; Sir Hugh Browe; John Massy. C 76/62, m. 18; E 101/36/32, m. 3; E 101/36/39, m. 7.

[37] Sir John Assheton; Sir Hugh Browe; John Massy; Richard Vernon. C 76/65, mm. 23, 28; E 101/39/9, m. 4.

[38] Sir John Assheton; Thomas Legh; William Hilton. C 76/67, mm. 17, 18.

[39] Sir Hugh Browe; Robert Danyell; John Frodesham; John Holand; John Massy; Robert Pilkington; Sir Ralph Vernon; E 101/31/11, no. 2 m. 2; C 76/55, m. 22; C 76/57, m. 21; C 76/71, m. 14; E 101/40/33, m. 1; E 101/41/5, mm. 1d, 10d, 11, 16.

[40] Sir John Assheton; John Massy. S. K. Walker, 'John of Gaunt and his Retainers, 1361–99' (D. Phil, Oxford, 1986), p. 266; C 76/70, m. 28.

[41] On the utility of such an approach, see Ayton, 'Military Service and the Dynamics of Recruitment', pp. 45–57; Bell, 'The Soldier, "hadde he riden, no man ferre"', pp. 210–17; Bell et al., *The Soldier*, pp. 167–70.

[42] Robert Fishlake (5); Sir William Berdewell (4); Robert Lymworth (4); William Plumstead (4). *PCM*, I, pp. 429–35; 390–2; 413–21; 478–80.

in the Lancastrian military retinue to St. Malo (1378), Scotland (1385) and Spain (1386).[43] Yet, he was also in Gascony in 1369, on Gaunt's *chevauchée* in 1373, on two naval expeditions in 1372 and 1388, and on the Flemish Crusade in 1383.[44] And the fewer campaigns a deponent mentioned, sometimes the greater the gaps left to fill. The esquire, John Roger, who outlined only his participation on Gaunt's Spanish enterprise, provides a perfect illustration, since his war record, by chance, survives in considerable detail in other military records.[45] This reveals that by the time he journeyed to Spain at the age of 30, he was already something of a military veteran. He had first been armed as a teenager in Gascony in 1369, and had subsequently served in Brittany in 1375, at St. Malo in 1378, and in Gascony again in 1383, following up his Spanish service with participation as a member of the Earl of Arundel's naval force in 1388.[46]

Addressing the shortcomings of the Court of Chivalry testimony, though, is to some extent a matter of perspective. Our wider knowledge of the careers of the knightly élite naturally lends itself to a 'glass half-empty' approach, since one can often uncover through other sources just how little a knightly deponent actually revealed in his testimony about his own campaigning experiences.[47] Taken as a 'glass half full', however, the greatest strength of the surviving testimony may in fact lie in the evidence it provides about the careers in arms of militarily-active lesser gentry, whose comparatively lowly rank often renders them, in the traditional military records of the Crown, as mere numerals in the retinue lists of greater men.[48] Their brief

---

[43] *PCM*, I, pp. 423–4.
[44] C 76/52, m. 16; C 76/56, m. 25; E 101/32/20, m. 1; E 101/41/5, m. 1; C 76/67, m. 16.
[45] *PCM*, I, pp. 397–9.
[46] C 61/82, m. 8; E 101/35/6, m. 1; E 101/36/69 m. 9d; C 61/96, m. 10; E 101/41/5, m. 13.
[47] See above, n. 41. See also, Bell, 'The Soldier, "hadde he riden, no man ferre"', pp. 214–15.
[48] The most serious shortcoming is the relative absence of muster rolls, especially prior to 1369, without which, one is reliant upon letters of protection and grants of pardon. Letters of protection were usually acquired only by men of sufficient substance that their property required guarding in their absence, whilst grants of pardon were naturally limited only to those possessing criminal records. Bell et al., *The Soldier*, pp. 4-22. Historians have consequently been forced to improvise. E.g., Ayton sought to overcome these deficiencies through a detailed examination of horse restoration accounts for individual expeditions. A. Ayton, *Knights and Warhorses. Military Service and the English Aristocracy under Edward III* (Woodbridge, 1994).

testimonies provide an invaluable insight into years of soldiering that would otherwise have gone unrecorded.⁴⁹ The testimony can also fill in gaps for campaigns that, for various reasons, are comparatively poorly documented. Most obviously, across both sets of defendants, we have 30 men who detailed their participation on Richard II's Scottish expedition of 1385, for which the nominal data is relatively patchy.⁵⁰

If one digs deeper beneath the bald figures of military service, moreover, one finds in the war records of Grosvenor's and Hastings' deponents ample evidence of regional differences in the character of the English military experience for men of the northwest and eastern counties (borne from the fact that both defendants selected witnesses with whom they were familiar, and who consequently largely hailed from their respective regional strongholds). Amongst Hastings' witnesses, due to his father, Sir Hugh Hastings III's, distinguished career as a Lancastrian banneret, it is possible to gain an impression of the extent of continuity within the ranks of John of Gaunt's wartime retinue. Half of the 22 deponents who accompanied Gaunt to Spain in 1386 had been with him in Scotland the previous year.⁵¹ More impressively still, almost half of Hastings' total number of militarily active witnesses (19 out of 39 men) served more than once beneath the Lancastrian banner, with particular continuity apparent from the siege of St. Malo (1378) to the campaigns in Scotland (1385) and Spain (1386).⁵² Simon Walker long ago demonstrated the presence of an inner core of regular Lancastrian wartime followers, around whom less stable elements could dip in and out of Gaunt's military retinue as opportunity dictated.⁵³ At least half of Sir Edward Hastings' testators – and certainly almost all of those knights who spoke for him – fitted this

---

⁴⁹ E.g., Thomas, Lord Morley's witness, John Raven. C 47/6/1, no. 6. On Raven's absence from the traditional military records, see Ayton, 'Knights, Esquires and Military Service', p. 90.

⁵⁰ On the surviving nominal data for the Scottish campaign of 1385, see G. P. Baker, 'The English Way of War, 1360–99' (PhD, Hull, 2011), pp. 149–78. See also, A. Curry, A. R. Bell, A. King, and D. Simpkin, 'New Regime, New Army? Henry IV's Scottish Expedition of 1400', *EHR*, 125 (2010), pp. 1382–413.

⁵¹ Sir William Berdewell; Sir Robert Berney; Thomas Clifford; Sir Thomas Erpingham; Sir John Geney; Sir Robert Morley; Robert Poley; John Reymes; Sir Ralph Shelton II; Sir John Wilton; Sir John Wiltshire. *PCM*, I, pp. 390–2; 474–6; 500; 439–42; 425; 421–2; 495–6; 444–5; 423–4; 497–8; 401–4.

⁵² This impressive degree of military continuity amongst Hastings' testators was first addressed by Keen. Keen, 'Grey v. Hastings', p. 182.

⁵³ S. K. Walker, *The Lancastrian Affinity, 1361–1399* (Oxford, 1990), pp. 39–80.

bill. Yet, as we shall see in Chapter 2, these military commitments did not necessarily reflect broader membership of the Lancastrian affinity in peacetime, whilst the careers in arms of several of Sir Edward's lesser testators will allow us to tease out the character of the Hastings family's personal affinity within their native East Anglia.

Grosvenor's body of militarily active witnesses from the same phase of the war provides a useful point of comparison. With Lord Scrope monopolising the support of the knightly élite of the northern shires, Grosvenor was left to acquire his testators largely from amongst those Cheshire and Lancashire gentry with whom he enjoyed a personal connection. Many were the heads of distinguished northwestern families, but none were quite of the same stamp as Scrope's more eminent witnesses, and few were of sufficient standing that their influence held much sway beyond the region between the Dee and Ribble from whence they hailed.[54] Their military careers were not all that different in intensity from those who spoke for Hastings. Both groups, after all, largely comprised gentry 'socio-professionals' who served on an intermittent basis. The bulk of Grosvenor's testators were in arms for at least ten, and, in some cases, for more than 20 years. Most were in their thirties or early-to-mid forties at the time of their depositions and had first been armed either on the Rheims expedition of 1359–60 or the Gascony campaign of 1369. For many, long-term semi-regular soldiering had become the order of the day. The esquire John Massy, for example, served at least five times during the Hundred Years War's second phase;[55] Richard Vernon's career in arms stretched from Gascony in 1369 to Scotland in 1400;[56] and, perhaps most impressively, Sir Hugh Browe campaigned on at least seven occasions in addition to his years in garrison service and was still in the saddle as late as 1403, more than three decades after his military debut.[57]

---

[54] Vale, 'The Scropes', pp. 95–105; Bennett, *Community, Class and Careerism*, pp. 12–16. This is not to imply, as Morgan has rightly cautioned, 'that the Grosvenors were somehow unworthy opponents, knights from the periphery'. Morgan, 'Sir Robert Grosvenor', p. 82.

[55] *Scrope v. Grosvenor*, I, p. 287; E 101/36/39, m. 7; E 101/39/9, m. 4; C 76/70, m. 28; E 101/41/5, m. 16.

[56] *Scrope v. Grosvenor*, I, pp. 285–6; E 101/42/39, m. 1.

[57] *Scrope v. Grosvenor*, I, pp. 256–7; C 76/57, m. 10; E 101/36/32, m. 3; C 76/65, m. 28; E 101/40/33, m. 1; E 101/41/5, m. 10d; Morgan, *War and Society in Medieval Cheshire*, p. 217.

If the intensity of their careers in arms was similar, a key difference lay in the fact that Grosvenor's witnesses traversed the military landscape far more widely than did Hastings': unsurprisingly so, since the Northwest was a poorer, less agriculturally fertile, and less peaceable region than East Anglia, which naturally made the soldier's life enticing to those below the ranks of the knightly élite.[58] Hastings' deponents served almost exclusively in France during the 1370s and on two large-scale expeditions to Scotland and Spain in the mid 1380s.[59] Grosvenor's deponents, by contrast, are to be found in all sorts of different locations. Most significantly, garrison service – a non-factor for Hastings' supporters – was crucial to the military careers of a number of Grosvenor's men. Much has been made of Sir Hugh Browe's assertion – when he was summoned to depose for Lord Scrope – that he had never seen the Scropes bearing the disputed arms on *chevauchées* or other grand voyages because he had been 'in the garrisons…of France', mainly as captain of Derval in Brittany.[60] It has subsequently been shown that Browe's claim rested, to say the least, upon a case of selective memory, and that he had in fact served on a variety of shorter expeditions during the 1370s and 1380s.[61] Nonetheless, there is no denying his exertions as captain of Derval,[62] and he was hardly the only Grosvenor witness to follow this career path. Indeed, more than half of Grosvenor's militarily active testators (20 of 38 soldiers) held positions in garrisons and/or standing forces at some point during their careers. Nine garrisoned castles in Scotland, Wales or English-occupied France.[63] For some – like

---

[58] Bennett, *Community, Class and Careerism*, pp. 162–91.
[59] See above, pp. 28–30.
[60] *Scrope v. Grosvenor*, II, p. 266. Bennett, *Community, Class and Careerism*, pp. 167, 182, 188; Morgan, *War and Society in Medieval Cheshire, 1277–1403* (Chetham Society, 3rd Series, 34, Manchester, 1987), pp. 129–30; Keen, *Origins of the English Gentleman*, pp. 62, 80–1; Sumption, *The Hundred Years War III*, pp. 736–7; Ayton, 'Military Service and the Dynamics of Recruitment', p. 53.
[61] Bell, 'The Soldier, "hadde he riden, no man ferre"', pp. 214–15.
[62] Jean Froissart, *Chroniques*, ed. S. Luce et al. (Paris, 1869–1975), VIII, p. 150.
[63] Sir Hugh Browe; Sir Owen Glyn Dwr; Thomas Halghton; William Hilton; Sir John Massy of Puddington; John Massy; Richard Massy of Rixton; Robert Pilkington; Richard Vernon. *Scrope v. Grosvenor*, I, pp. 256-7; 254-5; 308; 309; 255; 296; 302; 285-6. E 101/39/39, m. 1; C 76/60, m. 4; C 76/60, m. 35; C 76/65, m. 2; C 76/72, m. 27; E 101/34/29, m. 10i; C71/68, m. 1; C 76/61, m. 18; E 101/37/5, m. 1.

William Hilton and Richard Massy[64] – this service was intertwined with participation on shorter expeditions, reminding one of the degree of overlap between the garrison soldier and his 'socio-professional' colleague. For others, however, garrison service clearly became their primary means of self-support, at least for a few years. Browe spent the early 1370s fighting with his uncle, Sir Robert Knolles, in Brittany, whilst members of the Massy family, for six years in the 1380s, were to be found in the garrisons of Cherbourg, Berwick and Calais.[65] Additionally, six of Grosvenor's testators later became members of Richard II's bodyguard.[66]

Hastings' and Grosvenor's militarily active deponents also, naturally enough, had their wartime careers shaped by the political societies of the northwest and eastern counties in which they dwelt. A few of Hastings' supporters had moved from John of Gaunt's service into Henry of Bolingbroke's, in one noteworthy case going so far as to accompany him into exile in 1398.[67] Several were well rewarded for their loyalty after the usurpation, and indeed only one East Anglian knight is known to have raised arms against Bolingbroke in Richard II's hour of need.[68] Amongst Grosvenor's witnesses, a fractured political environment of 'haves' and 'have nots', both before and after 1399, sent many militarily active Cheshire men off on different paths during the early years of Lancastrian rule.[69] The interwoven character of war and politics in the wake of the truce with France and the change of dynasty is perhaps best illustrated by the fact that in 1403, whilst prominent

---

[64] Hilton served with the Cherbourg Garrison in the mid 1380s, but had earlier campaigned in Gascony twice (1369 and 1378) and had undertaken Bishop Despenser's Flemish Crusade in 1383. Massy was stationed at Berwick, but also served at least twice in France. C 76/60, m. 35; C 61/82, m. 11; C 61/91, m. 5; C 76/67, m. 18; C 71/68, m. 1; C 76/56, m. 26; C 61/95, m. 1.

[65] Froissart, *Chroniques*, ed. Luce, VIII, p. 150; C 76/65, m. 2; E 101/39/39, m. 1; C 76/72, m. 27.

[66] Hugh Coton; Arthur Davenport; Sir William Legh; John Maynwaryng; Robert Toft; Richard Vernon. E 101/42/10, mm. 1, 3d. On King Richard's Cheshire bodyguard, see Morgan, *War and Society in Medieval Cheshire*, pp. 198–207.

[67] Edmund Barry; John Reymes; Sir Robert Berney; John Payn. *PCM*, I, pp. 393, 444, 474, 502. Sir Thomas Erpingham was the deponent who accompanied Bolingbroke into exile. *PCM*, I, p. 439; H. Castor, *The King, the Crown, and the Duchy of Lancaster: Public Authority and Private Power, 1399–1461* (Oxford, 2000), pp. 64–5.

[68] Castor, *The King, the Crown, and the Duchy of Lancaster*, pp. 62–72.

[69] Bennett, *Community, Class and Careerism*, pp. 209–15; Morgan, *War and Society in Medieval Cheshire*, pp. 185-218.

Lancastrians (who would later speak for Hastings) were peacefully buttressing the new regime in the eastern counties, two of Grosvenor's more distinguished witnesses, Sir John Massy of Puddington and Sir Hugh Browe, were dying at the battle of Shrewsbury – Massy in the royalist army, Browe in Hotspur's.[70] This raises the question of what impact this combination of internecine strife, Anglo-French peace, and a change of royal dynasty had upon the military communities of the Northwest and East Anglia? Simply put, despite these upheavals, to what extent did the 80-odd militarily active families who spoke for Sir Robert Grosvenor and Sir Edward Hastings maintain their martial traditions into the early French wars of Henry V?

The Grosvenor and Hastings Testimony: Family Military Traditions
It is tempting to view family traditions of military service amongst the English gentry between 1389 and 1415 in light of the English military experience during the earlier decade-long truce that followed the Treaty of Brétigny in 1360.[71] It has been well documented that there developed an impressive degree of continuity of personnel from the campaigns of the 1350s into those of the 1370s.[72] A range of factors favourable to ongoing military careerism were at play here. Most obviously, the Treaty of Brétigny lasted a mere nine years, whilst a significant sector of English military society never stopped fighting. English gentry – especially younger sons and those from minor families – continued bearing arms throughout the 1360s in a variety of theatres. Some remained across the Channel after the Rheims campaign (1359–60), finding employment with the Free Companies ravaging the Languedoc and other parts of the collapsing French realm.[73] Others crusaded in Prussia and the eastern Mediterranean.[74] Others still, accompanied Edward, the Black Prince on his Spanish venture in 1366–7.[75] Moreover, the 1360s was for the royal court of Edward III a decade of hubris in

---

[70] Morgan, *War and Society in Medieval Cheshire*, pp. 215–17.
[71] J. Sumption, *Trial By Fire: The Hundred Years War II* (London, 2001), pp. 445–585.
[72] Ayton, 'Military Service and the Dynamics of Recruitment', pp. 45–57.
[73] K. Fowler, *Medieval Mercenaries I: The Great Companies* (Oxford, 2001).
[74] T. Guard, *Chivalry, Kingship and Crusade: The English Experience in the Fourteenth Century* (Woodbridge, 2013).
[75] P. E. Russell, *The English Intervention in Spain and Portugal in the Time of Edward III and Richard II* (Oxford, 1955), pp. 83–171; Sumption, *The Hundred Years War II*, pp. 504–85.

which the king and his aging aristocracy rested upon the laurels of their hard-won chivalric reputations and enjoyed the fruits – material and otherwise – of the Crécy-Poitiers era.[76] This atmosphere would have gone a long way towards encouraging the young warrior gentry of the 1350s to continue seeking martial outlets where they could find them, whilst simultaneously making the prospect of a military career enticing to those even younger gentry who reached fighting age shortly after 1360.

Matters proved very different a generation later between the second and third phases of the Hundred Years War. Although the Truce of Leulinghem was only established in 1389, in practice Anglo-French conflict had been petering out since the early 1380s,[77] with the last great military operations of the epoch comprising John of Gaunt's Castilian venture of 1386 and the large-scale naval expeditions of 1387 and 1388.[78] Military opportunities for gentry socio-professionals were thereafter relatively few and far between. This, of course, is to define 'military opportunities' very narrowly. Fighting a-plenty persisted within the British Isles itself as the realm descended into turmoil. Richard II led two expeditions into Ireland in 1394 and 1399.[79] Henry IV marched a much larger force into Scotland in 1400.[80] Border skirmishing between the Scots and their northern English neighbours continued unabated, occupying the great Marcher families and the gentry of the northern shires.[81] Additionally, the Welsh rose up under Grosvenor's witness, Owain Glyn Dwr,[82] and civil unrest within England after the Revolution of 1399 led to a series of hard-fought campaigns, and even the occasional pitched battle.[83] And, all the while, English garrisons at

[76] W. M. Ormrod, *Edward III* (New Haven, 2011), pp. 414–97.
[77] On the Truce of Leulinghem, see Sumption, *The Hundred Years War III*, pp. 774–833.
[78] Goodman, *John of Gaunt*, pp. 111–43; Bell, *War and the Soldier*.
[79] D. Biggs, *Three Armies in Britain: The Irish Campaign of Richard II and the Usurpation of Henry IV, 1397–1399* (Leiden, 2006), pp. 65–71.
[80] Curry et al., 'New Regime, New Army?', pp. 1382–413.
[81] J. A. Tuck, 'War and Society in the Medieval North', *Northern History*, 21 (1985), pp. 33–52; A. Goodman, 'Introduction', in *War and Border Societies in the Middle Ages*, ed. A. Goodman and J. A. Tuck (London, 1992), pp. 1–29; A. King and D. Simpkin (ed.), *England and Scotland at War, c.1296–c.1513* (Leiden, 2012).
[82] R. R. Davies, *The Revolt of Owain Glyn Dwr* (Oxford, 1995); Chapman, *Welsh Soldiers*, pp. 109–26.
[83] M. J. Bennett, *Richard II and the Revolution of 1399* (Gloucester, 1999); Morgan, *War and Society in Medieval Cheshire*, pp. 207–18.

home and abroad still required manning and mercenary employment remained open to the ambitious few, who chose to try their luck in France, Italy and the Low Countries.[84]

Yet, these numerous martial outlets offered few prospects of profit or advancement and the price of being on the losing side in a civil war was higher than most gentry – certainly those living far from the action – were prepared to pay. This is reflected in the war records of Grosvenor's and Hastings' witnesses after 1389. A minority ended up extending their careers in arms into the scattered theatres mentioned above. At least three deponents accompanied Richard II to Ireland,[85] whilst six of Grosvenor's Cheshire men were in Richard's pay as members of the royal bodyguard in 1398.[86] Others, notably Thomas Stanton, and the aforementioned Sir John Massy and Sir Hugh Browe, became embroiled in the internecine strife that followed the usurpation.[87] Moreover, at least ten men across both sets of deponents, including Sir Edward Hastings himself, followed Henry IV into Scotland in 1400.[88] It was in this period that the regional divide in military experience between the Northwestern and East Anglian gentry became starker

---

[84] J. Rickard, *The Castle Community: The Personnel of English and Welsh Castles, 1272–1422* (Woodbridge, 2002); D. J. Cornell, 'Northern Castles and Garrisons in the Later Middle Ages' (PhD, Durham, 2006); A. R. Bell, 'The Fourteenth-Century Soldier: More Chaucer's Knight or Medieval Career Soldier?', in *Mercenaries and Paid Men. The Mercenary Identity in the Middle Ages*, ed. J. France (Leiden, 2008), pp. 301–15; Bell, 'The Soldier, "hadde he riden, no man ferre"', pp. 209–18.

[85] Sir Simon Felbrigg; Thomas, Lord Morley; John Reymes. J. D. Milner, 'Sir Simon Felbrigg KG: The Lancastrian Revolution and Personal Fortune', *Norfolk Archaeology*, 37 (1978), p. 85; *CPR, 1396–9*, pp. 525, 538, 545; *HPC, 1386–1421*, IV, p. 203. Significantly more testators may well have served on these expeditions. However, the records are sufficiently patchy that the names of very few have been recovered. Biggs, *Three Armies*, pp. 65–71. Certainly, those with strong Ricardian connections would likely have undertaken at least one of these expeditions. C. Given-Wilson, *The Royal Household and the King's Affinity: Service, Politics and Finance in England, 1360–1413* (New Haven, 1986), pp. 282–6.

[86] Hugh Coton; Arthur Davenport; Sir William Legh; John Maynwaryng; Robert Toft; Richard Vernon. E 101/42/10, mm. 1, 3d. See also, Biggs, *Three Armies*, pp. 73–6.

[87] Bell et al., *The Soldier*, pp. 169–70; Morgan, *War and Society in Medieval Cheshire*, pp. 215–17.

[88] Geoffrey Boidell; Sir Simon Felbrigg; Sir Edward Hastings; Sir William Legh; John Massy; John Payn; William Plumstead; Sir Ralph Shelton; Robert Toft; Richard Vernon. E 101/41/1, mm. 1, 38, 50; E 101/42/16, mm. 13, 37d; E 101/42/29, m. 1; E 101/43/4, m. 26.

than was ever the case during the Hundred Years War's second phase. A significant body of Grosvenor supporters remained active in the Crown's ongoing struggles with the Irish, Scots and Welsh, or became involved in the internecine bloodshed of the early years of Lancastrian rule.[89] By contrast, Hastings' East Anglian deponents saw virtually no military action beyond the occasional stand-alone expeditions launched by Richard II and Henry IV.[90]

Additionally, the fact that the Truce of Leulinghem lasted 26 years would have made it far less likely that Grosvenor's and Hastings' surviving militarily active deponents – men largely born between the mid 1340s and mid 1360s – would still have been fit to return to arms under Henry V in 1415.[91] And this certainly proved to be the case. Unsurprisingly, none of the Grosvenor witnesses who recalled the Gascony campaign of 1369 were on the field at Agincourt, whilst, such was the passage of time, that even Grosvenor's younger deponents failed to return to the fray.[92] Amongst Hastings' East Anglian contingent, whose depositions had been provided as recently as 1408–9, only two men – the distinguished Norfolk Garter Knights, Sir Thomas Erpingham and Sir Simon Felbrigg – without a doubt were present at the battle of Agincourt.[93] The experience of such trusty old hands would have proven invaluable to the English cause. Certainly, we know that Erpingham – then 60 years of age, with over four decades of military service beneath his belt – was assigned a crucial

---

[89] Morgan, *War and Society in Medieval Cheshire*, pp. 185–208; Bennett, *Community, Class and Careerism*, pp. 162–91.

[90] Aside from the above East Anglian contributions to the Irish and Scottish campaigns of the era, the Hastings' witnesses, Sir Thomas Hengrave and Hamo Claxton, undertook military service beneath the command of Thomas, Duke of Clarence, respectively in 1406 and 1412. C 76/95, m. 8; C 76/90, m. 18. On Clarence's French expedition of 1412–13, see J. D. Milner, 'The English Enterprise in France, 1412–13', in *Trade, Devotion and Governance: Papers in Later Medieval History*, ed. D. J. Clayton, R. G. Davies and P. McNiven (Gloucester, 1994), pp. 80–101.

[91] Sumption, *The Hundred Years War III*, pp. 774–833.

[92] Sir John Assheton; Sir Hugh Browe; Arthur Davenport; Thomas Davenport; Sir Owen Glyn Dwr; John Hanmere; Sir John Massy of Puddington; John Maynwaryng; Sir Ralph Vernon. *Scrope v. Grosvenor*, I, pp. 275–6; 256–7; 271–2; 263; 255; 259; 274; 271. Assheton, Browe and Massy had all died in the intervening years. Of the rest, only Thomas Davenport and John Hanmere, who would have been in their mid-fifties in 1415, could have potentially participated. The others, if still alive, were in their seventies and eighties.

[93] E 101/45/3, m. 1.

role, according to the French chroniclers, in the drawing up of the English battle formation and in the leadership of the iconic archers.[94] Notwithstanding the presence at Agincourt of such older men, if our broader sample of Grosvenor and Hastings witnesses provide any sort of indication, it is clear that the vast majority of Henry V's gentry participants in 1415 were getting their first taste of combat on French soil, yet were not necessarily lacking in military experience, having (especially amongst the gentry of the Northwest) honed their fighting skills within the British Isles over the previous two decades.

Royal expectations that the gentry would serve their king in his wars, active Crown-driven strategies designed to maximise gentry participation, and the gentry's own family traditions of military service, collectively explain why so many (especially younger) gentry answered the royal call to arms in 1415.[95] This high level of commitment is borne out within the ranks of our Court of Chivalry witnesses. More than half of those who deposed for Sir Robert Grosvenor – 22 of 38 men – had identifiable descendants who participated on the Agincourt campaign. These ranged from eldest sons taking up the mantle of their fathers and grandfathers – like the heirs of the Dutton, Massy and Legh families[96] – to a host of cadets, including numerous scions of great Cheshire families who served as archers.[97] The same was true of Sir Edward Hastings' deponents, where 24 (of 39) militarily active

---

[94] Curry, 'Sir Thomas Erpingham', pp. 71–3.

[95] On gentry participation in 1415, see Curry, *Agincourt: A New History* (Gloucester, 2005), pp. 58–68. See also, www.agincourt600.com. The Agincourt expeditionary force was the largest English army sent to France since Edward III's expedition in 1359–60. The English army at Agincourt may have been as large as 9,000 men, whilst the army of 1359-60 that marched upon Rheims enjoyed an approximate strength of 10,000 men. Curry, *Agincourt*, p. 192; Ayton, *Knights and Warhorses*, p. 10. For an example of a royal initiative designed to maximise gentry military service, see a discussion of the pressure brought to bear upon royal and ducal annuitants to fulfil their military obligations, especially when the king himself was leading an expedition. Curry et al., 'New Regime, New Army?', p. 1390. On the longer-term origins of the gentry's family traditions of military service, see D. Simpkin, *The English Aristocracy at War, from the Welsh Wars of Edward I to the Battle of Bannockburn* (Woodbridge, 2008).

[96] Laurence Dutton; William Dutton; John Massy; Nicholas Massy; Sir William Legh. E 101/45/18, m. 2; E 101/45/7, m. 1; BL, MS Harley 782 f. 84; E 101/46/24, m. 4; E 101/44/30/no3, m. 1.

[97] E.g., John, Nicholas and William Dutton and Emond, John and William Danyell. E 101/45/13, mm. 1, 3, 4; E 101/45/7, m. 1; E 101/46/36, m. 2.

witnesses could count descendants who were members of the Agincourt army, including sons of nine of Hastings' 17 knightly supporters.[98]

Most of these families had been armed in the king's wars since the 1330s or 1340s, if not since the reign of Edward I, and were thus entering at least their fourth consecutive generation of military commitment.[99] The Hemenhales of Norfolk may stand for the rest. Sir John Hemenhale (c.1292–1347) was already a middle-aged man when the Hundred Years War began in 1337.[100] He nonetheless campaigned at least three times during the war's first seven years.[101] His son, Ralph (c.1317–1382), followed in his father's footsteps from a young age, serving on at least five expeditions and participating at the battle of Crécy (1346).[102] Ralph's sons upheld their family's wartime commitment during the 1370s and 1380s, including the young, and relatively obscure, David Hemenhale, who described before the Court his campaigning experiences in Brittany and Scotland, as well as at the siege of St. Malo (1378).[103] Consequently, when David's nephew, Robert, joined Henry V's army in 1415, he was following a very long family military tradition indeed.[104] The close ties enjoyed by both the Northwestern and East Anglian gentry with Henry V were undoubtedly strong contributing factors in facilitating this high degree of commitment, yet neither proved a regional anomaly. At least 95 descendants of Scrope and Morley testators were likewise present on the Agincourt expedition, and these men were drawn from a much wider pool of gentry, in Scrope's case spread liberally throughout the northern shires, with contingents from the West Country, the Midlands, and East Anglia, and in Morley's case encompassing a much broader cross-section of the gentry of the eastern counties than Sir

---

[98] E 101/45/13, m. 2; E 101/44/30/no3, m. 3; E 101/45/3, m. 1; E 101/45/4, m. 2; E 101/47/1, m. 1; Curry, *Agincourt: A New History*, pp. 282–6.

[99] Simpkin, *The English Aristocracy at War*; Ayton, 'Edward III and the English Aristocracy', pp. 173–206.

[100] Blomefield, *History of Norfolk*, III, pp. 121–2.

[101] C 76/14, m. 11; C 76/15, m. 20; C 76/19, m. 19.

[102] *Treaty Rolls Preserved in the Public Record Office. Volume 2: 1337–39*, ed. J. Ferguson (London, 1972), p. 319; C 76/14, m. 3; C 76/15, m. 32; C 76/17, m. 26; *Crecy and Calais from the Original Records in the Public Record Office*, ed. G. Wrottesley (London, 1898), p. 96; C 76/38, m. 17.

[103] *PCM*, I, pp. 458–64. David's contemporaries, Sir Robert and Ralph, also bore arms during these years. E 101/36/39, m. 5; E 101/40/33, m. 15.

[104] E 101/46/16, m. 1.

Edward Hastings could muster.[105] In total, then, at least 141 members of the Agincourt expeditionary force in 1415 were the descendants of militarily active nobles, knights and esquires, who had provided vignettes of their military careers in the Hundred Years War's first two phases before the Court of Chivalry.[106]

Interestingly, too, it appears that the traditional recruitment networks of the localities, much-studied in a fourteenth-century context,[107] remained important sources of manpower and were actively mobilised for the Agincourt expedition.[108] The retinue composition of our two renowned Agincourt veterans from *Grey v. Hastings*, Sir Simon Felbrigg and Sir Thomas Erpingham, neatly underscore the point. Felbrigg had been one of the few Norfolk gentry intimately tied to the Ricardian Court in its later years. He had risen high in Richard II's household, becoming the royal standard-bearer and accompanying his sovereign to Ireland. Despite this, Felbrigg's lifelong friendship with Erpingham, who was his neighbour in northeast Norfolk, appears to have shielded him from a significant fall from grace. In 1398, Erpingham – a long-time Lancastrian retainer – had accompanied Henry of Bolingbroke into exile and Felbrigg had acted as one of the caretakers of Sir Thomas' estates. When the tables were turned the following year, Erpingham repaid the favour and Felbrigg was integrated into Norfolk's new governing circle remarkably quickly for a man who had been on the wrong side of a dynastic overthrow.[109]

---

[105] *Scrope v. Grosvenor*; C 47/6/1.

[106] This figure is drawn from those families who provided war-related testimony on behalf of Scrope, Grosvenor, Morley and Hastings. *Scrope v. Grosvenor*; C 47/6/1; *PCM*.

[107] A. Goodman, 'The Military Subcontracts of Sir Hugh Hastings, 1380', *EHR*, 95 (1980), pp. 114–20; S. K. Walker, 'Profit and Loss in the Hundred Years War: The Subcontract of Sir John Strother, 1374', *BIHR*, 58 (1985), pp. 100–6; Morgan, *War and Society in Medieval Cheshire*, pp. 150–4; A. Ayton, 'Sir Thomas Ughtred and the Edwardian Military Revolution', in *The Age of Edward III*, ed. J. S. Bothwell (York, 2001), pp. 122–5.

[108] On the degree of continuity and change at an institutional level within late medieval English armies, see Ayton, 'English Armies in the Fourteenth Century', pp. 303–19; A. Curry, 'English Armies in the Fifteenth Century', in *Arms, Armies and Fortifications in the Hundred Years War*, ed. A. Curry and M. Hughes (Woodbridge, 1994), pp. 39–68; Bell et al., *The Soldier*.

[109] Castor, *The King, the Crown, and the Duchy of Lancaster*, p. 67; *CFR, 1422–30*, p. 130; C 139/23/31.

Felbrigg attended Henry V in 1415 accompanied by thirteen men-at-arms.[110] Nine were fellow Norfolk men, including three young men – John Reymes II, Oliver Shelton and Robert White – whose fathers had all spoken alongside him and Erpingham in Sir Edward Hastings' defence and who had all grown up as his neighbours in northeast Norfolk. Felbrigg had engaged in the private affairs of his recruits' fathers, and together they collectively enjoyed shared campaigning memories, political authority, and business ties dating back to the 1380s.[111] Felbrigg was, in short, heading to war with the sons of several of his oldest and closest friends and associates in his train.[112]

The composition of Sir Thomas Erpingham's military retinue points in the same direction. He had spoken on behalf of both Scrope and Hastings, on the former occasion providing evidence at Plymouth prior to embarking with John of Gaunt for Spain (continuing the family connection before the Court, his paternal uncle, William, spoke for Lord Morley the following year).[113] Erpingham's life, however, had undergone a sea change between his two appearances before the Court. In the 1380s, he was merely a young knight in the Lancastrian military retinue. By the time he spoke for Sir Edward Hastings, he was the pre-eminent figure in his native Norfolk, providing a physical link between shire and Crown, where he sat on the king's council and acted as steward of the royal household.[114] Erpingham indented to serve on the Agincourt campaign with 20 men-at-arms (he ended up serving with 23 men). Only one was a knight, but that knight was the son and heir of his fellow testator, Sir Alexander Goldingham,[115] and, when constructing his retinue, Erpingham, like Felbrigg, engaged the services of the children of some of his oldest friends and associates. Beyond Goldingham, his young military followers included the sons

[110] Felbrigg indented to serve with 12 men-at-arms and 36 archers, though he ended up mustering with 13 men-at-arms. Milner, 'Sir Simon Felbrigg KG', p. 88. For his retinue in 1415, see E 101/45/3, m. 1

[111] E 101/45/3, m. 1; Walker, *The Lancastrian Affinity*, pp. 270, 279, 284; *PCM*, I, pp. 423–4, 443–4; *Testamenta Vetusta*, ed. Sir N. H. Nicolas (London, 1826), I, pp. 245–6; *HPC, 1386–1421*, III, p. 251, IV, p. 830; Castor, *The King, the Crown, and the Duchy of Lancaster*, pp. 59, 62–3.

[112] For a fuller discussion of East Anglian inter-gentry solidarities, see pp. 114–30.

[113] On Scrope's East Anglian support base, see Caudrey, 'War, Chivalry and Regional Society', pp. 120, 129-30. For William Erpingham's testimony, see C 47/6/1, no. 39.

[114] Castor, *The King, the Crown, and the Duchy of Lancaster*, pp. 64–81.

[115] E 101/44/30/no3, m. 3; *Scrope v. Grosvenor*, I, p. 70; II, pp. 227-9.

of Sir John Geney, Sir William Calthorp, Sir John Strange and William Bressingham.[116] Each of these families had enjoyed private connections with Erpingham in peace and, as their testimony before the Court of Chivalry revealed, had, like him, contributed to the campaigns of the 1370s and 1380s, sometimes in his direct company.[117]

Two lessons may be drawn from Felbrigg's and Erpingham's military ties in 1415. Firstly, the well-worn local recruitment networks of the fourteenth century remained largely intact at this stage. Felbrigg and Erpingham – although viewed here through the prism of the Court of Chivalry – acquired their gentry participants by utilising local bonds of kinship, friendship and association in much the same fashion as the Yorkshire man Sir Thomas Ughtred in the 1340s,[118] the Cheshire man Sir Ralph Mobberley in the 1350s,[119] or the Northumbrian Sir John Strother in the 1370s.[120] Secondly, if our small sample of 141 Court of Chivalry descendants provide any sort of indication, the strong family military traditions of the English gentry – much discussed by historians in a fourteenth-century context[121] – remained alive and well in 1415, even if relatively few men with direct experience fighting in France had personally survived the quarter-century of peace to return to arms under Henry V.

This section has addressed the patterns of military service undertaken by Sir Robert Grosvenor's and Sir Edward Hastings' testators before the Court of Chivalry and has more broadly considered their war records in the context of family military commitments. Yet, war making, from a personal standpoint, is ultimately a qualitative experience and if one pauses to look more closely at the careers in arms of a select few individual deponents, it becomes apparent how far removed their war records – as bland statements of participation – were from their overall military experiences. What motivated these gentry to bear arms

---

[116] Three of these young men, Thomas Geney, John Calthorp and Hamo Strange, were knighted on the campaign. Leonard Strange and Reynold Bressingham served Erpingham as men-at-arms. E 101/44/30 no3, m. 3; Bell et al., *The Soldier*, pp. 108–9.

[117] *Scrope v. Grosvenor*, II, p. 220; *PCM*, I, p. 425; C 76/98, m. 12; *HPC, 1386-1421*, II, pp. 719-20, IV, pp. 500-2; Curry, 'Sir Thomas Erpingham', p. 77.

[118] Ayton, 'Sir Thomas Ughtred', pp. 122–5.

[119] Morgan, *War and Society in Medieval Cheshire*, pp. 150–4.

[120] Walker, 'Profit and Loss', pp. 100–6.

[121] Simpkin, *The English Aristocracy at War*; Ayton, 'Edward III and the English Aristocracy', pp. 173–206.

and what role soldiering played in their wider careers is the subject to which we shall now turn.

Knights, Esquires and Gentlemen: Contextualising Military Careerism

One of the chief difficulties when assessing the military careerism of the fourteenth-century English gentry – whether knights, esquires or gentlemen – is that they were members of a heavily militarised society, yet were not military professionals in the modern sense of the term.[122] Although an armigerous soldier would be recognised in battle by his coat-of-arms, this was merely an individual marker of identification, inextricably linked to his personal and family honour.[123] Similarly, armies were recruited in piecemeal fashion via indentures made between combatants and the Crown, and although there was a strong element of national oversight (such as pay accounts and muster reviews to check for absentees), each captain was ultimately responsible for the attendance, arms and accouterment of his men, whether he be an esquire with a handful of followers, or a magnate with hundreds of gentry and ordinary soldiers in his train.[124] Moreover, military commitments were invariably short-term, usually six months or one year, only occasionally longer. Even soldiers who served on a continuous basis had to regularly re-contract and potentially move to a new theatre whenever military employment dried up in their previous location.[125]

---

[122] D. J. B. Trim, 'Introduction', in *The Chivalric Ethos and the Development of Military Professionalism*, ed. D. J. B. Trim (Boston, 2003), pp. 1–38; A. King, 'The English Gentry and Military Service, 1300–1450', *History Compass*, 12 (2014), pp. 759–69; Ayton, 'The Military Careerist', pp. 4–23.

[123] Jones, *Bloodied Banners*, pp. 20–1.

[124] Ayton, 'English Armies in the Fourteenth Century', pp. 303–19; Curry, 'English Armies in the Fifteenth Century', pp. 39–68. On the complexities of the varying relationships between captains and those who indented to serve with them, see Goodman, 'The Military Subcontracts of Sir Hugh Hastings', pp. 114–20; Walker, 'Profit and Loss', pp. 100–6; Morgan, *War and Society in Medieval Cheshire*, pp. 150–4; Ayton, 'Sir Thomas Ughtred', pp. 122–5.

[125] J. C. Bridge, 'Two Cheshire Soldiers of Fortune: Sir Hugh Calveley and Sir Robert Knolles', *JCAS*, 14 (1908), pp. 112–231; S. K. Walker, 'Janico Dartasso: Chivalry, Nationality and the Man-At-Arms', *History*, 84 (1999), pp. 31–51; Ayton, 'Nicholas Sabraham', pp. 75–120.

All of this smacks readily of a lack of professionalisation.[126] Yet, medieval armies – as is apparent before the Court of Chivalry – were stocked with military professionals: men of all ranks who knew well how to wield their weapons and behave courageously and responsibly in skirmish, siege and battle.[127] The surviving records of English-held garrisons, for example, reveal significant numbers of soldiers who evidently made war their full-time vocation and sought to live from its wages and profits.[128] Amongst the medieval gentry at large, however, assessing motivation is complicated by the fact that military service was, to a significant degree, the *raison d'être* of the knightly class, whose values spread downward into the squirearchy over the course of the fourteenth century.[129] The term 'socio-professionals' has been coined to describe military participants of this stamp: those 'who served as a by-product of their social status',[130] and to distinguish them from that other sort of gentry soldier, who undertook a military career on a full-time basis as his primary means of income and subsistence. Before the Court of Chivalry, we encounter both types of gentry soldiers, with plenty of wriggle room in between. Even limiting our discussion to these neat brackets, knights, esquires and gentlemen remained permanently subject to royal policy and the military needs of the Crown, whilst bearing arms for a variety of very specific and usually highly personal reasons. This is what needs to be teased out from their testimony, because categorising deponents by the length, breadth or intensity of their careers in arms can only tell us so much. It obscures the personal incentives and external pressures that drove them to serve, as well as masking the ways in which military service fitted into their wider lives and shaped their overall career trajectories. This may best be illustrated through a handful of case studies of individual deponents,

---

[126] From the perspective of most early modernists, the professionalisation of military society in Europe took place between c. 1470 and c. 1620. Trim, 'Introduction', pp. 14–23.

[127] Prestwich, *Armies and Warfare*, pp. 334–46.

[128] On the composition and organisation of a medieval garrison, as well as a discussion relating to the professionalisation of garrison service, see D. Grummitt, *The Calais Garrison: War and Military Service in England, 1436–1558* (Woodbridge, 2008), pp. 44–118. See also, A. Curry, 'Military Organization in Lancastrian Normandy 1422–1450', 2 vols. (PhD thesis, CNAA, Teesside Polytechnic, 1985); Cornell, 'Northern Castle Garrisons'.

[129] Keen, *Origins of the English Gentleman*, pp. 71–86. Bell et al., *The Soldier*, pp. 95–138.

[130] Bell et al., *The Soldier*, p. 20.

whose war records appear superficially similar, yet whose paths to a successful career in arms were anything but homogenous.

A good starting point might be to begin with the testimony of the distinguished West Country baron, Guy, Lord Brian, whose deposition on behalf of Richard, Lord Scrope, incidentally underscores the perils of relying upon the Court of Chivalry material in isolation.[131] Brian told the Court that he was over 60 years of age and had first been armed at Stanhope Park (1327). He deposed that he had seen Geoffrey Scrope (uncle of the plaintiff) bearing the disputed arms with a label at the battle of Buironfosse and at Ourney St. Benoit in Flanders (1339); that he had seen Geoffrey's son, Henry, subsequently armed with the same arms, though he did not specify where; and that he had later seen the plaintiff, Lord Richard, bearing the disputed arms with the Duke of Lancaster in the Pays-de-Caux (1369). Were Brian an obscure esquire, known only from this thumbnail career profile, his overall war record would doubtless be open to intense speculation, for his testimony detailed four decades in arms, yet mentioned only three expeditions. Fortunately, Brian was one of the more distinguished figures of his generation, whose complete military record is both easily traceable and thoroughly impressive. Beyond the three expeditions he mentioned, he additionally served in Scotland in 1356 and 1370, in France in 1359–60, in Brittany in 1375, and in Ireland in 1380.[132] Although he missed most of the picture-book *chevauchées* of the high Edwardian age, this was merely the result of being preoccupied with military and diplomatic duties elsewhere. By July 1330, he had become an esquire of the royal household, and later the royal standard-bearer, in which capacity he served King Edward at the siege of Calais in 1347. He was additionally appointed governor of St. Briavel's Castle in Gloucestershire, and spent much of the 1350s engaged in high level diplomacy in Flanders and Scotland, later serving as steward of the royal household between 1359 and 1361.[133] He was also consistently active in the war at sea, leading naval expeditions as Admiral toward the West in 1370 and 1371, mustering for Edward III's abortive campaign of 1372, and last

---

[131] *Scrope v. Grosvenor*, I, pp. 76–7; II, pp. 245–55.

[132] *Scrope v. Grosvenor*, II, pp. 245–50.

[133] E 101/398/14; Rickard, *The Castle Community*, pp. 222–4; *CPR, 1358–61*, p. 47; *CPR, 1361–4*, p. 18; *CPR, 1370–4*, pp. 34, 61; *CCR, 1369-74*, pp. 216–17, 226; E 101/393/11, f. 76.

seeing service in Ireland in 1380 at the age of 70 years.[134] His martial reputation and track record of loyal service to King Edward was rewarded with election to the Order of the Garter in 1369.[135]

Part of what makes Brian's career so fascinating is that he engaged in all types of military service. He (nominally at least) held a garrison post and served at sea, as well as on shorter land expeditions; he participated in both siege and battle; and he campaigned in three different military theatres over a career in arms that lasted fifty-two years. At the heart of it all, however, lay a lifetime of service to the Crown – specifically to Edward III – as Brian worked his way up from esquire to standard-bearer to steward of the royal household, received grants, annuities and offices from his sovereign, and was entrusted with diplomatic missions on Edward's behalf. Brian was undoubtedly a fine exemplar of a 'socio-professional' soldier as defined above, in so far as his regular bouts of campaigning may best be understood as one of many functions he performed in the service of his sovereign.[136]

The war record of another Scrope deponent, the Norfolk knight, Sir Stephen Hales, highlights the ways in which superficially similar careers could arise from markedly different origins.[137] By the early 1380s, both Hales and Brian were members of the young Richard II's household,[138] yet the paths they had traversed to reach this ascent had been anything but similar. In these years, Brian was holding a largely inactive (one might even say emeritus) position within the household he had served near-continuously for over half a century.[139] Hales, by contrast, was one of a number of Richard's knights who had made his career in the service of the king's late father, Edward, the Black Prince.[140] And it had all begun in the wars with France. For Hales,

[134] E 101/30/21, m. 1 (1370); E 101/31/11, no. 2 m. 1 (1371); E 101/32/16, m. 1 (1372). For Brian's service in Ireland, see *Scrope v. Grosvenor*, II, p. 249.

[135] H. E. L. Collins, *The Order of the Garter 1348–1461: Chivalry and Politics in Late Medieval England* (Oxford, 2000), p. 290.

[136] Though beholden to Edward III, Brian appears to have been a man of independent character. He twice disagreed with King Edward over questions of ecclesiastical patronage during the 1360s and, notwithstanding his sovereign's ongoing favour, he increasingly detached himself from the royal court amidst the turmoil of the 1370s. Given-Wilson, *The Royal Household*, pp. 156–7.

[137] *Scrope v. Grosvenor*, I, p. 163; II, pp. 369–70.

[138] Given-Wilson, *The Royal Household*, pp. 282, 285.

[139] Given-Wilson, *The Royal Household*, pp. 156–8, 162.

[140] Given-Wilson, *The Royal Household*, pp. 280–6.

military service enabled him to escape the obscurity of lesser gentry life in west Norfolk. After making his military debut as a teenager at the sea-battle of Winchelsea in 1350, he soon found his way into the Prince's military retinue and remained heavily involved in his campaigns over the next 20 years. He appears to have been largely absent from Norfolk throughout this period, and we know that he served, at the very least, on the Gascony campaigns of 1355–7, the Rheims expedition of 1359–60, and the Spanish enterprise of 1366–7, culminating in the battle of Nájera, and he was probably in Aquitaine with the Prince for much of the early 1360s.[141] Although he served in France one last time in 1369,[142] his impressive career in arms effectively came to a close with the Prince's retirement from the field in poor health in the early 1370s. And it was at this point that Hales – entering his forties and now knighted with powerful friends and a 100-mark annuity from the Prince[143] – re-entered the world of Norfolk county society with gusto, becoming the shire's most active administrator of the 1370s and 1380s. He represented Norfolk in nine Parliaments in as many years, was appointed sheriff in 1377, and sat on an impressive 26 local commissions, acting in his time as a J.P., a commissioner of array and *oyer* and *terminer*, and as one of the more zealous prosecutors of the perpetrators of the Peasants' Revolt of 1381.[144] Hales' position in the household of the young Richard II reflected the boy-king's early reliance upon his father's old retainers and it was in this capacity that Hales saddled up one last time in 1385 for the royally-led Scottish expedition on which he saw Lord Scrope bearing the disputed arms.[145]

The parallels between Hales' and Brian's careers are readily apparent. Although Brian undeniably maintained a leading presence in his native Dorset,[146] it was through his court connections that he attained his lofty position in English society, and his bouts of military service were consequently undertaken merely at steady intervals over the course of his entire adult life. Hales, meanwhile – a man of comparatively humble origins – built his career with sword in hand, yet was fortunate enough to find steady military employment with the Black Prince, whose near

[141] *Scrope v. Grosvenor*, I, p. 163; II, pp. 369–70; H. J. Hewitt, *The Black Prince's Expedition 1355–1357* (Manchester, 1958), p. 204.
[142] *Scrope v. Grosvenor*, I, p. 163; II, pp. 369–70.
[143] *CPR, 1377–81*, p. 413.
[144] *HPC, 1386–1421*, III, p. 267.
[145] Given-Wilson, *The Royal Household*, pp. 280–6; *Scrope v. Grosvenor*, I, p. 163.
[146] See below, pp. 113–14.

constant mobilisation of his military retinue during the 1350s and 1360s indirectly turned Hales (and most middling and lesser gentry in the Prince's retinue) into near full-time soldiers. Once the Prince was no longer fighting, Hales returned to Norfolk and openly milked his martial reputation, princely annuity, knightly rank, and friends in high places, to reinforce his newly-acquired status as a member of Norfolk's county élite by serving energetically in shire administration. Both men carved out war records of impressive length. Yet, whilst Brian intertwined military service with his domestic/administrative responsibilities, for Sir Stephen Hales, political achievement was the pay-off for a youth spent in arms.

If Brian and Hales were contrasting figures with superficially similar war records, the shades of grey that coloured the gentry soldier's military experience become greyer still the deeper one penetrates the individual careers of those who gave evidence before the Court. The career in arms of another East Anglian, Sir William Berdewell – who spoke, a generation apart, on behalf of Thomas, Lord Morley and Sir Edward Hastings – underscores these complexities.[147] Berdewell was a cadet of a family that hailed from near Bury St. Edmunds in Suffolk, and with few prospects to his name he appears to have turned to war as his full-time vocation, much in the style of the young Stephen Hales.[148] Yet, whilst Hales found his way into the Black Prince's retinue, which granted him steady military employment and eventual long-term reward, Berdewell became the type of middling gentry career soldier who moved from one retinue to the next, undertaking a nomadic lifestyle in which he was rarely out of arms. Between 1378 and 1387, he served on seven identifiable expeditions in nine years. He campaigned under Robert, Lord Willoughby in John of Gaunt's force that besieged St. Malo in 1378, was on Sir John Arundel's ill-fated voyage the following year, and served in Brittany in 1380 in the force commanded by the Earl of Buckingham.[149] In 1383 he was retained by the Norfolk baron, John, Lord Clifton, to serve, with a small retinue of his own, on the Bishop of Norwich's disastrous Flemish Crusade.[150] Two years later, he was part of the enormous army that accompanied Richard II into Scotland. The year after that, he joined John of Gaunt's expedition to

---

[147] C 47/6/1, no. 93; *PCM*, I, pp. 390–2.
[148] Blomefield, *History of Norfolk*, I, pp. 253, 298–302, 427.
[149] *PCM*, I, pp. 390–2; E 101/39/7, no. 1 m. 1.
[150] *HPC, 1386–1421*, II, p. 125.

Spain. And in 1387 he was contracted to serve with a handful of men under Thomas, Lord Camoys in the fleet commanded by the Earl of Arundel.[151]

Berdewell's war record contains all the hallmarks of the 'landless younger son' who turned to soldiering for the sake of income and served wherever he could under whichever commander would take him.[152] Around 1388, however, his fortunes took a sudden and dramatic turn for the better, when a succession of male relatives passed away, making him almost overnight the head of his family's senior branch and a significant East Anglian landowner.[153] As such, just shy of his thirtieth birthday, after a decade of near continuous soldiering, Berdewell settled down into the sedentary life of a substantial country gentleman, acting thereafter as an MP, J.P., commissioner of array and tax collector in his native Suffolk.[154] He simultaneously became an active player in the East Anglian land market, gradually expanding his holdings through marriage and purchase, whilst developing close ties not only with his fellow East Anglian gentry, but also with Michael de la Pole, Earl of Suffolk, who granted him an annuity of £20.[155]

Had Berdewell not fortuitously inherited his family's fortune in his late twenties, his track record up to that point suggests that he would have continued serving in whichever military theatres were available. His acquisition of his family's inheritance, in fact, could not have come at a better time, for it coincided with the truce years between the Hundred Years War's second and third phases, when opportunities for gainful military employment became comparatively scarce. The fact that he never bore arms again might lead one to suspect that his military career had represented a last resort for a young gentleman of meager means, which he readily abandoned when given the chance. Yet, upon his death in 1434, he left to his surviving son, Robert, a wide array of mementoes from his days in the saddle: his basilard, all of his gilt armour, and his best girdle, whilst his sword hung on the north wall of Berdewell Church for centuries after his death.[156] Berdewell began

---

[151] C 47/6/1; *PCM*, I, pp. 390–2; E 101/41/5, m. 7.

[152] On this type of soldiering, see Bell et al., *The Soldier*, pp. 117–25, 167–77. A useful discussion of 'military careerism', with a regional focus upon Cheshire, is provided in, Bennett, *Community, Class and Careerism*, pp. 162–91.

[153] Blomefield, *History of Norfolk*, I, pp. 298–302.

[154] *HPC, 1386–1421*, I, p. 125.

[155] Blomefield, *History of Norfolk*, I, p. 301; BL, Add. Ch. 15537; JUST 1/1516 m. 3d.

[156] SRO (Bury St. Edmunds), Reg. Osbern, ff. 211–12; *HPC, 1386–1421*, I, p. 127.

his adult life seeking to live from the wages and profits of war, yet he simultaneously hailed from that very genteel background in which young men 'served as a by-product of their social status'.[157] Unlike his senior relatives, he did not enjoy the luxury of serving intermittently in the king's wars for the twin purposes of social networking and shoring up his chivalric reputation. Yet, his actions upon his death bespeak those of a man thoroughly imbued with the culture of soldiering for these very reasons. Berdewell, one may surmise, did not turn his back on the martial vocation the moment he acquired his inheritance. He now no longer needed to make a living from war, but one may fairly posit that had the Hundred Years War's second phase continued throughout the 1390s and 1400s, Berdewell would have gone on bearing arms, now on an intermittent basis, in between engaging in those domestic affairs that came to characterise his later career.[158]

It is worth noting that both Berdewell and Sir Stephen Hales began their careers in arms as mere esquires with minimal landed wealth before their promotions into the knightly class. Before the Court of Chivalry, the testimony of dozens of other highly militarily active esquires and gentlemen, who never rose to Hales' or Berdewell's heights, have provided historians with a fascinating glimpse into the careers of England's lesser gentry military community.[159] Despite the fact that such men survive only sporadically in other types of military records, and were distinctly a step or two down the social ladder from the knightly élite, their testimony, when assessed on an individual basis, makes plain that their priorities were not necessarily all that different from the knightly class above them.

Like their knightly contemporaries, one encounters amongst these esquires and gentlemen men who had forged careers in arms rooted in personal circumstance. On the one hand, there were soldiers like the Yorkshire esquire, John Rither, who described a military record stretching from the battle of Buironfosse in 1339 to the Gascony expedition in 1369. Over these three decades, Rither fought at the battles of Sluys (1340), Morlaix (1342) and Crécy (1346), and the sieges of Tournai (1340) and Rennes (1356–7), as well as serving in Scotland and Ireland, campaigning in Spain, where he participated at the

[157] Bell et al., *The Soldier*, p. 20.
[158] On the impact of royal policy in shaping military opportunities, see J. N. N. Palmer, *England, France and Christendom, 1377–99* (London, 1972).
[159] On sub-knightly military participants more generally, see Bell et al., *The Soldier*, pp. 95–215.

battle of Najéra (1367), and undertaking a *Reise* into Prussia in the early 1360s, which brought him to the siege of Wellon in Lithuania.[160] Rither appears very much the quintessential career professional who moved from one retinue to the next in the style of the young William Berdewell, and likely developed into the type of experienced lieutenant so valued by bannerets and knights who served intermittently with comparatively small personal retinues.[161] Where a man like Rither differed from Berdewell was in his lack of substance – material and social – beyond the military sphere. Rither, by his old age in the 1380s, was undoubtedly well known to the gentry of his native Yorkshire for his numerous feats of arms.[162] Over the years, he would have proven a valuable recruit for their retinues, for he would presumably have enjoyed access to recruiting networks of his own amongst his fellow career soldiers.[163] Yet, he was not a man of any political significance or domestic standing. He never worked in shire administration. He was never knighted. And we know precious little about his non-military career.[164] One should be wary, however, of simply linking the shape of Rither's career in arms directly to his station as a parish-level notable, for other testators, born into the same social milieu, ended up carving out equally lengthy careers in arms, but in very different fashion.

[160] *Scrope v. Grosvenor*, I, pp. 144–50; II, pp. 351–4.

[161] E.g., See the vital role played by the obscure man-at-arms, Jankyn Nowell, in the retinue of Sir Hugh Hastings III in Brittany in 1380. Nowell personally provided one-twelfth of Hastings' retinue and was paid a slightly higher wage. Goodman, 'The Military Subcontracts of Sir Hugh Hastings', pp. 116–17. On Nowell's career, see Fowler, *Medieval Mercenaries*, pp. 20–1; Bell et al., *The Soldier*, pp. 130–1.

[162] Richard, Lord Scrope specifically requested that Rither be allowed, on account of his age, to provide his deposition at his home in Scarborough, since he was too infirm to make the trip to York. One may infer from this that Scrope was well aware of Rither's martial record and was determined to secure his potentially valuable testimony, regardless of the inconvenience. Nicolas, 'The Scrope and Grosvenor Controversy', pp. 389, 392.

[163] Walker, 'Profit and Loss', p. 104.

[164] Sir Harris Nicolas' biography of Rither simply states: 'He was probably a younger branch of the ancient family of Rither near Selby in Yorkshire, but he has not been identified; nor can any thing be said with certainty respecting his marriage or descendants'. *Scrope v. Grosvenor*, II, p. 352. A John Rither did hold an annuity from John of Gaunt between 1361 and 1394. This may have been the same man (and could account for his presence on Scrope's behalf), but may just as likely have been his son, or some other near kinsman. Walker, *The Lancastrian Affinity*, p. 279.

Rither's contemporary, William Thweyt – a younger son from a minor Norfolk family – provides just such a contrast.[165] Thweyt campaigned extensively under the Ufford earls of Suffolk and their kin in Scotland and France during the 1330s and early 1340s.[166] Amidst these numerous military ventures, however, he found steady employment and a regular wage as Sir Ralph Ufford's deputy constable at Corfe Castle in Dorset, and not long thereafter as the marshal of Ufford's forces in Ireland.[167] Thweyt disappears entirely from the records of the 1350s and 1360s, re-emerging only on the Gascony expedition of 1369 when he was in late middle age. This has led Andrew Ayton to speculate that Thweyt may have spent these years fighting as a mercenary in France or Italy, and it is entirely possible that he did just that.[168] Equally, he may very well have spent these years serving quietly in a garrison somewhere in English-held territory, whose records have not survived, or he may even have returned home to his obscure life as a member of Norfolk's parish gentry, sufficiently far enough down the social ladder that no record of his domestic activities have been recovered. Although Rither and Thweyt were men of similar rank, who enjoyed broadly conterminous careers in arms that stretched well into middle age, war-making played starkly contrasting roles in their lives. Rither essentially became a sword for hire in an age when plenty of English captains were hiring. Thweyt, at a far less exalted level than Sir Stephen Hales, made a career in magnate service, one in which his martial expertise made him the perfect candidate for running a garrison in the absence of its nominal commander.

The contrasts between John Rither's and William Thweyt's military experiences hint at how varied the lives of lesser gentry career soldiers could be. Historians have naturally tended to fixate upon those lesser gentry deponents who carved out spectacular war records across

---

[165] Thweyt's career has been carefully reconstructed by Ayton. Ayton, 'William de Thweyt', pp. 731–8.

[166] Thweyt was present at the siege of Berwick and the battle of Halidon Hill (1333); he served on the Roxburgh campaign (1334–5); he was in Gascony in 1337–9 and Brittany in 1342–3, and at the battles of Sluys (1340) and Crécy (1346), and the siege of Calais (1347). As late as 1369, he was serving in Gascony under Sir William Morley. C 47/6/1, no. 92; C 61/49, m. 17; C 76/18, m. 9.

[167] Ayton, 'William de Thweyt', pp. 733–5.

[168] Ayton, 'Military Service and the Dynamics of Recruitment', p. 53.

a range of military theatres.¹⁶⁹ This, on the one hand, is entirely understandable, since the testimony of a man like Rither highlights the potential depth of the lesser gentry's military experience and the extent to which martial prowess, most of the time, did not lead to promotion into the knightly class, but rather bred a generation of reliable, battle-hardened subordinates.¹⁷⁰ On the other hand, most of those esquires and gentlemen who spoke before the Court described careers in arms far less spectacular than Rither's, in which soldiering – as was the case for most knightly 'socio-professionals' – played a comparatively limited role in their lives. The example of the Norfolk esquire, Hugh Curson, who spoke on behalf of Thomas, Lord Morley, bears this out.¹⁷¹

Curson enjoyed a brief, albeit incredibly active, military career that began under the distinguished Norfolk banneret, Sir John Norwich, in the force commanded by Henry of Grosmont, Earl of Derby, in Aquitaine in 1345, and extended into the Crécy-Calais campaign that followed.¹⁷² His testimony – much like that of Grosvenor witnesses recalling the Gascony campaign of 1369 – reminds one of just how much action a soldier could see on a single expedition. Over a period of nine months, Curson participated at the siege of Langon, the capture of Bergerac, the battle of Auberoche, the siege of La Reole, on Edward III's march through Normandy, and finally, at the battle of Crécy.¹⁷³ Unlike Rither or Thweyt, however, this appears to have marked the full extent of Curson's career in arms. Yet, his military retirement did not herald his disappearance into obscurity. At Bintree, just northwest of Norwich, he was a tenant of the Lords Morley and, over the ensuing decades, his family developed increasingly close ties with their mighty neighbour.¹⁷⁴ Hugh Curson's son, William, acted as a feoffee and executor for William, third Lord Morley (father of our Court of Chivalry defendant), and his grandson, John, would go on to provide securities in Chancery for the Morleys and achieve an

---

[169] E.g., Keen, 'Chaucer's Knight', pp. 106–11; Ayton, 'Knights, Esquires and Military Service', pp. 94–6; Sumption, *The Hundred Years War III*, pp. 735–7; Barber, *Edward III and the Triumph of England*, pp. 379–80; Bell et al., *The Soldier*, pp. 167–70; Ayton, 'Nicholas Sabraham', pp. 95–120.

[170] Ayton, 'Knights, Esquires and Military Service', pp. 94–6; Keen, *Origins of the English Gentleman*, pp. 71–86.

[171] C 47/6/1, no. 99; *PCM*, I, pp. 444–5.

[172] C 47/6/1, no. 99.

[173] C 47/6/1, no. 99; C 76/22, m. 7d.

[174] *CIPM*, XIII, p. 328.

immensely advantageous marriage with the Morley's family friends, the prestigious Feltons of Litcham.[175] John Curson, indeed, rose into the knightly class, and although his military record is unclear, we know that he entrenched himself as a member of Norfolk's governing élite and not only represented his native shire in Parliament, but was also nominated to sit on special tribunals to oversee cases before the Court of Chivalry, which suggests a military background.[176] It was in the context of this longstanding relationship with the Lords Morley that Hugh Curson in his old age testified on Lord Thomas' behalf before the Court, recalling those occasions in the mid 1340s when he had seen the defendant's grandfather, Lord Robert, bearing the disputed arms. In short, Hugh Curson was a man of immense military experience, even though most (possibly all) of that experience was crammed into a single year's campaigning. He was not – as the cliché goes – a 'landless' young man who drifted in search of military opportunity, but one who enjoyed a small landed stake in his native shire and who went on to make the most of his local connections back home, enabling his immediate descendants to reap the benefits.

The shape of Hugh Curson's career would have been influenced, to a significant degree, by the fact that, as a Norfolk man, he hailed from a peaceable and economically prosperous part of the realm. For gentry of similar standing living in a less hospitable and less commercially-successful climate – as we have seen from the Grosvenor testimony – matters proved very different, for the Scots and Welsh posed a far more immediate threat and most of the magnates and barons of the region were heavily involved in the ongoing defence of the northern border.[177] Through Richard, Lord Scrope's witnesses, one may gain a powerful sense of the way in which England's northern gentry were drawn, at the Crown's behest, into the war with Scotland. At least 138 of Scrope's militarily active deponents fought against the Scots at least once (and most more than once), the majority describing their participation on specific expeditions.[178] To cite but a single, pertinent example of the potential military focus of the northern gentry, one comes across the Yorkshire knight, Sir Randolph Pygot, who was 46 years old at the time of his deposition, had been in arms for 20

---

[175] *CPR, 1370–4*, p. 419; Lambeth Palace Library, Reg. Sudbury, f. 102; *CCR, 1381–5*, p. 420; *CP*, V, pp. 292–4.

[176] *HPC, 1386-1421*, II, pp. 719–20.

[177] See above, n. 81.

[178] *Scrope v. Grosvenor*.

years, yet had never served beyond the sea.[179] His every expedition had taken place against the Scots in an age when English armies were journeying to France at least once a year. This stands in stark contrast to the evidence provided by Lord Morley's predominantly East Anglian deponents, which revealed a pattern of semi-regular soldiering in France from the battle of Sluys in 1340 to the Rheims campaign in 1359–60, and, for younger men, from the Rheims campaign to Richard II's Scottish expedition in 1385.[180] This feature of the disputes – the role of regionalism – will be explored at greater length in Chapter 3.

Finally, as the team behind the Soldier Project has reminded us, the one noteworthy omission amidst this wealth of military data presented before the Court of Chivalry is the role of garrison service.[181] The war records of the Scropes, Grosvenors, Morleys and Hastings, although stretching across several generations and a range of military theatres, were essentially limited to land expeditions and occasional forays into the war at sea. None undertook the longer-term commitment of garrison service and hence there was no need for their deponents to mention any garrison service they might have performed.[182] Andrew Ayton, for instance, had to move well beyond William Thweyt's deposition on behalf of Lord Morley to uncover his career as deputy constable of Corfe Castle, and Guy, Lord Brian likewise saw no reason to mention his garrison appointment in his deposition.[183] Yet, small hints of the ways in which garrison communities intermingled with English military society at large can be gleaned from the testimony, and, unsurprisingly, what evidence exists on this score largely derives from the northern shires where the manning of castles was a matter of immediate military necessity.

---

[179] *Scrope v. Grosvenor*, I, p. 119; II, p. 314.

[180] *Scrope v. Grosvenor*, I, p. 119; Ayton, 'Knights, Esquires and Military Service', pp. 91–5.

[181] Bell et al., *The Soldier*, pp. 3–4.

[182] E.g., William Biset focused in his testimony upon his campaigning experiences under William Bohun, Earl of Northampton, during the first phase of the Hundred Years War. Biset continued his career in arms under Northampton's son, Humphrey, Earl of Hereford, between 1369 and 1373. After the latter's death, however, he appears to have belatedly moved into the service of the Percy family, under whom he served extensively in garrisons in the Scottish Marches. *Scrope v. Grosvenor*, I, pp. 125–6; C 76/52, m. 20; E 101/31/15, m. 1; C 71/57, m. 8; C 71/58, m. 3; C 71/60, m. 10; C 76/78, m. 14; BL, Cotton Roll XIII 8, m. 3. On Biset's career, see Bell et al., *The Soldier*, p. 119.

[183] Ayton, 'William de Thweyt', pp. 733–5; *Scrope v. Grosvenor*, I, pp. 76–7.

The obvious and well-worn example is that of the Cheshire knight, Sir Hugh Browe, whose assertion – that he had never seen the Scropes armed because he had been employed solely in garrisons during the wars and campaigns in France and had not participated on any great expeditions – long ago captured the attention of historians.[184] Browe's testimony, despite its shortcomings (alluded to above), implicitly revealed the world of the garrison soldier, who dwelt in a community largely comprising full-time careerists, men seemingly distinct from those 'socio-professionals' who bore arms intermittently and usually only on the grandest of occasions.[185] Yet, as the more nuanced approach of recent scholars has made clear,[186] although such men undeniably existed and were crucial to the effective functioning of English military society at an everyday level, the line between socio-professionals and full-timers was heavily blurred. The testimony of another northerner, far more obscure than Sir Hugh Browe – the Yorkshire esquire, John Neuland – hints at the fluidity between these two worlds.[187] Neuland participated on two Scottish expeditions in 1383 and 1385. He also saw Sir William Scrope bearing the disputed arms with a difference in Gascony in 1369. Yet, when he confessed before the Court that he could remember no other battles or journeys on which he had seen the Scropes bearing their arms because he was in garrison service, one might have assumed that he would have been found manning fortifications on the northern border or stationed at a Scottish castle under English control. Instead, he outlined his service in garrisons in Normandy, Brittany and Burgundy.[188] One may surmise from this that he had journeyed to Gascony in 1369 and that he had subsequently remained across the Channel, serving in garrisons across a variety of French theatres throughout the 1370s, before returning home in the early 1380s, just in time to be recruited for the two recent Scottish

---

[184] On Browe, see Bennett, *Community, Class and Careerism*, pp. 167, 175, 182, 187–9; Morgan, *War and Society in Medieval Cheshire*, pp. 129–30; Keen, *Origins of the English Gentleman*, pp. 50, 62; Sumption, *The Hundred Years War III*, pp. 735–7; Bell, 'The Soldier, "hadde he riden, no man ferre"', pp. 214–15.

[185] Matters were hardly this clear cut. On garrison culture and the complexities of defining military professionalism within late medieval garrisons, see Grummitt, *The Calais Garrison*, pp. 92–118.

[186] Curry, 'Military Organizaton'; Cornell, 'Northern Castle Garrisons', Grummitt, *The Calais Garrison*; Bell et al., *The Soldier*, pp. 87–94, 117–38.

[187] *Scrope v. Grosvenor*, I, p. 138; II, p. 343.

[188] *Scrope v. Grosvenor*, I, p. 138.

expeditions on which he had participated. If this timeline is accurate, then Neuland's role as a garrison soldier was essentially a matter of opportunity, for the English in the 1370s were fighting a defensive war to maintain their gains from the Treaty of Brétigny and there was in consequence plenty of English-held territory under threat and requiring skilled defenders.[189] Once he returned home, it would have been just as natural for a man of his military experience to become embroiled in the efforts of the northern aristocracy to keep the Scots at bay.

This section has sought to illustrate the subtleties of the role war-making played in the lives of the English gentry during the final two-thirds of the fourteenth century. Appraising patterns of recruitment and participation are naturally pivotal to the study of English armies from an institutional perspective, for they reveal the challenges faced by the Crown, nobility and knightly élite in their efforts to put substantial contingents in the field. Yet, quantifying the gentry's military careers, and dividing participants into neat categories, according to the length, breadth or intensity of their careers in arms, or the type of soldiering they performed, can prove deeply misleading from an individual standpoint. Men with superficially similar war records were often motivated to bear arms for vastly different reasons. The personal circumstances of individual gentry – rooted in their family's pre-existing military traditions; their socio-economic position; whether they lived in a heavily militarised part of the realm; their membership of a magnate's affinity; the martial inclinations of their lord; and, quite simply, the availability of military opportunities, as well as the type and location of those opportunities – all played a role in shaping the career trajectories of individual gentry and proved crucial considerations when weighing up whether or not to bear arms in the king's wars. The value of the Court of Chivalry material is that it provides a convenient avenue for engaging with the personal circumstances of a range of gentry soldiers: from occasional participants to full-time careerists; from barons, bannerets and knights at the apex of county society, to obscure parish gentry; and from men heavily aligned with a single magnate affinity to those who fought in numerous retinues as their careers unfolded. There has been a marked (and perfectly understandable) tendency to focus upon the patterns of military service revealed in the surviving depositions. Yet, one military

---

[189] Sumption, *The Hundred Years War III*.

career was not necessarily typical of others. As the above case-studies have shown, John Rither, William Thweyt and Hugh Curson were not entirely of a type. Nor were Guy, Lord Brian, Sir Stephen Hales and Sir William Berdewell, or Sir Hugh Browe, Sir Randolph Pygot and John Neuland. The superficial similarities between their careers-in-arms masked a tremendous diversity of motives, influenced, at every turn, by a range of endogenous and exogenous factors.

Conclusion

Historians have long been aware of the rich sources of military testimony provided before the Court of Chivalry. This testimony has been catalogued, quantified, and investigated by means of individual case study. The length, breadth and intensity of deponents' military careers has been scrutinised in considerable depth, with special emphasis placed upon those who served regularly across a variety of theatres from their youths to the cusp of old age, reinforcing just how heavily militarised the English gentry became during the fourteenth century. One aim of this chapter has been to delve a little deeper into the wider careers of these martially-inclined witnesses, pinpointing more precisely the role military service came to play in their lives. By adopting this approach, it becomes clear the extent to which superficially similar war records could develop from vastly different origins and for markedly different reasons. A point to be particularly stressed is that, despite the undoubted martial enthusiasm of many of those who deposed, the careers spotlighted above indicate just how crucial was the weight of exogenous factors in shaping the gentry's patterns of military service. The military policies of the Crown, or the martial zeal of the particular magnate a testator served, created a series of preconditions that provided individual gentry with greater opportunities to develop their military pedigrees, whilst royal expectations that the gentry would answer their sovereign's call to arms made refusal all the harder for those inclined to stay at home.

The wealth of military testimony that survives has additionally enabled historians to explore the continuities and changes inherent within English military society between the 1330s and the 1380s. Building upon this body of scholarship, a second aim of this chapter has been to illustrate that the surviving testimony may prove equally useful when considering the linkages between the second (1369–1389) and third phases (1415–1453) of the Hundred Years War. It has been demonstrated that the war records of Sir Robert Grosvenor's and Sir Edward Hastings' witnesses were shaped, to a significant degree, by the character of the military societies of the Northwest and East Anglia in which they respectively dwelt, emphasising what will be a recurring theme in this study – the role of regionalism in shaping English military identity. Specifically, it has been shown that Grosvenor's witnesses, and their immediate descendants, enjoyed greater opportunities to continue bearing arms on a regular basis during the truce years of the 1390s and 1400s than their East Anglian contemporaries, who undertook barely any military service during these years. The 26-year Truce of Leulinghem (1389) brought to a close the military careers of almost every surviving Court of Chivalry witness. Nonetheless, the impressive participation of their sons, nephews, and other younger kinsmen, on the Agincourt campaign of 1415 underscores that their family military traditions were still very much alive as the third phase of the Hundred Years War began.

Thus, despite the impact of a generation-long truce, significant continuities remained between the English armies of the fourteenth century and that which fought the battle of Agincourt. Further exploring these continuities will be a theme to which we shall return towards the conclusion of this study. First, though, the military careers of our testators must be situated in their proper social and cultural context. Accordingly, Chapters 2 and 3 take this large body of witnesses and examine the social networks they formed, exploring what motivated them to speak before the Court and, more generally, what types of vertical and horizontal ties shaped their relationships, both with the protagonist they were defending, and with each other. In so doing, one may build upon the case studies detailed in the second half of this chapter, directly exploring how military and county society intersected in the mid-to-late fourteenth and early fifteenth centuries.

2

Lordship

We saw in the previous chapter that a great many testators before the Court of Chivalry became heavily involved in the Hundred Years War over the course of the fourteenth century. As late as the 1370s and 1380s, numerous witnesses who spoke for Sir Robert Grosvenor and Sir Edward Hastings participated on multiple expeditions, quite often spending more than a decade campaigning at intervals. Although few were still in arms by 1415, their descendants continued upholding their families' martial traditions to an impressive degree, providing a clear measure of continuity between the war's fourteenth and early fifteenth century phases. One of the more significant structural developments that shaped English armies after 1369 was the evolution of the 'supersized' retinue, in which small numbers of magnates contracted with the Crown to bring ever-larger contingents of troops.[1] With Edward III too old, Edward, the Black Prince too ill, and Richard II too young, to personally command the English war effort, the dominant figure in English military society during this epoch was John of Gaunt, Duke of Lancaster. His military retinue became not only the backbone of the English expeditionary forces dispatched across the Channel during the 1370s, but also formed the basis of his private military strength as he sought to acquire the throne of Castile by force in the mid 1380s.[2]

The Lancastrian affinity, with its voluminous documentary records, and with the powerful and controversial figure of Gaunt at its head, has long been a focal point for scholars of later medieval England, and a number of distinguished studies have thoroughly conveyed its

---

[1] J. Sherborne, 'Indentured Retinues and the English Expeditions to France, 1369–80', *EHR*, 79 (1964), pp. 718–46; A. Ayton, 'Armies and Military Communities in Fourteenth-Century England', in *Soldiers, Nobles and Gentlemen: Essays in Honour of Maurice Keen*, ed. P. Coss and C. Tyerman (Woodbridge, 2009), pp. 218–19; Bell, *War and the Soldier*, pp. 9–28; Ayton, 'The Military Careerist', pp. 4–23.
[2] Walker, *The Lancastrian Affinity*, pp. 39–80.

significance.³ With their preponderance of Lancastrian deponents, the bonds respectively enjoyed by Richard, Lord Scrope and the Hastings of Elsing with John of Gaunt have been widely acknowledged. Yet, the intricacies of the Lancastrian affinity's role in *Scrope v. Grosvenor* and *Grey v. Hastings* have hardly been the subject of serious scrutiny.[4] This is somewhat surprising, for the wider character of the Lancastrian affinity – as an institution directed from above by Gaunt; as a major employer that drew together hundreds of gentry; and as a creator and reinforcer of inter-gentry solidarity – is indirectly laid bare before the Court, where we essentially encounter it at two distinct moments in its history: on the cusp of Gaunt's Spanish enterprise in 1386, and a near-decade after his death in 1407. It remained a vibrant and powerful institution between these dates, yet one that underwent significant change as Gaunt aged and eventually passed away, and as his son and heir, Henry of Bolingbroke, seized the throne, thereby bringing his father's affinity into the royal fold.[5] Scrope's and Hastings' testators, as we shall see, reveal two markedly different shades of the magnate–gentry experience within the Lancastrian affinity, even though they were largely men of the same generation and recalled the same expeditions.

Of course, neither Scrope nor Hastings relied exclusively upon their Lancastrian ties when mounting their defence. Both men mined their personal connections within their native shires, eliciting support from a variety of kin, friends and longstanding associates. They also – albeit on a much smaller scale and in more localised fashion – maintained their own private affinities of tenants, servants and regular military followers, and, when their cases came before the Court of Chivalry, they were not backward in drawing upon the support these men could offer. Thomas, Lord Morley and Reginald, Lord Grey notably did the same thing. Yet, this dimension to the Court's proceedings has likewise been given short shrift in the existing scholarship, mostly because the numbers of witnesses officially tied to the various protagonists was very

[3] R. Somerville, *History of the Duchy of Lancaster*, 2 vols. (London, 1953–70); Walker, *The Lancastrian Affinity*; Goodman, *John of Gaunt*.
[4] Vale, 'The Scropes', pp. 95–105; Keen, 'Grey v. Hastings', pp. 168–9.
[5] Castor, *The King, the Crown, and the Duchy of Lancaster*, pp. 22–31.

small.[6] These ties, however, are undeniably important for the light they shed upon the bonds of direct and indirect lordship – at a level below that of the higher nobility – that drew many lesser gentry to testify. This chapter, then, addresses the issue of lordship through the prism of the Court of Chivalry, beginning with an in-depth exploration of the Lancastrian connections enjoyed by Richard, Lord Scrope and Sir Edward Hastings, before turning to the realm of local lordship by assessing the vertical ties utilised by Hastings, Morley and Grey, as they set about mounting their defence. With a view to broadening the discussion beyond the Lancastrian sphere, attention will also be paid to the retinues of Edward, the Black Prince and the Bohun earls of Northampton and Hereford, whose former retainers spoke in significant numbers for Scrope and Morley, long after their lords had passed away.

The Lancastrian Affinity I: The Scrope Testimony

The character of lordship in later medieval England has long proven a deeply contentious and hotly debated issue. For some historians, lordship represented the primary means of organising society, with the gentry actively seeking, and competing for, lordly patronage. Others have emphasised gentry independence centred upon the shire, with attention paid to the shire's role as a political community with its own identity and corporate existence.[7] Moreover, after initially

---

[6] Ayton, 'Knights, Esquires and Military Service', pp. 93–4; Vale, 'The Scropes', pp. 102–3; Bennett, *Community, Class and Careerism*, pp. 82–3, 166; Morgan, *War and Society in Medieval Cheshire*, pp. 127–30; Morgan, 'Sir Robert Grosvenor', pp. 78–81, 86–90.

[7] For overviews of the scholarly literature, usually advocating one side of the debate or the other, see J. M. W. Bean, *From Lord to Patron. Lordship in Medieval England* (Manchester, 1989); R. Virgoe, 'Aspects of the County Community in the Fifteenth Century', in *Profit, Piety and the Professions in Later Medieval England*, ed. M. A. Hicks (Gloucester, 1990), pp. 1–13; M. Rubin, 'Small Groups: Identity and Solidarity in the Late Middle Ages', in *Enterprise and Individuals in Fifteenth-Century England*, ed. J. Kermode (Gloucester, 1991), pp. 132–50; C. Carpenter, 'Gentry and Community in Medieval England', *Journal of British Studies*, 33 (1994), pp. 340–80; M. A. Hicks, *Bastard Feudalism* (London, 1995); G. L. Harriss, *Shaping the Nation: England 1360–1461* (Oxford, 2005), pp. 187–206. The pioneering studies of bastard feudalism were: K. B. McFarlane, 'Parliament and 'Bastard Feudalism'', *TRHS*, 4th Series, 26 (1944), pp. 53–79; K. B. McFarlane, 'Bastard Feudalism', *BIHR*, 20 (1945), pp. 161–80.

focusing upon the affinity through the framework of private military indentures, historians have come to appreciate that retaining primarily reflected a lord's need for service in peace rather than war, although the recruitment of gentry contractually obligated to fulfil a military function was still important, as we saw in the previous chapter.[8] What is also abundantly clear is that even though magnates sought to establish a collective identity amongst their retainers through the distribution of livery, the fostering of interpersonal relationships, and the forging of a sense of chivalric *esprit de corps* within their military retinues, the magnate–gentry dynamic was ultimately a personal bond between a lord and his retainer, which could take on a variety of forms.[9]

Firstly, living in closest proximity to their lord were his household attendants, essentially his employees. These included administrators, advisors, and menial servants, as well as knights and esquires who lived with their lord, ate his food, and acted as members of his riding retinue. Secondly, there were his indentured retainers: men generally employed in peace and war, although sometimes, especially in the case of highly active knights, their services were only required for military expeditions. Thirdly, every lord needed estate officials to oversee his lands, some of whom were knights and esquires fulfilling their peacetime obligations to their lord. In their midst were to be found an assortment of other associates: men, for example, whose relationship with their lord was purely tenurial, or who simply served him informally as a matter of family tradition. Collectively, this complex group of followers, amongst whom there was considerable overlap in terms of their personnel, duties and rewards, formed the inner core of their lord's affinity. Alongside this inner core worked a host of 'well-willers' whose relationship to the affinity in question was transient, short term, and usually task specific. Such men included experienced lawyers and administrators who acted as councillors or estates officials for a variety of great lords, and soldiers who drifted from one magnate military retinue to the next.[10]

This aptly described 'sea of varying relationships'[11] was held together by various means on an individual basis, ranging from written contract

[8] G. L. Harriss, 'Introduction', in *England in the Fifteenth Century: Collected Essays of K. B. McFarlane* (London, 1981), pp. x–xi.
[9] Harriss, 'Introduction', pp. xi–xiii.
[10] Harriss, 'Introduction', pp. xi–xxiii; Harriss, *Shaping the Nation*, pp. 189–90.
[11] G. A. Holmes, *The Estates of the Higher Nobility in Fourteenth-Century England* (Cambridge, 1957), p. 79.

to verbal agreement. England's magnates possessed considerable wealth (John of Gaunt more than any of his contemporaries), yet even their purses were far from bottomless, meaning that they had to manage their employment policies carefully. Indentures of retainer – the most formal bond available – bound a knight or esquire to his lord, with fees specified and expectations of the relationship outlined. Others served on a less formal basis, though often receiving miscellaneous fees and benefits. Foremost amongst a magnate's retainers were his annuitants (those who drew an annual fee). This was generally a reward for past, and in expectation of future, service. This most desirous of outcomes could guarantee its recipient a steady income for the rest of his days. Finally, the livery badge – especially for a magnate of Gaunt's stature, with his iconic *SS* device – contained strong chivalric overtones, advertising a retainer's allegiance to his lord, thereby making their bond public knowledge. The lord–retainer relationship, then, was essentially a package deal from which both sides hoped to prosper and which comprised a range of interlocking relationships of various types, some of which were more stable and longer-term than others.

One relationship that was undoubtedly stable was that between Richard, Lord Scrope and John of Gaunt. In 1385–6 – at the time Scrope challenged Grosvenor before the Court of Chivalry – John of Gaunt commanded the largest and most powerful magnate affinity in the realm. His household in 1381 contained a permanent strength of 115 employees, rising to over 150 by the early 1390s; in 1382, he could call upon the services of 173 indentured retainers, comprising seven bannerets, seventy knights and ninety-six esquires; and, over his thirty-eight years as Duke of Lancaster, he had 315 known annuitants on his books.[12] Even in parts of the realm peripheral to his interests, he enjoyed an enormous landed stake and wielded considerable influence. In Norfolk, for instance, far from his strongholds in the North of England, his estates were valued at over £900 per annum, dwarfing the Norfolk inheritance enjoyed by the neighbouring Earl of Suffolk.[13]

It was Lord Scrope's good fortune to have a man such as Gaunt in his corner. He had been one of Gaunt's military mentors – part of a coterie of distinguished bannerets and knights allotted to supervise the young prince as he cut his military teeth during the 1350s and 1360s. Scrope had served alongside Gaunt on the Rheims expedition

---

[12] Walker, *The Lancastrian Affinity*, pp. 11–14.
[13] Walker, *The Lancastrian Affinity*, pp. 183–4.

in 1359–60, on the Black Prince's Spanish campaign in 1366–7, and in France a second time in 1369. In November 1367, Scrope was retained by Gaunt, receiving the large annuity of £40. Although bonds of lordship, duty and service were a notable feature of their relationship, Scrope's ties with Gaunt were, without a doubt, more those of a friend or close associate than a mere employee. They shared pious interests and exchanged expensive gifts and Scrope continued serving as an experienced hand on Gaunt's later expeditions, accompanying him to France a third time in 1373 and to Scotland twice in the 1380s.[14] Scrope's friendship, moreover, would have proven a boon to Gaunt in a more general sense, for he moved in the highest circles of government, acting at various times during the 1370s and 1380s as treasurer and chancellor of the royal household, and was well liked by the English aristocracy at large, as evidenced by the fact that he survived the tumults of the Ricardian age, despite having been one of the government's leading figures.[15]

In light of their longstanding relationship, and his duties as a 'good lord' maintaining his loyal retainer, it is unsurprising that Gaunt leapt to Lord Richard's defence when his case came before the Court of Chivalry. Aside from providing his own deposition – in which he asserted the Scrope family's right to the disputed arms dating back to the Norman Conquest, and provided personal testimony of the favourable verdict accorded Lord Richard in *Scrope v. Carminowe* on the Rheims campaign in 1359–60 – Gaunt also drew the vast majority of his closest retainers and regular military followers to speak on Scrope's behalf.[16] Fifty-eight of his annuitants deposed for Scrope, as well as numerous gentry – such as Sir Edward Hastings' father, Sir Hugh Hastings III – who possessed strong Lancastrian ties but, as far

---

[14] Goodman, *John of Gaunt*, pp. 288–90.

[15] Given-Wilson, *The Royal Household*, pp. 74, 142, 158, 173, 302. Scrope's son, William – an avid Ricardian – was executed in the wake of the Revolution of 1399, yet Lord Richard was spared any punishment by Henry of Bolingbroke, who specifically exempted him from forfeiture on the grounds that he had 'always accounted him a loyal knight'. *CP*, XI, p. 541.

[16] *Scrope v. Grosvenor*, I, pp. 49–50; One of the pillars of Scrope's defence was that he had successfully defended his arms, *azure a bend or*, against the Cornish esquire, Thomas Carminowe, whom he had encountered bearing the same arms on the Rheims campaign. It was ultimately decided that both men should be allowed to keep their arms on the grounds that Cornwall had once been a separate kingdom. Stewart-Brown, 'The Scrope and Grosvenor Controversy', pp. 15–16.

as we know, were never officially on Gaunt's long-term payroll.[17] Those who testified included all of the biggest names in Lancastrian service, notably Gaunt's past, present and future chamberlains, Sir Robert Swillington, Sir Richard Abberbury and Sir Walter Blount, as well as other miscellaneous officeholders ranging from his Hertford constable, Edward Beauchamp, to his chief steward in the North, Sir John de la Pole.[18] Scrope's remaining Lancastrian testators comprised a veritable rollcall of gentry who had made their mark alongside him in Gaunt's military retinue, men such as Sir Walter Urswick and Sir Edmund Pierrepoint.[19]

Each of the above retainers campaigned with Gaunt at least once, whilst fulfilling a range of peacetime functions. Swillington, Blount and Urswick may stand for the rest. Swillington fought beside Gaunt at least four times, beginning as far back as 1359, when Gaunt was still a teenager and yet to inherit the Duchy of Lancaster.[20] Blount bore arms in the Lancastrian military retinue five times over 26 years.[21] Urswick campaigned consistently with Gaunt between 1367 and 1373 and, shortly after providing his deposition, followed him to Spain.[22] Swillington enjoyed tenurial relations and family ties with the house of Lancaster that long pre-dated Gaunt's accession to lordship over the Duchy,[23] whilst he and Blount, despite being independently wealthy, significantly enhanced their fortunes under Lancastrian patronage. Swillington, from Yorkshire, purchased and married his way into Derbyshire and Leicestershire society, and Blount, the younger son of a Worcestershire family, inherited the Mountjoy estates in Staffordshire.[24] All three men roundly displayed their loyalty to Gaunt when the opportunity arose: Urswick, for instance, remained resolutely by Gaunt's side when the peasant mob set their sights upon

---

[17] *Scrope v. Grosvenor*.
[18] *Scrope v. Grosvenor*, I, pp. 203–4; 166–7; 58; 57; 83; Walker, *The Lancastrian Affinity*, pp. 285–7.
[19] *Scrope v. Grosvenor*, I, pp. 51; 153–4.
[20] C 76/38, m. 13; C 81/912 (40); C 81/942 (3); C 71/60, m. 2.
[21] C 81/925 (20); *JG Reg*, I, nos. 969, 1670; C 76/62, m. 18; C 76/70, m. 19; C 61/104, m. 5.
[22] C 61/79, m. 4; C 76/52, m. 15; C 61/83, m. 2; C 81/947 (11); C 81/1034 (61); *Scrope v. Grosvenor*, I, p. 51.
[23] C. Beanlands, 'The Swillingtons of Swillington', Thoresby Society, *Miscellanea*, 15 (1909), pp. 204–5.
[24] CP 25 (1)/39/39; JUST 1/1488 m. 63.

him during the Revolt of 1381.[25] All, too, were long-time recipients of exceptionally handsome annuities, with Urswick and Blount receiving well over £100 per annum from Gaunt's treasury.[26] Although these men were unusual in their physical proximity to Gaunt and in their positions amongst his most trusted advisers, all three were, in a broader sense, wholly typical of the vast majority of Lancastrians who defended Scrope, in so far as they enjoyed an official, paid position as retainers within the Lancastrian affinity and combined participation in Gaunt's military retinue with the performance of peacetime duties.

Beyond these exceptional individuals, the bald figures bear out just how extensive was the presence before the Court, on Scrope's behalf, of gentry from the inner core of the Lancastrian affinity, with a long history of serial participation in Gaunt's military retinue. Forty-six of the 58 Lancastrian annuitants who deposed for Scrope had prior experience fighting beneath the Lancastrian banner, and the vast majority were notably active soldiers. Thirty-three of them had campaigned with Gaunt for over a decade, and 22 had fought alongside him since the late 1360s. Equally impressive was the intensity of their military service, with a high degree of individual continuity from one expedition to the next. More than three-quarters had campaigned with Gaunt on multiple occasions, and one-third – a core body of 15 knights – had served with him four or more times.[27] These were, in short, gentry who were well accustomed to mapping out strategies, sharing a campfire and enduring the hardships of life on campaign in each other's company. In the context of Scrope's defence, they were men possessing a stock of shared memories of occasions when they had seen Lord Richard bearing the arms, *azure a bend or*, in the Lancastrian military retinue.[28]

Yet, one may also detect, upon closer inspection, the fluid character of Gaunt's affinity and the extent to which his real strength, as the realm's pre-eminent magnate, derived from his ability to make short-term Lancastrian employment appear enticing to those on the fringes of his affinity and military retinue. This becomes readily apparent if one considers Scrope's Lancastrian support base in the context of Gaunt's imminent departure for Spain. A vast array of Lancastrian retainers gave their depositions at Plymouth, where

[25] *The Anonimalle Chronicle 1333 to 1381*, ed. V. H. Galbraith (Manchester, 1927), p. 153.
[26] *CPR, 1367–70*, p. 77; DL 43/15/6 m. 7; *JG Reg*, I, no. 1042; *CPR, 1396–9*, p. 547.
[27] *Scrope v. Grosvenor*.
[28] Caudrey, 'War, Chivalry and Regional Society, p. 135.

Gaunt's army was awaiting embarkation.²⁹ Yet, by no means every one of these committed Lancastrians went on the fight in Spain. This was, perhaps, to be expected, since Scrope essentially required testators who could recall long-past occasions when he had borne his family's arms beneath Gaunt's banner, and many of those capable of providing relevant testimony would have been influential middle-aged men by 1386, preoccupied with their own domestic responsibilities, and unable to dedicate their time to a speculative enterprise of conquest whose end-date was uncertain.

To cite four prominent examples of such men: Sir John Godard had been a member of the Lancastrian military retinue since the Spanish expedition of 1366–7 and had participated on almost all of Gaunt's subsequent campaigns, including Richard II's recent march into Scotland in 1385. By the time Gaunt sailed for Spain the following year, however, Godard had been appointed to the bench in the East Riding and was sitting as an MP for Yorkshire.³⁰ In similar vein, Sir Robert Constable, who had fought regularly under Gaunt between 1373 and 1385, was currently serving as Yorkshire's sheriff.³¹ And it was not merely the acquisition of high-profile posts in shire administration that kept such trusty old hands at home. Sir Richard Roucliffe, for instance, had testified for Scrope alongside his son, Sir David. Yet, whilst Sir David went to Spain, Sir Richard was prevented from adding to his 20 years of Lancastrian military service, because he was busily serving Gaunt in an entirely different capacity as steward of the important Duchy honour of Pickering.³² Lastly, providing an example from the fringes of the Lancastrian affinity, Sir Richard Tempest, who had joined Gaunt on his two recent expeditions to Scotland, did not continue on to Spain, because he had, in the interim, been appointed co-commander of the English garrison at Roxburgh Castle, where he would subsequently spend the late 1380s enhancing his military reputation against the Scots.³³

---

²⁹ *Scrope v. Grosvenor*, I, pp. 49–73.
³⁰ *Scrope v. Grosvenor*, I, pp. 171–2; *HPC, 1386–1421*, accessed at historyofparliamentonline.org
³¹ *Scrope v. Grosvenor*, I, pp. 135–6; *Lists of Sheriffs for England and Wales* (PRO Lists and Indexes, 9, 1898), p. 162.
³² *Scrope v. Grosvenor*, I, pp. 65, 143–4; II, p. 215; Somerville, *Duchy of Lancaster*, I, pp. 378, 533.
³³ *Scrope v. Grosvenor*, I, p. 198; II, pp. 473–4; *Cal. Scots. Docs.*, IV, nos. 235, 340, 360, 528.

As the absence of these veterans makes plain, the Scrope depositions indirectly reveal a significant generational shift within the Lancastrian military retinue,[34] with the result that Gaunt's soon-to-depart Spanish army, although heavily stocked with paid retainers, was nonetheless in some ways a new construct, with the places of numerous Lancastrian stalwarts filled by a host of younger gentry, newly retained, who had never (or only recently) fought with Gaunt, together with a handful of equally young barons looking to cut their military teeth.[35] And the figures bear this out. Only 28 of those Lancastrian annuitants who deposed for Scrope – fewer than half – are known to have journeyed to Spain.[36] By contrast, almost two-thirds were veterans of the five expeditions on which the young Gaunt had participated between 1367 and 1373.[37] A core group of 14 gentry campaigned with Gaunt at least three times during these years, and, as we have seen in the cases of Blount, Urswick and Swillington, some served on four, or even on all five, of these occasions.[38] The Lancastrian army that crossed to Spain in 1386 was thus impressive on paper, but was relatively inexperienced as a military contingent. Several of the highly active veterans of the 1367–73 campaigns were noticeably absent and a significant number of gentry, for whose services Gaunt had been prepared to pay handsomely, had no proven track record of Lancastrian service. It might perhaps be in this context that Sir Hugh Hastings III – father of the defendant in *Grey v. Hastings* – was promoted to the rank of banneret for the expedition, despite, as far as we know, never having been an indentured retainer or annuitant of the Duchy.[39] The fact that he had campaigned with Gaunt on four previous occasions, was a cadet of the Earl of Pembroke, and

[34] The surviving military records for Gaunt's Spanish force are patchy in several respects. Incomplete muster rolls, and a resultant reliance upon surviving letters of protection and attorney, means that some of those Lancastrian stalwarts unaccounted for, may in fact have participated. However, as the above examples of Sir John Godard, Sir Robert Constable, Sir Richard Roucliffe and Sir Richard Tempest illustrate, there were plenty of good reasons for distinguished middle-aged Lancastrians to stay at home. For the expedition's surviving letters of protection and attorney, used in conjunction with Nicolas' second volume of *Scrope v. Grosvenor*, see, C 76/70.

[35] E.g., The young Richard, Lord Poynings and Robert, Lord Scales. *Scrope v. Grosvenor*, I, pp. 50, 67.

[36] *Scrope v. Grosvenor*, C 76/70.

[37] *Scrope v. Grosvenor*, C 61/79; C 76/52; C 61/83; C 76/55; C 76/56.

[38] See above, pp. 69–70.

[39] Blomefield, *History of Norfolk*, IX, p. 513.

was the son and grandson of distinguished Lancastrian bannerets, was evidence enough to ensure his promotion in an army relatively bereft of trusty old hands.[40]

So, turning to the depositions themselves, how did this generational shift, and indeed Gaunt's current focus upon Spain, affect the composition of Scrope's witness list? On the one hand, the presence of so many distinguished members of the Lancastrian affinity reflect the fact that Gaunt undeniably mobilised the more prominent members of his Spanish army to testify for Scrope, with his official annuitants alone comprising almost one quarter (23%) of Scrope's total witnesses.[41] Yet, a clear distinction should be drawn between those Lancastrian retainers about to depart for Spain, and the minority of older gentry of long Lancastrian affiliation, who provided depositions, but remained at home. The former generally contributed comparatively little hard evidence in Scrope's defence. Many were young and inexperienced soldiers, often poorly acquainted with Scrope. Doubtless, they admired his reputation, but there was scant personal connection involved. Consequently, they could provide relatively little to his defence beyond sheer weight of numbers on the witness stand (in an age in which the heaping of witnesses was useful in and of itself).[42] By contrast, if one turns to the testimony of older Lancastrian witnesses, it becomes abundantly clear that many enjoyed close personal ties with the Scrope family and would have spoken on Lord Richard's behalf regardless of John of Gaunt's interest in the case.

A handful of examples drawn from Scrope's contemporaries, who were fellow Northerners in Lancastrian pay, may serve to illustrate the point. Sir Robert Neville of Hornby had fought in Gaunt's retinue

[40] The deaths on campaign of several of Gaunt's closest and most experienced lieutenants would only have served to exacerbate these tensions. Sir John Marmion, Sir Thomas Morieux and Hastings himself all lost their lives, together with the young Lords Fitzwalter and Scales. *CIPM*, XI, nos. 377, 406, 414, 482; Goodman, *John of Gaunt*, pp. 125–6; Walker, *The Lancastrian Affinity*, p. 203.

[41] Precisely why so many depositions were taken at Plymouth is unclear. Gaunt may well have made himself available only at this time, whilst his force was mustering for departure. This was quite possibly a strategic decision, made in the knowledge that his presence before the Court of Chivalry, and overt support for Scrope, would have prompted most of the notables about to accompany him to Spain to likewise testify. Equally, with so many Lancastrians mustering for the expedition, it might simply have been a convenient location to interview as many of them as possible before they departed overseas. *Scrope v. Grosvenor*, I, pp. 49–73.

[42] E.g., *Scrope v. Grosvenor*, I, p. 50.

alongside Lord Richard since the Rheims campaign of 1359–60, seeing action across three different theatres.[43] Sir Robert Swillington – whom we have already encountered – claimed to have been in arms for 45 years and not only recalled numerous expeditions in Scrope's direct company beneath the Lancastrian banner, but could cast his mind back further still, to the siege of Vannes (1342) and the battle of Crécy (1346), where he saw Lord Richard's Masham cousins bearing the disputed arms with a difference.[44] Sir Andrew Lutterell likewise outlined Scrope possession of the arms dating back to the siege of Tournai (1340) and enumerated later occasions on which he had personally served with Lord Richard in the Lancastrian military retinue.[45] Sir John Scargill – one of Scrope's few older companions that accompanied Gaunt to Spain – described various occasions when he had seen the Scropes campaigning with the disputed arms and claimed that his father had told him of even longer-ago expeditions when they had done so, asserting also that the arms had belonged to the Scropes since time immemorial.[46] Sir Ralph Hastings described seeing Lord Richard at the battles of Neville's Cross (1346), Winchelsea (1350) and Nájera (1367), and, in similar vein to Scargill, he argued that the disputed arms had belonged to the Scropes since the time of the Norman Conquest.[47] Finally, of slightly more recent vintage, the esquire Conan Aske pointed in his deposition to service alongside Lord Richard in Spain (1367), France (1373) and on both recent expeditions into Scotland (1384, 1385).[48]

These testators all shared longstanding Lancastrian ties with Lord Scrope. Yet, Gaunt's active interest in the case notwithstanding, these men very obviously deposed independently on Lord Richard's behalf, for they enjoyed personal relationships with him and his family stretching back decades, often pre-dating their mutual service to the Duchy of Lancaster. Swillington and Scrope, for instance, were neighbours in the North Riding and had been Gaunt's tenants in his adolescent guise as Earl of Richmond, and it would have been in this context that they had entered his service so early, even before

---

[43] *Scrope v. Grosvenor*, I, pp. 106–7.
[44] *Scrope v. Grosvenor*, I, pp. 203–4.
[45] *Scrope v. Grosvenor*, I, p. 243.
[46] *Scrope v. Grosvenor*, I, p. 65.
[47] *Scrope v. Grosvenor*, I, pp. 103–4.
[48] *Scrope v. Grosvenor*, I, p. 131.

he inherited the Duchy.[49] The Scargills had engaged in private land transactions with the Scropes for decades.[50] Sir Robert Neville, Sir Ralph Hastings and Conan Aske had all witnessed grants for Lord Richard on multiple occasions across more than 20 years,[51] and, of even closer proximity, Neville and Lutterell were Lord Richard's kinsmen, having married into the family of his Masham cousins.[52]

Richard, Lord Scrope's intimate personal connections with this small sample of fellow Yorkshire gentry reminds one of the extent to which the Lancastrian core of his witness list shaded, almost imperceptibly, into the more personal ties with kin, friends and associates to whom he also turned for support.[53] Regular military participation beneath Gaunt's banner and joint domestic responsibilities as some of his leading northern retainers was something that these gentry shared and which would doubtless have strengthened their pre-existing bonds. Yet, their intimacy with the Scrope family derived as much from their mutual status as members of Yorkshire's county élite, as it did from shared Lancastrian service,[54] and they would likely have spoken in Lord Richard's defence regardless of Gaunt's interest in the case. In this regard, Scrope's Lancastrian connections before the Court of Chivalry had far more in common with those of Sir Edward Hastings than has traditionally been assumed. How gentry networking, overlaid by Lancastrian bonds, played its part in enabling Hastings to secure his support base is the subject to which we shall now turn.

The Lancastrian Affinity II: The Hastings Testimony

Sir Edward Hastings, like Richard, Lord Scrope, relied heavily upon his Lancastrian ties when he came before the Court of Chivalry in 1407. However, barely out of his teens and with only a single campaign to his name, he entirely lacked Scrope's resources and reputation.[55] Hastings, nonetheless, milked his family's impressive Lancastrian pedigree for

---

[49] C 136/73/8; *CIPM*, VIII, no. 546; Walker, *The Lancastrian Affinity*, p. 27.
[50] Vale, 'The Scropes', Appendix, nos. 136, 139, 173.
[51] Vale, 'The Scropes', Appendix, nos. 222, 237, 275, 308, 334.
[52] Vale, 'The Scropes', p. 102.
[53] See below, pp. 98–114.
[54] *HPC, 1386-1421*, I, pp. 728–34.
[55] See above, pp. 5–6.

all it was worth. He was the heir to three consecutive generations of Lancastrian bannerets and his family were tenants of Lancaster. His great-grandfather, Sir Hugh Hastings I, had been held in the highest esteem by Gaunt's father-in-law, Henry of Grosmont, who named him as an executor of his will and likely helped construct the magnificent memorial brass tomb that commemorated Sir Hugh upon his death in 1347.[56] Sir Edward's grandfather, Sir Hugh II, maintained the family's tradition of Lancastrian military service, in 1366 becoming the first banneret to be officially retained by the young Gaunt.[57] Of greatest significance to Sir Edward's chances of winning his case, his father, Sir Hugh III, although never officially a Lancastrian retainer, remained Gaunt's tenant and still served him on at least five expeditions over more than 15 years during the 1370s and 1380s.[58]

Sir Edward, then, despite his youth and lack of personal achievement, had plenty of Lancastrian credit in the bank. It is in consequence entirely unsurprising that almost all of his 39 militarily active testators had campaigned at least once beneath the Lancastrian banner and most were men who had carved out the bulk of their careers in arms in Gaunt's military retinue.[59] This is partly to be explained by the fact that Hastings, possessing limited reach, largely sought witnesses amongst his father's old East Anglian comrades, and this region – especially northeast Norfolk, where he was born and raised – enjoyed strong Lancastrian connections both before and after 1399, initially as a recruiting ground for Gaunt, and later as a regional pillar of Henry IV's young regime. Indeed, by the time Hastings' case came before the Court of Chivalry, Norfolk was governed by a clique of gentry loyal to the house of Lancaster, with pre-existing ties to Gaunt. The central figure – one might justifiably say, the leader – of this clique, was Sir Thomas Erpingham, whom we encountered briefly as an Agincourt

---

[56] Goodman, *John of Gaunt*, p. 214; L. Dennison and N. Rogers, 'The Elsing Brass and its East Anglian Connections', in *Fourteenth Century England I*, ed. N. Saul (Woodbridge, 2000), pp. 167–93.
[57] Sir Hugh's indenture, dated 1366, is published in Walker, *The Lancastrian Affinity*, pp. 294–5.
[58] Goodman, *John of Gaunt*, p. 214; *PCM*.
[59] Eighteen testators described multiple occasions when they had served beneath the Lancastrian banner. *PCM*, I, pp. 390–2; 397–9; 401–4; 413–21; 421–2; 423–4; 425; 427–9; 429–35; 439–42; 444–5; 458–64; 474–6; 478–80; 495–7; 497–8; 500–1.

veteran in the previous chapter.[60] Erpingham proved adept at gradually expanding Norfolk's governing circle to include all of its most important gentry families, regardless of their pre-existing Lancastrian affiliations.[61] Several prominent figures from within this governing clique deposed for Sir Edward Hastings, but it seems highly unlikely that Erpingham mobilised old East Anglian Lancastrians on Hastings' behalf. Erpingham's relations with these gentry, unlike Gaunt's with his paid retainers in *Scrope v. Grosvenor*, were essentially horizontal, though undoubtedly influenced by the knowledge that he had friends in high places.[62] Moreover, Hastings' Lancastrian supporters were, on the whole, of a rather different stamp to Scrope's supporters. Despite their track record of Lancastrian military service, only six of them had been officially retained by Gaunt, or employed in his administration.[63]

The war memories outlined before the Court on Hastings' behalf were naturally nowhere near as diffuse as those provided by Scrope's far more numerous witnesses. Speaking as they were, a generation on from *Scrope v. Grosvenor*, the earliest memories these men could conjure up were of the battle of Crécy (1346), the siege of Rennes (1356–7), and the Rheims expedition (1359–60), whilst a few also described Sir Hugh Hastings II's crusading activities in the 1360s.[64] Most, as we saw in Chapter 1, recalled a succession of ducal campaigns spread over a period of two decades, on which Sir Edward's father (and, in the early years, his grandfather) had participated.[65] These memories were bookended by the Spanish ventures of 1366–7 and 1386–8 and in between encompassed the Gascony campaigns of 1369 and 1370, the Earl of Pembroke's defeat off La Rochelle in 1372, Gaunt's *chevauchée* across northern France in 1373, the siege of St. Malo in 1378, Sir John Arundel's naval disaster in 1379, the Earl of Buckingham's Brittany

[60] Erpingham had earlier deposed before the Court of Chivalry on behalf of Richard, Lord Scrope, in 1386. *Scrope v. Grosvenor*, I, p. 59; II, pp. 194–6.

[61] Castor, *The King, the Crown, and the Duchy of Lancaster*, pp. 62–72.

[62] P. J. Caudrey, 'War and Society in Medieval Norfolk: The Warrior Gentry, c. 1350–c. 1430' (PhD, Tasmania, 2010), pp. 93–9.

[63] Edmund Barry; Sir Robert Berney; Sir Thomas Erpingham; Sir John Geney; William Plumstead; John Reymes. NRO, NRS 15171, m. 2; DL 29/289/4744, m. 4; *JG Reg* II, no. 338; *JG Reg*, II, p. 12; DL 42/15, f. 125v; NRO, NRS 3344, m. 2.

[64] Only three witnesses could recall the first phase of the Hundred Years War. *PCM*, I, pp. 426–7; 429–35; 453–5; 533.

[65] The specific character of the case naturally shaped the military memories of those who deposed. *Grey v. Hastings* was much more focused upon family connections and inheritance rights than *Scrope v. Grosvenor*. See above, pp. 5–7.

expedition in 1380, and Richard II's Scottish campaign in 1385.⁶⁶ Gaunt was present on all but three of these occasions and Sir Hugh Hastings II and/or Sir Hugh Hastings III was a member of his retinue each time he took the field. By its very nature, then, as a series of recollections of occasions when Sir Edward's immediate ancestors had borne the disputed Pembroke arms with a difference, the vast majority of war-related testimony centred upon participation in the Lancastrian military retinue.

The contours of Hastings' deponents' wider careers may serve to exemplify just how varied the ties of Lancastrian 'well-willers' (even within knightly ranks) could be. The career of Sir Ralph Shelton II was indicative on many of his fellow Hastings supporters. Shelton, as we have seen, campaigned with Gaunt on four occasions, on the *chevauchée* of 1373, at the siege of St. Malo, and later in Scotland and Spain.⁶⁷ His Lancastrian military ties, though, were far from exclusive. He was in Aquitaine with the Earl of Suffolk in 1369, served at sea under the Earl of Hereford in the early 1370s and the Earl of Arundel in the late 1380s, and undertook Bishop Despenser's crusade to Flanders in 1383.⁶⁸ His family possessed no pre-existing Lancastrian affiliations: indeed, his eponymous father, having been knighted at the battle of Crécy (1346), became a retainer of Gaunt's brother, Edward, the Black Prince, in whose retinue he suffered capture at the battle of Poitiers (1356).⁶⁹ Sir Ralph II, moreover, in his private life, proved a knight of wide-ranging association. Through his father, he was close to the family of the Black Prince's leading Norfolk retainer, Sir Thomas Felton, and witnessed deeds for various barons and knights, most notably Walter, Lord Fitzwalter.⁷⁰ He also became close to three of his Lancastrian neighbours in northeast Norfolk, Sir John Strange, Erpingham, and the lawyer, William Winter, whilst his stepmother was the widow of Gaunt's Suffolk banneret, Sir John Plays of Chelsworth.⁷¹ Shelton was thus a knight with a few noteworthy kin, friends and associates within the Lancastrian affinity, and this may well have smoothed his path into Gaunt's military retinue. Yet, military service was Shelton's only

⁶⁶ Keen, 'Grey v. Hastings', pp. 181–2.
⁶⁷ C 76/56, m. 25; *PCM*, I, pp. 423–4.
⁶⁸ C 76/52, m. 16; E 101/32/20, m. 1; E 101/41/5, m. 1; C 76/67, m. 16.
⁶⁹ *CPR, 1345–8*, p. 474; *CCR, 1354–60*, p. 334.
⁷⁰ *CPR, 1381–5*, p. 557; *HPC, 1386–1421*, IV, p. 356.
⁷¹ *HMC, Thirteenth Report*, IV, pp. 424–7; NRO, NCC Reg. Harsyk, f. 240; *CCR, 1389–92*, pp. 331–2; NRO, NCC Reg. Heydon, f. 117.

identifiable connection with Gaunt and, given his active career in arms, one may surmise that unlike many of those Lancastrian soldiers cited above as Scrope witnesses, Shelton served in the Lancastrian military retinue primarily because he was seeking regular military employment and Gaunt happened to command the largest, most stable, and most active retinue available.

The shape of Shelton's career in Lancastrian service was matched by many of Hastings' other deponents, since knights and esquires who could recall multiple occasions when Hastings' ancestors had borne the disputed arms in war were naturally those best placed to defend his claim. What one encounters before the Court, then – especially if one fleshes out the recollections of these testators by identifying, from other military records, additional occasions on which they had campaigned – is a sample of gentry who were members of a distinctive local military community in the eastern counties, centred in northeast Norfolk.[72] Some were Gaunt's retainers, but most served at regular intervals under whichever magnate was available. The fact that Gaunt campaigned so often naturally led many of these gentry to serve in his retinue more than once. The careers in arms of Sir John Wiltshire, Simon Burgh and Robert Poley, for example, closely resemble those of Shelton.[73] Indeed, exclusive Lancastrian service was almost non-existent, even amongst Gaunt's fully-fledged retainers. Even that highest-profile of Lancastrians, Sir Thomas Erpingham, first bore arms under the Ufford earls of Suffolk and only entered Gaunt's service in the late 1370s.[74]

Yet, one must not overemphasise the homogeneity of the military careers carved out by Hastings' largely 'socio-professional' deponents, for the diffuse character of the Lancastrian military experience was also indirectly on display before the Court. Many of Hastings' deponents were very much the type of gentry soldier who merely supplemented a magnate's military retinue, fleshing out its inner core. Gaunt actively courted their services, sometimes going to the extreme of sending out letters individually, inviting prospective participants to join him.[75] As such, whilst a man like Sir Ralph Shelton II would eventually have become something of a familiar face and someone to be counted on, through his regular appearances beneath the Lancastrian banner,

---

[72] See below, pp. 127–30.
[73] *PCM*, I, pp. 401–4; 427–9; 495-7.
[74] Curry, 'Sir Thomas Erpingham', p. 60.
[75] *JGReg, 1379–83*, II, nos. 775–80.

several of his fellow testators dipped in and out of Gaunt's military retinue in far more haphazard fashion.

Sir Simon Felbrigg's participation on Gaunt's Spanish enterprise hints strongly at how the system worked. If any expedition required the services of potential short-term recruits, this was it. Gaunt's 'way of Spain' was a large-scale, privately funded military venture, requiring far more manpower than even his inner core of retainers could possibly muster.[76] Moreover, despite being tentatively disguised as a campaign in the national interest, the wrangling of Parliament over the preceding years makes plain the reluctance of England's political class to fund Gaunt's vaulting ambition.[77] As such, the Lancastrian affinity, to an even greater degree than on traditional expeditions to France or Scotland, was forced to spread its tentacles via Gaunt's retainers into the latter's stockpile of friends and associates. And a young man like Felbrigg, loosely attached through family tradition to the Earl of March, and yet to complete his rise into Richard II's inner circle of chamber knights, would have appeared a perfect target.[78] As we saw in the previous chapter, Felbrigg was born and raised in northeast Norfolk in the heartland of Gaunt's East Anglian power base and was one of the few younger greater gentry of the region who had not found his way onto Gaunt's payroll.[79] As such, in an atmosphere in which his Lancastrian neighbours and close friends, Sir Thomas Erpingham, Sir Robert Berney and John Reymes, were all signing up for Gaunt's 'way of Spain', it is unsurprising that Felbrigg was enticed to follow suit, thereby joining the ranks of that unstable array of men-at-arms, who clung on a campaign-by-campaign basis to the outer reaches of the Lancastrian military retinue.[80] Felbrigg's contribution proved a one-off event. At the opposite extreme, his fellow testator, Sir William Berdewell – fighting as a career professional – served in equally informal fashion, yet, by the sheer regularity with which he bore arms, he ended up fighting for Gaunt three times across the seven campaigns he undertook between 1378 and 1387.[81]

[76] Goodman, *John of Gaunt*, pp. 111–43.
[77] Harriss, *Shaping the Nation*, pp. 414–19.
[78] Given-Wilson, *The Royal Household*, pp. 201–2; Milner, 'Sir Simon Felbrigg: KG', pp. 84–6.
[79] See above, pp. 43–4.
[80] Caudrey, 'War and Society in Medieval Norfolk', pp. 93–9; *PCM*, I, pp. 439–42; 443–4; 444–5; 474–6.
[81] *PCM*, I, pp. 390–2.

All of this points to the starkly indirect character of Lancastrian influence on Sir Edward Hastings' behalf. Despite his grandfather's and great-grandfather's exalted positions within the Lancastrian affinity, what we largely find in Sir Edward's defence before the Court are an assortment of East Anglian knights and esquires who served with varying degrees of regularity in the Lancastrian military retinue, but with few exceptions, were never active members of Gaunt's peacetime affinity. As such, the composition of Sir Edward's witness list – in a local, East Anglian context – throws the role of indirect lordship into sharp relief, revealing the extent to which his deponents' friendships and associations had flourished loosely, for the best part of two generations, beneath the Lancastrian umbrella.

Sir Edward himself, notwithstanding his youth and his family's relatively recent migration from Yorkshire to Norfolk, was very much a part of this East Anglian community. Distinguished knights from the region, including Shelton, Erpingham, Berdewell and Sir Thomas Gerbergh, attested to having fought alongside his father, Sir Hugh Hastings III, at least three times during the 1370s and 1380s, and vividly recalled Sir Hugh's exploits at St. Malo and Brest.[82] Other locals, including Sir Thomas Hengrave, John Reymes, Thomas Stanton and Robert Fishlake, had all served in the Hastings' personal retinue.[83] Additionally, a host of deponents from northeast Norfolk – Shelton, Erpingham, Felbrigg, Berney, Reymes, Sir Miles Stapleton, Sir John Geney, Sir William Calthorp and Edmund Barry – had all been Sir Edward's adult neighbours as he approached his majority during the 1390s.[84] The Hastings' standing in Norfolk, moreover, is underscored by the fact that this was the only shire, upon the death of the last Earl of Pembroke, whose inquisition post mortem found that the Earl's estates rightfully devolved to their family, rather than the Greys of Ruthin.[85] For one so young and inexperienced, Sir Edward Hastings did a remarkable job of mining his personal connections with his father's old East Anglian friends and associates.

In short, the vast majority of Sir Edward Hastings' testators hailed from the East Anglia of his birth and were part of an interrelated social network, one of whose common features – as they themselves avowed

---

[82] *PCM*, I, pp. 423–4; 439–42; 390–2; 496–7.
[83] *PCM*, I, pp. 492; 444–5; 486–7; 429–35.
[84] Castor, *The King, the Crown, and the Duchy of Lancaster*, pp. 59–81.
[85] Caudrey, 'War, Chivalry and Regional Society', p. 131.

before the Court – was personal familiarity with the Hastings family and an appreciation of the splendid deeds in arms of Sir Edward's immediate ancestors. If *Scrope v. Grosvenor* enables the historian to glimpse the Lancastrian affinity at its peak, engaged in a very obvious act of maintenance, *Grey v. Hastings* reveals the extent to which Lancastrian military leadership in the 1370s and 1380s left a lasting legacy of inter-gentry solidarity in Hastings' native East Anglia that significantly outlived John of Gaunt.

Other Magnate Affinities

No other magnate in these heraldic disputes enjoyed an influence upon the Court of Chivalry's proceedings to match that achieved by John of Gaunt in *Scrope v. Grosvenor*. The latent influence of lordship, however – so apparent amongst Sir Edward Hastings' witnesses – is evident across all three cases. Each protagonist extended their reach into gentry communities that were, to varying degrees, recruiting grounds for individual magnates. As such, it is no surprise that a small, but by no means insignificant, body of witnesses detailed in their testimony the retinues in which they had fought. In the context of the cases themselves, these snippets were effectively descriptive flourishes, for witnesses were invited (but were not obliged) to talk about their own careers, and most of the military testimony consequently related nothing more than occasions when the testator in question had seen the protagonist's family bearing the disputed arms in a military setting.[86] Nonetheless, the fortuitous survival of these more detailed depositions makes it possible to probe more fully – beyond the Lancastrian affinity – the role of lordship before the Court.

Historians have largely approached this theme from a socio-military perspective, with an emphasis upon the character of retinue construction in wartime. As Andrew Ayton has emphasised, a great many witnesses who provided information about the lords under whom they fought revealed variously: (1) a career in arms moving from one retinue to the next; (2) a period of extensive military service under one lord, interrupted by his decline or death, which necessitated the search for a new military employer; and (3) a lifelong attachment to a single magnate affinity, made possible by long-lived lords and

---

[86] Caudrey, 'War, Chivalry and Regional Society', pp. 126–7.

male heirs who successfully maintained their father's followings.[87] This approach to the issue of lordship before the Court of Chivalry has been well covered in the existing scholarship, and it is not the intention here to retrace old ground. Rather – picking up where we left off with Sir Edward Hastings – let us turn our attention to those steps taken by Richard, Lord Scrope and Thomas, Lord Morley to acquire the support of gentry from other magnate affinities to speak in their defence.

Both Scrope and Morley recruited witnesses who had served in all manner of military retinues. Morley's testators included gentry who had served in a military capacity under the Earls of Warwick, March and Suffolk, the Lords Willoughby, Zouche and Latimer, and even the bannerets, Sir John Norwich, Sir Bartholomew Burgherssh and Sir William Kerdiston.[88] These deponents were few in number and diverse in allegiance. By contrast, a significant group across both witness lists were former followers respectively of Edward, the Black Prince and the Bohun earls of Northampton and Hereford.[89] What is especially striking is that all three of these magnates were some years dead by the time gentry formerly in their employ provided their testimony.[90] It is, in consequence, worth considering why these gentry spoke before the Court, what they revealed, and how they had moved on into the next phase of their careers in the wake of their lord's passing.

The Bohuns and the Black Prince had long been associated with the Scropes and Morleys. William Bohun, Earl of Northampton – one of Edward III's leading commanders and most trusted companions – enjoyed a powerful recruiting reach throughout northern England, centred upon his possession of the lordship of Annandale and the castle of Lochmaben on the Western Scots March.[91] With his military retinue containing a substantial northern contingent, it comes as no surprise

---

[87] Ayton, 'Knights, Esquires and Military Service', pp. 93–4; Ayton, 'Military Service and the Dynamics of Recruitment', pp. 45–55. See also, Bell et al., *The Soldier*, pp. 23–53.

[88] C 47/6/1, nos. 5, 34, 39, 93, 14, 30, 38, 96, 12.

[89] Ayton briefly addressed the Bohun connection on Lord Morley's behalf. Ayton, 'Military Service and the Dynamics of Recruitment', p. 52.

[90] Some of these men had been officially retained by the Black Prince and the Bohun earls. Other merely moved within the orbit of their affinity. See below, pp. 85–90.

[91] A. Ayton, 'The Crécy Campaign', in *The Battle of Crécy, 1346*, ed. A. Ayton and P. Preston (Woodbridge, 2005), p. 56; Ormrod, *Edward III*, pp. 23, 231; Holmes, *The Estates of the Higher Nobility*, pp. 20, 22.

that Richard, Lord Scrope's elder brother, William, had forged his brief, albeit intensive, career in arms beneath Northampton's banner during the early 1340s.[92] Lord Richard's Masham cousin, Geoffrey, had been heavily involved in the English crusading movement in the 1360s, as had the young Earl of Hereford.[93] Northampton and Hereford had also regularly campaigned in the company of Thomas, Lord Morley's father and grandfather, and the Scropes, Morleys and Bohuns had all been stalwarts of the Edwardian regime since its inception.[94] Hereford's eldest surviving daughter, Eleanor, moreover, had married the Duke of Gloucester, who was one of Thomas, Lord Morley's closest friends, whilst his younger daughter, Mary, subsequently wed Henry of Bolingbroke.[95] Edward, the Black Prince, for his part, as the dominant figure in English military society during the 1350s and 1360s, and as an active recruiter of gentry from both the northern and eastern counties, naturally drew numerous future Scrope and Morley witnesses into his military retinue.[96] Indeed, Thomas, Lord Morley's father had first borne arms on the Prince's Gascony expeditions in the mid 1350s, whilst Richard, Lord Scrope himself had accompanied the Prince to Spain with John of Gaunt in 1366–7, as had his cousin, William, who lost his life there.[97] Scrope, moreover, remained a pivotal figure in the minority government of Richard II, and although far from a favourite of the young king, he nonetheless maintained regular contact with a number of Richard's household knights who had been former followers of either the Prince or Hereford.[98]

Scrope was thus able to bring together in his defence at least ten deponents, ranging from distinguished knights to mere esquires, who identified one or more occasions when they had campaigned under

[92] Rosenthal, *Telling Tales*, p. 82.
[93] Guard, *Chivalry, Kingship and Crusade*, pp. 236, 220.
[94] C 47/6/1. Ormrod, *Edward III*, pp. 291, 293–4, 304, 450, 503, 529, 553.
[95] A. Goodman, *The Loyal Conspiracy* (London, 1971), pp. 101–2; Walker, *The Lancastrian Affinity*, p. 104.
[96] D. S. Green, 'The Household and Military Retinue of Edward the Black Prince' (D.Phil, Nottingham, 1999), Appendix, pp. 1–39.
[97] *Foedera*, III, i, p. 325; *CP*, XI, pp. 539–41; *Scrope v. Grosvenor*, I, pp. 374, 400.
[98] Given-Wilson, *The Royal Household*, pp. 158, 173, 283–6.

Northampton.⁹⁹ Some were more closely aligned with the Bohuns than others. The relatively obscure Roger Culwyn, for example, merely detailed his service under Northampton at the sea-battle off Winchelsea in 1350.¹⁰⁰ At the opposite extreme, William Hesilrige could recall an extended bout of campaigning beneath Northampton's banner, beginning at the siege of Vannes (1342), stretching into the ensuing Brittany expedition, where he fought at the battle of Morlaix (1342), and culminating in the battle of Crécy and the siege of Calais (1346–7).¹⁰¹ Those who could recall service under Northampton were generally older men and their testimony almost exclusively focused upon the campaigns of the 1330s and 1340s, with few mentioning any military commitments later than the battle of Winchelsea.

Notwithstanding this, some degree of continuity between the retinues of father and son is evident amongst Scrope's and Morley's body of testators, revealing a small core of followers who moved into Hereford's service after Northampton's death in 1360. William Biset, for instance, having served under Northampton in his youth in the 1340s and 1350s, returned to arms under Hereford on at least three occasions during the second phase of the Hundred Years War.¹⁰² Sir Richard Waldegrave and Nicholas Sabraham made the same transition, in Sabraham's case having served with Northampton as far back as the French campaigns of the mid 1340s.¹⁰³ Others were amongst Hereford's closest retainers in peace as well as war. Waldegrave and Sir William Lucy were members of his household, accompanying him on his three crusades to Prussia, Egypt and Syria, and acting with him in his private affairs back in England.¹⁰⁴ Sir John Clanvowe,

---

⁹⁹ William Biset, Roger Culwyn, Sir William Flamville, William Hesilrige, Sir Robert Marney, John Rither, Nicholas Sabraham, Sir John St. Quintin, Sir Richard Waldegrave, Sir Richard le Zouche. *Scrope v. Grosvenor*, I, pp. 125–6; 237–8; 176–7; 126–7; 170–1; 144–50; 124–5; 167–8; 165–6; 189–90.

¹⁰⁰ *Scrope v. Grosvenor*, I, pp. 237–8.

¹⁰¹ *Scrope v. Grosvenor*, I, pp. 126–7.

¹⁰² *Scrope v. Grosvenor*, I, pp. 125–6; C 76/52, m. 20; E 101/31/15, m. 1.

¹⁰³ *Scrope v. Grosvenor*, I, pp. 165–6; 124–5. Ayton has recently reconstructed Sabraham's lengthy career in arms, arguing that he likely first saw service in Brittany in 1345. After Northampton's death, Sabraham undertook extensive bouts of crusading during the 1360s, almost certainly serving under Hereford in Prussia during the winter of 1362–3 and at the siege of Alexandria in 1365. Ayton, 'Nicholas Sabraham', pp. 95–120.

¹⁰⁴ *Scrope v. Grosvenor*, I, pp. 165–6, 77–8; Guard, *Chivalry, Kingship and Crusade*, p. 141.

although unspecific about his own military record in his deposition, was likewise an annuitant of Hereford's and a member of his inner circle.[105] Similarly, amongst Morley's testators, Sir Thomas Mandeville 'the son' held estates from Hereford, whilst Sir John Burgh was in receipt of a 40-mark annuity from the Earl.[106] This body of evidence, though impressionistic, hints at the strong level of stability that existed within the Bohun family's inner core of retainers and regular military followers, whilst the noteworthy number of testators, who merely described occasional military service in their retinues, reminds one of how enticing the very active Bohuns were as military employers over consecutive generations.

Edward, the Black Prince, meanwhile, had been an even more substantial military employer of Scrope's and Morley's Court of Chivalry testators. Thirty-five gentry, known to have fought at least once beneath his banner, provided depositions on Scrope's behalf.[107] The reasons for this connection are not hard to find. Many were called to testify because they could recall Lord Richard fighting with the disputed arms at the battle of Nájera (1367). Moreover, given the size of the Prince's following during the 1350s and 1360s, it would only have been natural that miscellaneous older gentry brought together in Scrope's defence had coincidentally fought in the Prince's company at least once or twice. Importantly, too, the presence of former followers of the Prince was tremendously helpful to Lord Richard because they not only could uphold his armorial claim, they could disparage Sir Robert Grosvenor's counter-claim at the same time. Almost every long-term retainer of the Prince who spoke for Scrope asserted in his testimony that he had never heard of Sir Robert Grosvenor, nor could he recall any of the Prince's many Cheshire followers bearing the disputed arms.[108] This was, to some extent, a battle of memory between the Prince's Cheshire and non-Cheshire followers, for a significant number of Grosvenor's Cheshire supporters had either served personally in the Prince's retinue, or were immediate kinsmen

---

[105] *Scrope v. Grosvenor*, I, pp. 184–5; Guard, *Chivalry, Kingship and Crusade*, p. 142.
[106] C 47/6/1, nos. 47, 37; Holmes, *The Estates of the Higher Nobility*, p. 70n.
[107] *Scrope v. Grosvenor*; Green, 'Edward the Black Prince', Appendix, pp. 1–39.
[108] See pp. 166–7.

of older men who had done so.¹⁰⁹ Before the Court, then, to counter the claims of distinguished Cheshire families such as the Massys, Duttons and Leghs,¹¹⁰ Richard, Lord Scrope turned to the Prince's retainers from elsewhere. This explains, for instance, why Scrope's East Anglian supporters were effectively split down the middle, half being members of Gaunt's Spanish army, whilst the remainder – most notably, Sir William Wingfield, Sir Robert Morley, Sir John Brewes and Sir Stephen Hales – recounted, on the one hand, occasions when the Scropes had borne the disputed arms in the Prince's retinue, and, on the other, hinted at the obscurity of Sir Robert Grosvenor and, by implication, the insincerity of his claim.¹¹¹ Grosvenor, of course, was far from obscure to the gentry of the northwest. To the gentry of the eastern counties, though, he may well have appeared so.

More than 20 deponents tied in various ways to the Bohun family testified for Richard, Lord Scrope and Thomas, Lord Morley. Regular or occasional followers of the Black Prince across these two cases numbered closer to 50. Yet, by the mid 1380s, every one of these testators had been forced to find alternative employment. Humphrey Bohun had died suddenly in 1373 at the age of 32 and the Black Prince had finally succumbed to the ravages of ill-health in 1376.¹¹² The matter of shifting allegiances and the search for patronage was comparatively less urgent in the case of the Prince's retainers. He had been in physical decline since the late 1360s and his young son was anyway next in line to the throne.¹¹³ As such, a great many testators who had served the Prince in their youths had become knights and esquires of the Ricardian royal household by the time they spoke before the Court.¹¹⁴ Moreover, the bonds of inter-gentry solidarity that had developed across the Prince's campaigns continued to find expression long after his death.¹¹⁵

---

[109] Six Grosvenor deponents had served with the Prince at least once. *Scrope v. Grosvenor*, I, pp. 255–6; 262–3; 263–4; 311; 316; 320. More than a dozen others had older relatives who had served with the Prince. *Scrope v. Grosvenor*, I, pp. 255; 263; 271; 271–2; 275; 285–6; 286–7; 287; 288; 295–6; 296; 309; 319.

[110] *Scrope v. Grosvenor*, I, pp. 255; 255–6; 282–8; 296–8; 311; 313.

[111] Caudrey, 'War, Chivalry and Regional Society', pp. 133–4.

[112] Ormrod, *Edward III*, pp. 489, 549.

[113] Ormrod, *Edward III*, pp. 441, 500, 552, 558.

[114] Given-Wilson, *The Royal Household*, pp. 282–6.

[115] See below, pp. 125–6.

By contrast, the prospects facing the Earl of Hereford's retainers, in the wake of his sudden passing, were far less certain, which led to a scattering of the Bohun affinity as new employers were sought. Sir Richard Waldegrave, perhaps the highest profile Bohun retainer to speak before the Court, went on to reinforce his reputation in Richard II's household and as an incredibly active shire administrator.[116] Many merely followed the obvious avenues for future patronage that opened up before them. Most notably, Henry of Bolingbroke's marriage to Hereford's daughter, Mary, cleared a path for several of the late Earl's retainers to pass into Lancastrian service.[117] Sir William Lucy and Robert Fitzralph, for instance, became annuitants of Gaunt's and campaigned with him twice.[118] Most spectacularly, Sir Thomas Morieux ended up marrying Gaunt's bastard daughter, Blanche, and eventually was named marshal of the Lancastrian army for the Spanish expedition in 1386.[119] In similar fashion, several deponents – Sir John Gildesburgh, Sir Thomas Mandeville, Esmond Breton and Thomas Lampete – moved into the service of Gaunt's younger brother, Thomas of Woodstock, Duke of Gloucester, who, as we have seen, had married Hereford's other daughter, Eleanor.[120]

Significantly, though, many of these testators – especially Hereford's knightly retainers – actively maintained those ties of friendship and association that they had originally forged in their youths in Hereford's household and military retinue. The ongoing Bohun connections of Sir Richard Waldegrave provide a case in point.[121] A Suffolk knight, Waldegrave had served in the Bohun's household since the mid 1350s. He had campaigned at least once under Northampton, before carving out a distinguished career in arms under Hereford, which he explicated

---

[116] Given-Wilson, *The Royal Household*, p. 286; Keen, *Origins of the English Gentleman*, pp. 92-3.

[117] Walker, *The Lancastrian Affinity*, p. 104.

[118] *CPR, 1370-4*, pp. 283, 373; *JG Reg II*, nos. 41, 50; *JG Reg I*, no. 844; *Scrope v. Grosvenor*, I, p. 66; C 81/1032 (12).

[119] Goodman, *John of Gaunt*, pp. 357-8.

[120] *Scrope v. Grosvenor*, I, pp. 217-19; C 47/6/1, nos. 47, 44, 67; Goodman, *The Loyal Conspiracy*, p. 79. Lampete bore arms under Gloucester on at least three occasions. C 47/6/1, no. 67; C 76/61, m, 26; E 101/38/2, m. 1.

[121] On Waldegrave's career, see J. S. Roskell, 'Sir Richard Waldegrave', *Proceedings of the Suffolk Institute of Archaeology*, 27 (1957), pp. 154-75; Keen, *Origins of the English Gentleman*, pp. 92-3.

at length in his testimony before the Court.¹²² He simultaneously enjoyed a level of attachment to the Black Prince's widow, Joan, her son, Thomas Holland, Earl of Kent, and various future Ricardian courtiers, which saw him retained as a 'king's knight' in 1377.¹²³ Yet, throughout his life, his closest relationships arguably remained those with his old Bohun comrades, including several who like him testified before the Court. Sir John Burgh and Sir Richard Sutton were his kinsmen;¹²⁴ he became a feoffee for Sir Thomas Mandeville;¹²⁵ and he acted in various private business affairs with Sir John Gildesburgh, eventually become a trustee of his estates and assisting Gildesburgh's widow in a number of land transactions.¹²⁶ Waldegrave also remained on extremely close terms with Hereford's friend, Guy, Lord Brian, whose son married Waldegrave's stepdaughter, and whose position in the royal household may have helped facilitate Waldegrave's entry into courtly circles.¹²⁷ Finally, as the ultimate expression of Waldegrave's enduring Bohun connections, he remained on intimate terms with Hereford's widow, Countess Joan, and her brother, the Bishop of Ely, for years after Earl Humphrey's death.¹²⁸

Waldegrave – war veteran, crusader, courtier, twelve-time MP, and elected Speaker to the House of Commons – was an exceptional figure.¹²⁹ Yet, his later career, as outlined above, neatly illustrates the ways in which inter-gentry solidarities, when forged through bonds of shared service in a magnate affinity, could in the right circumstances continue to flourish well beyond the lifespan of the magnate in

---

[122] *Scrope v. Grosvenor*, I, pp. 165–6.

[123] *HPC, 1386-1421*, IV, pp. 736–7; Given-Wilson, *The Royal Household*, p. 286.

[124] C 47/6/1, nos. 37, 38; *CCR, 1377-81*, p. 359; *CIPM*, XIV, p. 227; CP 25(1)221/95/15.

[125] C 47/6/1, no. 47; *Feet of Fines for Essex: Volume 3: A.D. 1327–A.D. 1422*, ed. R. C. Fowler and S. C. Ratcliff (Essex Archaeological Society, 1929–49), III, pp. 201, 203.

[126] *Scrope v. Grosvenor*, I, pp. 217–19; *HPC, 1386–1421*, IV, p. 737.

[127] *Scrope v. Grosvenor*, I, pp. 76–7; *CFR*, XI, pp. 57–8; *Essex Feet of Fines*, III, p. 198; *CP*, II, pp. 361–2; *CCR, 1385–9*, pp. 302, 628; Given-Wilson, *The Royal Household*, pp. 156–8.

[128] E.g., *CCR, 1385–9*, p. 425; *Essex Feet of Fines*, III, pp. 201, 203.

[129] Keen specifically adopted Waldegrave as an outstanding exemplar of the 'socio-professional' knight, who combined military service with stints working in shire administration. Keen, *Origins of the English Gentleman*, pp. 92–3. It has even been suggested that Waldegrave may have been the model for Geoffrey Chaucer's knight. J. S. Roskell, *The Commons and their Speakers in English Parliaments 1376–1523* (Manchester, 1965), p. 129.

question. In the next chapter, we shall examine some of the ways in which these affinity-based social circles became integrated into other types of gentry communities, which collectively comprised the protagonists' support bases before the Court of Chivalry. First, though, it is worth lowering our sights from the large-scale affinities of princes, dukes and earls to consider the smattering of deponents before the Court who looked upon the protagonists themselves as their immediate lord.

Local Lordship

The three Court of Chivalry protagonists who most earnestly utilised their status as local lords when constructing their witness lists were Thomas, Lord Morley, Reginald, Lord Grey, and, in rather more limited fashion, Sir Edward Hastings.[130] Relatively few of Morley's or Hastings' deponents claimed kinship ties, or any sort of official bond of affinity, with their families. Sir John Strange rather ambiguously described himself as *d'alliance* with Lord Morley.[131] Despite being better known for his connections with Edward, the Black Prince, and later, John of Gaunt, Strange had begun his career in arms under Morley's late brother, Sir John, and by his own admission had subsequently remained close to the family.[132] The elderly esquire, Hugh Curson, was Morley's tenant, whilst Morley's neighbour, Sir Thomas Gerbergh, regularly bore arms in his military retinue in the early-to-mid 1380s.[133] Indeed, we encounter Gerbergh before the Court of Chivalry at the crossroads of his career, just prior to his rise as steward of the Duke of York.[134] Curson, similarly, had fought consistently in the retinue of Lord Thomas' grandfather, Robert, and his son and grandson, as

---

[130] The same was true of Richard, Lord Scrope, although his reach was wider and his testators were generally less forthcoming in describing the precise nature of their relationship with him. See below, pp. 98–114.

[131] C 47/6/1, no. 46. Strange may have enjoyed a distant familial connection with the Morleys. Certainly, he was a kinsman of the Morleys' longstanding associates, the Feltons of Litcham. Blomefield, *History of Norfolk*, X, p. 336.

[132] *CPR, 1374–7*, pp. 426, 440; C 139/23/31; *JG Reg* I, no. 853; *JG Reg*, II, p. 8; C 76/70, m. 11; C 47/6/1, no. 46. Sir John Morley served in Spain in 1366–7 and probably died not long after. *CP*, IX, p. 215.

[133] C 47/6/1, nos. 40, 99. *CIPM*, XIII, no. 328.

[134] *CPR, 1405-8*, p. 12.

we saw in the previous chapter, both acted regularly as feoffees and parties to land transactions involving the Morleys, indicative, one may surmise, of a level of trust achieved by a lesser gentry family who naturally looked to the Morleys as their 'good lord'.[135]

The Cursons were at one level atypical of the lesser gentry experience, in so far as they had risen steadily up the social ladder between the 1340s and the 1380s, becoming undeniably members of Norfolk's county élite by the turn of the fifteenth century.[136] Yet, in another sense, the type of vertical ties they enjoyed with the Morleys also finds expression in Lord Thomas' relations with several other, more obscure, esquires who testified in his defence. Although, as one might expect, a great many of Morley's sub-knightly deponents had borne arms beneath his family's banner at least once, a core group of six lesser gentry attested to having done so regularly.[137] All but one were distinguished old soldiers of immense military experience, whose war records dated back to the French expeditions of the early 1340s, and, in one instance, back still further to the Scottish wars of the 1330s, and who had fought under Robert, Lord Morley on at least three occasions across more than a decade.[138] The clearest expression of the Morleys' lordship over their lesser gentry neighbours, however, is to be found in the career of the one deponent from this group who was still actively in their employ at the time the case came before the Court: Oliver Mendham.[139] Mendham was well advanced in years by the time *Lovel v. Morley* began. He stated that he was 63 years old and that he had served under Lord Willoughby on the Rheims expedition in 1359–60. During the Hundred Years War's second phase, however, he fought beneath the Morley banner on five successive campaigns and attested before the Court that he was Lord Thomas' feed servant.[140] Mendham's career hints tantalisingly at the prospective bonds Robert, second Lord Morley, may have enjoyed with those five older, self-described Morley military followers who deposed on his grandson's behalf. One

---

[135] C 47/6/1, no. 99; *CPR, 1370–4*, p. 419; *CCR, 1381–5*, p. 420. On the levels of trust that could develop between greater and lesser gentry within the localities, see C. E. Moreton, 'A Social Gulf? The Upper and Lesser Gentry of Later Medieval England', *Journal of Medieval History*, 17 (1991), pp. 255–62.

[136] *HPC, 1386-1421*, II, p. 719.

[137] C 47/6/1, nos. 5, 10, 11, 20, 26, 59.

[138] C 47/6/1, no. 10.

[139] C 47/6/1, no. 26.

[140] C 47/6/1, no. 26.

of these men in particular, Thomas Rose, strongly gives the impression, through his participation with Lord Robert on expeditions as minor as a raid upon the Normandy coast, that their relationship, in the style of Mendham's, very likely extended beyond the military sphere.[141]

Sir Edward Hastings' witnesses reinforce this portrait of local lordship. Most of the 25 militarily active esquires who deposed for Sir Edward had seen his family bearing the disputed arms with a difference on more than one campaign, and a minority could recall enough such occasions that, even though they never explicitly said so, they very likely were serving at the time in the retinues of Sir Hugh Hastings II or Sir Hugh Hastings III. Thomas Pickworth, for instance, had been with Sir Hugh III when he survived the storm that destroyed Sir John Arundel's fleet in 1379, and he was with him again in Brittany the following year.[142] Thomas Swinborne and Robert Lymworth similarly recalled Sir Hugh III's exploits on three individual expeditions.[143] John Parker, who crusaded with Sir Hugh II in the early 1360s, probably enjoyed a personal connection with the Hastings family, for it seems unlikely that a man of his station crusaded on a whim unless he were a career soldier, for which no evidence survives.[144] In the case of another Hastings crusader, Robert Fishlake, there exist no such doubts. Aside from campaigning with Sir Hugh Hastings II in the eastern Mediterranean, Fishlake also fought in Sir Hugh Hastings III's retinue on four separate occasions between 1378 and 1385. He undertook this service as an archer, though he had probably become a man-at-arms by the time he spoke before the Court. In his lengthy testimony, he explained that he had dwelt with Sir Hugh III for 16 years prior to his death (i.e. from c. 1372) and that he had known the defendant, Sir Edward, since infancy.[145] Fishlake, in short, appears to have served Sir Hugh Hastings III in much the same fashion that Oliver Mendham, over the same time period, had served Thomas, Lord Morley. The Court's proceedings, then, reveal enticing snippets of lord–retainer relations within the locality, reminding one that the much-studied magnate–gentry dynamic was merely the top rung of a long ladder of

---

[141] C 47/6/1, no. 20.
[142] *PCM*, I, pp. 404–5.
[143] *PCM*, I, pp. 405-6, 413-21.
[144] *PCM*, I, p. 533.
[145] *PCM*, I, pp. 429–35. Fishlake's career has been addressed in the context of lesser gentry military careerism in Bell et al., *The Soldier*, pp. 167–9.

dependence and service to one's social superiors that percolated all the way down to the lesser gentry and below.[146]

The Morley and Hastings evidence on this score, however, is not particularly illuminating when it comes to fleshing out the character of local lordship. Robert Fishlake may provide a rarely detailed exemplar, but even here his testimony was essentially focused upon iconographic evidence and recollections of occasions when he had seen various Hastings bearing the disputed arms in a military setting, and the strength of his peacetime connections with their family arises almost as an aside designed to underscore the veracity of his testimony.[147] Fortunately, these blanks may, to some extent, be filled in, by turning to the depositions provided on behalf of Hastings' rival, Reginald, Lord Grey of Ruthin. Grey undoubtedly enjoyed a better claim to the Pembroke arms and inheritance than the cadet Hastings of Elsing.[148] As such, despite his family's distinguished war record, Grey's defence was centred upon matters of lineage and he did not require vast numbers of military testators, essentially because his family had never borne the arms, *or a manche gules*, in the lifetime of the Pembroke earls.[149] What his deponents consequently reveal, if only indirectly, is a taste of life in a local baronial household for lesser gentry for whom Grey was their lord and the focal point of the social circle in which they lived.

Their experiences were noticeably varied, reminding one that barons, bannerets and knights required an array of retainers for different purposes, albeit on a smaller scale than their magnate contemporaries. John Mortimer asserted that he had served in Lord Grey's retinue in Scotland in 1400 and was his retainer and fee holder;[150] Henry Howard had likewise been retained by Grey and had served him in Ireland;[151] and John Beche had been retained by Grey for the recent Welsh campaigns designed to pacify the Glyn Dwr rebels.[152] Even more telling is the civilian testimony, which provides the bulk of Grey's evidence, and which speaks to the longevity and continuity of personnel within the Grey family's affinity. At the more distinguished

---

[146] R. Horrox, 'Service', in *Fifteenth-Century Attitudes: Perceptions of Society in Late Medieval England*, ed. R. Horrox (Cambridge, 1994), pp. 61–78.
[147] *PCM*, I, pp. 429–35.
[148] Jack, 'Entail and Descent', pp. 2, 5.
[149] See above, pp. 5–7.
[150] *PCM*, I, pp. 275–7.
[151] *PCM*, I, p. 281.
[152] *PCM*, I, pp. 283–4.

end of things, John Harvey was an apprentice of the common law who acknowledged before the Court that he was a member of Grey's affinity and had served on his privy council.[153] Thomas Lound revealed that he had been a servant of Grey's father.[154] Roger Tunstall, the Mayor of Bedford, declared that in his youth he had lived with the Greys.[155] Reginald Ragour was a life retainer of both Grey and his father, and a distant kinsman of their family.[156] William Parker had been a servant of Grey's father and held from their family the office of Parker of Yardley Chase.[157] Finally, John Archer explained that he had been a servant of Grey's father and mother, that he had dwelt with them in their household, and that he held from them a life fee.[158]

These servants and retainers were wheeled out to testify because Grey required witnesses who could recall the matters of lineage pertinent to the case, and older men long in his employ and resident in his household would have been those best placed to revive memories of decades-old in-house meetings, conversations and pronouncements about the Grey family's armorial right. The purpose behind their testimony notwithstanding, one is left with the unmistakable impression that men like Lound, Tunstall, Ragour, Parker and Archer had been staples of the Grey household for decades and were amongst their oldest and most trusted servants. Military memories were not their priority, but the recollections of Mortimer, Howard and Beche reinforce that, in the same vein as Oliver Mendham and Robert Fishlake, the baronage and greater gentry provided wide-ranging employment for local lesser gentry and yeomen living in their immediate vicinity, for whom household and military service provided a steady income and the prospect of long-term reward. The character of lordship, as revealed before the Court of Chivalry, thus ran the gamut from John of Gaunt maintaining Richard, Lord Scrope, to Sir Edward Hastings utilising Lancastrian bonds of affinity in bringing his father's old companions to his defence, to the protagonists in all three cases turning to their own tenants, attendants, household servants and personal retainers, who were clearly expected to defend their lord in his hour of need.

[153] *PCM*, I, pp. 176–98.
[154] *PCM*, I, pp. 273–5.
[155] *PCM*, I, pp. 268–71.
[156] *PCM*, I, pp. 264–7.
[157] *PCM*, I, pp. 242–3.
[158] *PCM*, I, pp. 231–5.

Conclusion

The role of lordship before the Court of Chivalry was at its most direct in the steps taken by each protagonist to acquire testimony from men who had fought in their retinues or served in their households. This chapter, however, has essentially sought to illustrate that, beyond such ties, the role of lordship before the Court was rather more complex than has hitherto been assumed. Richard, Lord Scrope did, indeed, receive considerable aid from John of Gaunt in shaping his defence, yet, the greatest benefit he derived from his Lancastrian affiliations was indirect, in the form of access to fellow gentry who had likewise carved out their careers in Lancastrian service. As we shall see in Chapter 3, Scrope's inter-gentry solidarities flourished beneath (and beyond) the umbrella of Lancastrian lordship. The same was true of Sir Edward Hastings. Constructing his witness list as a young man, eight years after John of Gaunt's death, he enjoyed no active support from the Lancastrian affinity whatsoever. Consequently, the gentry connections he relied upon before the Court were almost wholly the result of localism, utilising the lingering bonds forged by many of his witnesses with his father, Sir Hugh Hastings III, primarily through shared service in their youths, a generation earlier, in the Lancastrian military retinue. The shades of grey between overt Lancastrian assistance and indirect Lancastrian influence are thus, in some measure, revealed before the Court. The significance of indirect influence, moreover, clearly extended to other affinities, notably those of Edward, the Black Prince and the Bohun earls of Northampton and Hereford, whose ties with Scrope and Morley broadly paralleled Sir Edward Hastings' ties with old Lancastrians. This chapter has examined the role of lordship before the Court. The next will address the tangentially-related theme of the protagonists' horizontal ties, highlighting, from a different perspective, how the bonds of lordship and inter-gentry solidarity overlapped and intersected.

3

Region, Locality and Community

Historians of the Court of Chivalry – with an eye towards the bigger picture – have quite understandably tended to focus upon the wider significance of the surviving testimony, rather than upon the specific character of the cases themselves.¹ Consequently, whilst *Scrope v. Grosvenor*, *Lovel v. Morley* and *Grey v. Hastings* have all broadly provided fascinating insights into the world of English war and society, the more straightforward question, of the relationship between the protagonists and their deponents, has been left largely unexplored. Only Sir Robert Grosvenor's witness list, piecing together the web of inter-gentry solidarities that prevailed in Cheshire and Lancashire, has been the subject of detailed scrutiny in this regard.² This oversight is perhaps surprising, especially for Richard, Lord Scrope and Thomas, Lord Morley, who, like Grosvenor, brought to their cause large bodies of identifiable witnesses from various backgrounds to speak on their behalf, thereby making it possible for the historian to reconstruct how their witness lists were formed and what networks they utilised in their construction. This line of enquiry, moreover, ties in very neatly with the impressive body of scholarship – emanating from the groundbreaking research of K. B. McFarlane³ – that has sought to unravel, through

---

¹ Keen, 'Chivalrous Culture', pp. 14–22; Ayton, 'Knights, Esquires and Military Service', pp. 81–104; Keen, *Origins of the English Gentleman*, pp. 25–70; Ayton, 'Military Service and the Dynamics of Recruitment', pp. 45–57; Bell, 'The Soldier, "hadde he riden, no man ferre"', pp. 214–15; Bell et al., *The Soldier*, pp. 117–20, 260–70.

² Stewart-Brown, 'The Scrope and Grosvenor Controversy', pp. 1–22; Bennett, *Community, Class and Careerism*, pp. 16–17, 76, 82–3, 166–7, 186; Vale, 'The Scropes', pp. 100–1; Morgan, *War and Society in Medieval Cheshire*, pp. 16, 129–32, 156, 168, 187; Morgan, 'Sir Robert Grosvenor', pp. 75–94.

³ McFarlane, 'Parliament and "Bastard Feudalism"', pp. 53–79; McFarlane, 'Bastard Feudalism', pp. 161–80. McFarlane essentially advocated that an investigation of the career patterns and personal connections and experiences of the nobility and gentry may help to illuminate our understanding of the institutional framework that bound together centre and locality in later medieval England.

case studies of individual regions, counties and localities, the everyday concerns, both public and private, of the English gentry.[4] By addressing the testimony in these terms, focusing upon the horizontal and vertical ties of the protagonists with their witnesses, one may gauge the ways in which the types of gentry networks investigated in county histories came into play in the formation of Scrope's and Morley's witness lists.

In so doing, however, it must be borne in mind that both witness lists were constructed within the parameters set by the judges before the Court. No evidence survives of how Scrope or Morley selected their deponents, but the instructions they received from the judges about the types of evidence they should provide, as well as the order in which the interviews were conducted, have all been preserved in the Court's proceedings.[5] To cite Scrope's case, which may stand for both,[6] he demanded from the judges early in the case (February 1386) that they inform him, 'in what manner he would be required to exhibit his right to the arms in question'. After further preliminaries, the Court reconvened in May 1386, at which point Scrope was given until January 1387 to oversee the interviewing of his witnesses by his nominated commissioners. The judges instructed that the evidence provided should be based

> upon the view of muniments, chronicles, tombs, and the testimony of abbots, priors, and other of Holy Church, and other honourable proofs, having notice of their ancestors and descent, and from tombs, paintings, glass windows, vestments, and other evidences, as also by the testimonies of lords, knights, and esquires of honour,

---

[4] E.g., N. Saul, *Knight and Esquires: The Gloucestershire Gentry in the Fourteenth Century* (Oxford, 1981); C. Richmond, *John Hopton: A Fifteenth-Century Suffolk Gentleman* (Cambridge, 1981); Bennett, *Community, Class and Careerism*; S. M. Wright, *The Derbyshire Gentry in the Fifteenth Century* (Chesterfield, Derbyshire Record Society, 8, 1983); N. Saul, *Scenes from Provincial Life: Knightly Families in Sussex 1280–1400* (Oxford, 1986); A. J. Pollard, *North-Eastern England during the Wars of the Roses: Lay Society, War, and Politics 1450-1500* (Oxford, 1990); C. Richmond, *The Paston Family in the Fifteenth Century*, 3 vols. (Cambridge, 1990, 1996; Manchester, 2000); S. Payling, *Political Society, in Lancastrian England: The Greater Gentry of Nottinghamshire* (Oxford, 1991); C. E. Moreton, *The Townshends and their World: Gentry, Law and Land in Norfolk, c. 1450–1551* (Oxford, 1992); E. Acheson, *A Gentry Community: Leicestershire in the Fifteenth Century, c.1422–c.1485* (Cambridge, 1992); C. Carpenter, *Locality and Polity: A Study of Warwickshire Landed Society, 1401–1499* (Cambridge, 1992).

[5] *Scrope v. Grosvenor*; C 47/6/1; *PCM*.

[6] Morley was acting upon very similar guidelines. C 47/6/1.

and gentlemen having knowledge of arms, and from none of the commons or other estate.[7]

How effective Scrope and Morley – distinguished barons, hailing from vastly different parts of the realm – were in meeting the judges' wide-ranging criteria tells us a great deal about their standing within gentry society, as well as the support networks, local, regional and national, that were at their disposal.

Finding Witnesses I: Richard, Lord Scrope

Richard, Lord Scrope and his ancestors had long resided at Bolton in northwest Yorkshire. Their family's fortune had been made during the reign of Edward II by Lord Richard's father and uncle, Henry and Geoffrey Scrope: royal justices, through whom the family's Bolton and Masham lines respectively descended.[8] By the time *Scrope v. Grosvenor* arose in 1385, Lord Richard had been raised to the peerage (in 1371) and was the lord of a vast cluster of estates centred around his ancestral home: his high standing in English society resting upon his family's achievements in war and administration, his membership of the Lancastrian affinity, and his recent stint as chancellor and steward of the royal household.[9] Such a well-credentialled and imposing figure unsurprisingly had little trouble acquiring widespread support when bringing Sir Robert Grosvenor to task before the Court of Chivalry. Yet, his national prominence notwithstanding, Scrope still relied most heavily upon the testimony of those gentry living in the broad vicinity of his Bolton estates.[10] In striking a balance between local and regional support, moreover, the formation of his witness list was complicated by Yorkshire's intricate topography. Even by the standards of the day, Yorkshire was an infamously fragmented shire. Geographical landmarks, notably rivers and mountains, proved more compelling demarcation points for the shire's residents than its crown-designated borders. Yorkshire was sub-divided into three distinct Ridings (East,

---

[7] Nichols, 'The Scrope and Grosvenor Controversy', pp. 389–90.
[8] Vale, 'The Scropes', pp. 8–37.
[9] Goodman, *John of Gaunt*, pp. 289–90; Given-Wilson, *The Royal Household*, p. 74; Vale, 'The Scropes', pp. 80–2, 115–19.
[10] One-third of Scrope's witnesses (82 out of 247 gentry) can conclusively be identified as Yorkshire men. *Scrope v. Grosvenor*.

West and North) and it was in the North Riding, with Richmondshire at its heart – bordered by the river Ure to the south, the river Swale to the north, the river Wiske to the east, and the Pennines to the west – that the Scropes of Bolton had long resided and enjoyed their greatest influence.[11]

The gentry of the North Riding consequently comprised the inner core of Lord Richard's support base: a fact easily obscured by the bevy of magnates, barons and knights from farther afield on his witness list, and by the fact that a significant proportion of these North Riding gentry were also members of the Lancastrian affinity.[12] Their Lancastrian credentials, though, were but one of numerous ties these gentry shared with Lord Richard. They largely hailed from knightly families who had long stood beside the Scropes at the apex of North Riding society.[13] Indeed, it was their prominence within the region that had initially enticed John of Gaunt to bring so many of them into his affinity in the first place.[14] Scrope's relationships with these families were often of long duration, those with fellow Lancastrians like Sir Robert Swillington and Sir John Scargill, as we saw in the previous chapter, long predating their mutual entry into Gaunt's service.[15] Lord Richard simultaneously enjoyed intimate ties with a host of other, non-Lancastrian, gentry from the North Riding, including most prominently, Sir Thomas Rokeby, Sir Robert Laton, Sir Thomas Boynton and Sir Gerard Lound.[16] Moreover, through a combination of his own high standing and his Masham cousins' influence in the East Riding, Lord Richard had additionally forged ties with Yorkshire's knightly élite at large, many of whom spoke in his defence. To cite but two distinguished examples, Sir Brian Stapleton and Sir Robert Roos, both better acquainted with the Scropes of Masham, described before the Court occasions when Lord Richard's uncle, Geoffrey, had

[11] Vale, 'The Scropes', p. 40.
[12] See above, pp. 68–70.
[13] On the political, social and cultural cohesion of the region and the independence and interconnectedness of its baronial and greater gentry families, see, Vale, 'The Scropes', pp. 38–53; Pollard, *Northeastern England*, pp. 86–100; A. J. Pollard, 'The Richmondshire Community of Gentry during the Wars of the Roses', in *Patronage, Pedigree and Power in Late Medieval England*, ed. C. D. Ross (Gloucester, 1979), pp. 37–59.
[14] Walker, *The Lancastrian Affinity*, p. 31.
[15] See above, pp. 69, 74–5.
[16] Vale, 'The Scropes', p. 103; *Scrope v. Grosvenor*, I, pp. 116; 110–11; 117; 108–9.

campaigned in France during the early stages of the Hundred Years War.[17]

Scrope's ties with his Yorkshire testators, however, were not strictly horizontal. Given his family's exalted position within northern society, it is entirely understandable that numerous lesser knights and esquires, especially those hailing from the North Riding, looked up to Lord Richard as their natural lord and as a potential fount of patronage. It would have been in this context that his deponents, Sir Randolf Pygot, Sir John Warde and Sir William Chauncy, campaigned as members of his military retinue.[18] John Conyers acquired the marriage of the St. Quintin heiress thanks to Lord Richard's intercession (and, indeed, the St. Quintins also spoke for him).[19] Simon Wensley, who held the living of Wensley Church – in the hundred in which the Scropes of Bolton had first achieved prominence in the thirteenth century – was Lord Richard's regular feoffee and witness.[20] Perhaps most impressively, Sir Robert Plumpton, a distant kinsman, attested to having borne arms beneath Scrope's banner, whilst Plumpton loyalty to the Scropes was such that a generation after *Scrope v. Grosvenor*, they unwisely threw in their lot with Lord Richard's bellicose cousin, Archbishop Scrope, when the latter rebelled against Henry IV in 1405, resulting in Plumpton and Scrope heads jointly decorating the walls of York.[21]

Lord Richard's Yorkshire deponents, moreover, were not merely close to him, but in many cases enjoyed intimate ties with each other, reinforcing just how intricately linked were the local social networks into which he was tapping. Scrope's great friend, Sir Robert Swillington, for example, oversaw Sir Robert Neville's estates, when the latter's father fell heavily into debt.[22] Sir Richard Tempest regularly

---

[17] *Scrope v. Grosvenor*, I, pp. 105; 106.

[18] *Scrope v. Grosvenor*, I, pp. 119; 118; 112.

[19] C. D. Ross, *The Yorkshire Baronage, 1399–1435* (Oxford, 1950), p. 227; *Scrope v. Grosvenor*, I, pp. 62–3.

[20] *Scrope Cartulary*, no. 41.

[21] *Scrope v. Grosvenor*, I, pp. 117–18; *Plumpton Correspondence: A Series of Letters, Chiefly Domestick, Written in the Reigns of Edward IV, Richard III, Henry VII and Henry VIII*, ed. T. Stapleton (CS, London, 1839), p. xxiii; *CPR, 1405–8*, pp. 45, 63, 70.

[22] *CCR, 1360-4*, p. 523; *CCR, 1364–8*, pp. 66, 358; *The Yorkshire Archaeological Society Records Series*, ed. M. J. Stanley-Price, vol. 120 (York, 1955), p. 61; W. Farrer and J. Brownhill, *The Victoria History of the County of Lancaster*, 8 vols. (London, 1906–14), VIII, p. 193.

joined his neighbour, Sir Ralph Ipres, in arbitrating local disputes.[23] Sir Ralph Hastings took fees from both Thomas, Lord Roos and John, Lord Neville.[24] The Rooses, Nevilles and Lutterells were all connected by marriage.[25] The Pygots and Wardes had engaged in private land transactions dating back almost a century,[26] as had the Askes and Scargills,[27] and the Laytons and Rokebys.[28] In similar vein, amongst Lord Richard's supporters in nearby Lancashire, Sir Richard Houghton, Sir William Melton and Sir Nicholas Harrington were collectively men of longstanding private association.[29] And this applied also to groups of testators living far from Scrope's northern power base, such as the 14 Norfolk and Suffolk gentry who testified on his behalf.[30]

None of this is to imply that Lord Richard's witness list comprised a series of harmoniously interlocking social circles that united in his defence. His reach stretched across the length and breadth of the realm and encompassed numerous individuals who were complete strangers: their memories of the Scrope family diverging sharply depending upon age, regional origin, and personal experience. Even when they were acquainted, by no means all deponents got along as well as those families cited above. Indeed, even amongst the tight-knit gentry community of the North Riding, hostilities could still arise. Sir Robert Constable and Sir John Saville, for example – both closely acquainted with the Scropes – fell into bitter dispute with one another in the late 1380s, with Constable eventually taking Saville to court, claiming that, as sheriff of Yorkshire, Saville had refused to pay him the money he was owed for his services as a member of parliament.[31] Even more spectacularly, in the late 1370s, Sir James Pickering – one of Lord Richard's self-appointed commissioners, and an intimate of several of his Lancashire witnesses – had accused another future Scrope deponent, Sir Thomas Roos of Kendal, of ambushing him with a force of armed followers purportedly 300-men strong.[32] Nonetheless,

---

[23] *Yorkshire Archaeological Society*, vol. 120, pp. 136–7.
[24] *Historic Manuscripts Commission*, ed. Bickley et al., I, p. 178; C 136/100/3.
[25] Vale, 'The Scropes', pp. 239–40.
[26] *Scrope Cartulary*, no. 108.
[27] *Scrope Cartulary*, nos. 136, 139, 173.
[28] *Scrope Cartulary*, nos. 291, 292.
[29] DL 37/3, m. 23; Walker, 'John of Gaunt and his Retainers, 1361–99', pp. 157–8.
[30] Caudrey, 'War, Chivalry and Regional Society', p. 120.
[31] CP 25(1)278/146/13; JUST 1/1500 rot. 18.
[32] *HPC, 1386–1421*, IV, pp. 77–80.

Constable, Saville and Roos, when pressed on Scrope's claim before the Court of Chivalry, agreed wholeheartedly that the arms, *azure a bend or*, were rightfully his, whilst Pickering, as one of those hand-picked by Scrope to collect the evidence on his behalf, presumably shared their view.[33]

Beyond his personal ties, the relative cohesion of Yorkshire military society in the fourteenth century also indirectly played its part in shaping Scrope's northern support base.[34] Most of Lord Richard's Yorkshire deponents, from knightly companions to lesser gentry military professionals, had spent their careers in arms intermittently defending their homeland from Scottish incursions. Hence, although many of these men had also fought in France and/or Spain, often in each other's company, it was their shared memories of Scrope participation against the Scots, dating as far back as the battles of Stanhope Park (1327) and Halidon Hill (1333), that formed a crucial component of their testimony.[35] Indeed, the war records of both Lord Richard and his Masham cousin, Henry, underscore the extent to which responsibility for dealing with the Scots was thrust upon the shoulders of the northern aristocracy.[36] In 1346, for example, Richard and Henry jointly cut their military teeth on Edward III's Normandy expedition that culminated in the battle of Crécy, yet were back in England within weeks, as members of the 4,000-strong Yorkshire contingent that repelled the Scots at the battle of Neville's Cross, after which victory the two young cousins were knighted.[37] Both were likewise at the relief of Berwick a decade later, Lord Richard once again abruptly returning from a bout of overseas campaigning to participate.[38] England's ongoing conflict with the Scots, and the Scrope family's active contribution towards the defence of the northern border, was crucial in shaping the wartime recollections of Scrope's Yorkshire deponents, both greater and lesser gentry, enabling Lord

---

[33] *Scrope v. Grosvenor*, I, pp. 135–6; 113; 132–4.

[34] See below, pp. 159–63.

[35] *Scrope v. Grosvenor*, I, pp. 142–5, 155–6.

[36] Tuck, 'War and Society in the Medieval North', pp. 33–52; Goodman, 'Introduction', pp. 1–29; A. King, 'Best of Enemies: Were the Fourteenth-Century Anglo-Scottish Marches a "Frontier Society"?', in *England and Scotland in the Fourteenth Century: New Perspectives*, ed. A. King and M. Penman (Woodbridge, 2007), pp. 116–35.

[37] *Scrope v. Grosvenor*, I, pp. 18, 113.

[38] *Scrope v. Grosvenor*, I, pp. 19, 114.

Richard – as we shall see in Chapter 4 – to bring to his cause large sections of Yorkshire's military community, who collectively possessed a shared body of memories of his family's martial endeavours.[39]

Importantly, too, it was not just Yorkshire's secular gentry who upheld Scrope's armorial claim. Lord Richard's influence extended well beyond this – as the judges had directed – to encompass the shire's ecclesiastical élite as well. The abbots and priors of more than a dozen religious houses (mostly located in the North Riding) spoke in his defence, each providing richly detailed iconographic and written evidence that purportedly proved Scrope possession of the disputed arms.[40] Lord Richard, for instance, unsurprisingly received support from his family's foundation abbey at St. Agatha's, located near his Bolton residence. The Scrope arms were strewn throughout the abbey upon tombs, sculptures, tablets and windows. Lord Richard's father and elder brother were both buried there, as he himself would be upon his own death in 1403, though not before bequeathing his testator, the Abbot John, a golden cup.[41] The Scropes were also amongst the Abbey of Jervaulx's early benefactors. The abbot produced muniments and charters detailing the donations Lord Richard's uncle, Geoffrey, had made to the abbey, whilst claiming that a certain Thomas Scrope – a thirteenth-century ancestor and former abbot – had installed a tablet in the abbey displaying the said arms.[42] The Abbot of Rievaulx likewise detailed the Scrope family's longstanding association with his abbey, telling the Court that the abbey held in its archives three undated charters from Lord Richard's father, Henry, granting them land and sealed with the disputed arms, together with other charters, dating back 70 years, that were similarly sealed.[43] Finally, the Abbot of Selby stated that the arms, *azure a bend or*, were displayed in the south aisle of his church, in a glass window at the altar of St. John the Baptist, explaining that they had been identified by his fellow monks as those of Scrope for as long as he could remember.[44] This array of churchmen,

---

[39] On the 'military community' as a theoretical construct, see Ayton, 'Armies and Military Communities', pp. 215–39.

[40] The Abbots of Selby, Rievaulx, Jervaulx, St. Agatha, Byland, La Roche and Covingham. The Priors of Gisburgh, Lanercost, Neuburgh, St. Mary, Marton and Berdenay. *Scrope v. Grosvenor*.

[41] *Scrope v. Grosvenor*, I, pp. 95–6.

[42] *Scrope v. Grosvenor*, I, pp. 94–5.

[43] *Scrope v. Grosvenor*, I, pp. 93–4.

[44] *Scrope v. Grosvenor*, I, pp. 91–3.

as we shall see, was perfectly placed to provide the Court with a combination of iconographic evidence, hearsay, and local history, leaving little doubt as to the Scrope family's status in the North Riding and the pride their family's deeds in war, tournament and government had brought to the region.

Lord Richard's connections in the North Riding – and, indeed, across Yorkshire gentry and ecclesiastical society more generally – heavily shaped the inner core of his witness list. In this regard, his approach hardly differed from that of his adversary, Sir Robert Grosvenor, who sought to rouse the gentry of the Cheshire–Lancashire borderlands in his defence.[45] What set Scrope apart from Grosvenor – and differentiated him from all the other protagonists in these surviving Court of Chivalry cases – was the breadth of support he received beyond his native power base. Quite simply, Lord Richard succeeded in accruing at least a few witnesses from virtually every single shire between York and London, stretching as far west as Devonshire and as far east as Norfolk, in the process granting his witness list a distinctly national flavour.[46]

Lord Richard's Lancastrian ties obviously played a significant role here, since they had brought him into close contact over the years with a miscellany of knights from all parts of the realm. Hence, to cite but a few noteworthy examples, Sir Walter Blount of Derbyshire, Sir Edmund Pierrepoint of Nottinghamshire, Sir John Deincourt of Lincolnshire, and Sir Thomas Morieux of Suffolk were all men of long acquaintance with Scrope through their mutual service as members of the Lancastrian affinity.[47] In similar fashion, Lord Richard's court connections – developed during his tenure as chancellor and steward of the royal household in the 1370s and 1380s – enabled him to tap into a geographically diverse body of eminent witnesses. Most prominently, Guy, Lord Brian – whose estates, as we have seen, lay principally in Gloucestershire and Dorset – had worked alongside Scrope as chamberlain of the royal household at the very time Lord Richard was serving as steward.[48] Other renowned high-flyers at the early Ricardian court who deposed for Scrope included Richard II's

---

[45] Bennett, *Community, Class and Careerism*, pp. 12–16; Morgan, 'Sir Robert Grosvenor', pp. 78–93.
[46] *Scrope v. Grosvenor*.
[47] *Scrope v. Grosvenor*, I, pp. 58; 153–4; 54; 56; Walker, *The Lancastrian Affinity*, pp. 264, 277, 268, 275.
[48] *Scrope v. Grosvenor*, I, p. 76; Given-Wilson, *The Royal Household*, p. 282.

long-serving under-chamberlain, Sir Simon Burley (of Hereford/ Kent), the chamber knights, Sir John Clanvowe (of Hereford) and Sir Lewis Clifford (of Devonshire), and, very famously, that giant of medieval English literature (and a native Londoner), Geoffrey Chaucer.[49] Additionally, a dozen of Richard II's 'king's knights', whose years of royal service overlapped with Scrope's, likewise testified on his behalf, including Sir Gerard Braybrooke (of Bedfordshire), Sir Edward Dalyngridge (of Sussex), Sir Richard Houghton (of Lancashire), Sir John Sully (of Devonshire), and Sir Richard Waldegrave (of Suffolk).[50]

Yet, it is important to recognise that whilst most of these court figures would have become personally familiar with Lord Richard during his tenure in royal high office, they were called to provide depositions essentially because – just like many of his older Yorkshire deponents – they had in their youths seen members of the Scrope family bearing the disputed arms in a military setting. Guy, Lord Brian, for instance, had witnessed Lord Richard himself, as well as his uncle Geoffrey and cousin Henry, fighting with the arms in France between 1339 and 1369.[51] Sir Simon Burley recalled seeing Lord Richard bearing the arms at the sea-battle off Winchelsea in 1350.[52] Sir Lewis Clifford claimed to have seen Lord Richard, and his cousin, Henry, bedecked in *azure a bend or* in France, Spain and Scotland.[53] Sir John Clanvowe swore that he had never seen any but the Scropes bearing the disputed arms on the many campaigns on which he had served.[54] Even Geoffrey Chaucer harked back to the brief military exploits of his young career, when he had been captured and ransomed on the Rheims expedition in 1359–60, claiming that he had seen both Lord Richard and his cousin, Henry, bearing the disputed arms, which, Chaucer asserted, had long been known to him by popular repute as those of Scrope.[55] And, providing perhaps the finest illustration of a courtly deponent whose testimony was worth its proverbial weight in gold, Sir Richard Waldegrave – known to Scrope through his active

---

[49] *Scrope v. Grosvenor*, I, pp. 206; 184–5; 183; 178–9; Given-Wilson, *The Royal Household*, p. 282.
[50] *Scrope v. Grosvenor*, I, pp. 192-3; 164-5; 74; 234-5; 165-6; Given-Wilson, *The Royal Household*, pp. 284-6.
[51] *Scrope v. Grosvenor*, I, p. 76.
[52] *Scrope v. Grosvenor*, I, p. 206.
[53] *Scrope v. Grosvenor*, I, p. 183.
[54] *Scrope v. Grosvenor*, I, pp. 184-5.
[55] *Scrope v. Grosvenor*, I, pp. 178-9.

political career as a Ricardian household knight, a Suffolk MP, and as Speaker of the House of Commons – could point to a militarily active youth in which he had campaigned in the company of four different members of the Scrope family across two French expeditions and the Earl of Hereford's Turkish Crusade.[56] Lord Richard thus utilised the court connections he had forged over the preceding 15 years to bring to his cause a range of distinguished and extremely well-connected knights, several of whom had in years past seen him or his kinsmen fighting with the disputed arms.

The clearest illustration of Scrope's unique advantage over Sir Robert Grosvenor, however, was in his ability to gather a significant body of magnates and barons to defend his armorial right. The active support he received from John of Gaunt and Henry of Bolingbroke has already been noted.[57] Beyond this, however, Scrope – through his own and Gaunt's influence – acquired the cooperation of almost two-dozen greater or lesser peers. Once again, his Yorkshire ties represented a natural first port-of-call. Thomas, Lord Roos of Helmsley and Henry FitzHugh, Lord of Ravensworth, stood alongside Scrope as the heads of the three dominant baronial families in the North Riding.[58] Lord Roos was connected by marriage to Scrope's Masham cousins, and all three had been heavily involved in each other's affairs for years.[59] FitzHugh had served Scrope as a witness in his private business, whilst Scrope had acted as one of the supervisors of Roos' heir's will.[60] All three men had additionally entered Lancastrian service around the same time. Scrope and FitzHugh had served together in France under Gaunt in 1359–60 and 1369, whilst Roos, having entered Gaunt's pay in 1366, had accompanied them on the latter expedition, and later saddled up with Scrope for the campaign of 1373.[61]

Other barons and magnates' sons were likewise members of this exalted circle on Northern peers with whom Scrope freely interacted. John, Lord Neville was on the friendliest of terms with Gaunt and

[56] Keen, *Origins of the English Gentleman*, pp. 92–3; *Scrope v. Grosvenor*, I, pp. 165–6.
[57] See above, pp. 67–9.
[58] Goodman, *John of Gaunt*, p. 288.
[59] Vale, 'The Scropes', p. 240.
[60] *Scrope Cartulary*, no. 285; *CP*, XI, pp. 101–2.
[61] C 76/38, m. 13; C 76/52, m. 13; *Scrope v. Grosvenor*, II, pp. 15–16; *CP*, V, pp. 420–1; *JG Reg, 1372–6*, nos. 945, 1185; Walker, *The Lancastrian Affinity*, pp. 31, 280–1.

acted as a feoffee for Scrope and as an executor for Lord Roos.[62] Hugh, Lord Dacre of Cumberland – renowned border fighter and warden of the West March – had served alongside Scrope in the Lancastrian affinity for years, as had Hugh, Lord Burnell, who cut his military teeth under Gaunt on the campaigns of 1369 and 1373.[63] Scrope was also well-connected with the powerful Percy family: Sir Henry Percy had acted as a witness in Scrope's private affairs, whilst Sir Thomas Percy, who testified on his behalf, had been part of Gaunt's inner circle since 1369.[64] Henry Percy, Earl of Northumberland, added his own influential voice to Scrope's defence, and, seven years later, joined him in overseeing Lord Roos' heir's will.[65] Additionally, beyond the North, one other magnate connection served Lord Richard particularly well. He had been extremely close to the much-admired William Ufford, second Earl of Suffolk, who had appointed him as one of his principle executors.[66] Suffolk had served alongside Scrope as one of Gaunt's leading lieutenants on the French expedition of 1373, whilst his uncle, Edmund, had been a longstanding Lancastrian retainer.[67] Despite Earl William's sudden death in 1382, Ufford influence remained strong on Lord Richard's behalf before the Court, with the Earl's cousin, Sir John Brewes, and nephew, Roger, Lord Scales, both testifying on his behalf: the former speaking confidently of his uncle, Robert Ufford, first Earl of Suffolk's, assertion that the arms, *azure a bend or*, were irrefutably those of Scrope.[68]

Beyond all of these personal ties, Lord Richard's wider support base was just as significantly shaped by the war records of his martially-inclined family: most obviously, his elder brother William's service with the Earl of Northampton between 1338 and 1344; his cousin Geoffrey's service with the Earl of Hereford, especially his fatal participation on the crusade of 1362; his father's and uncle's achievements in war and tournaments in the 1320s and 1330s; and his own martial exploits, often alongside his cousin, Henry, under Northampton (1346), the

[62] *Scrope Cartulary*, no. 222; *Early Lincoln Wills*, ed. A. Gibbons (Lincoln, 1888), p. 70.
[63] C 81/925 (4); C 76/55, m. 21; C 76/56, m. 27; *Scrope v. Grosvenor*, II, pp. 456–9.
[64] *Scrope Cartulary*, no. 719; *Scrope v. Grosvenor*, I, pp. 50-1; Goodman, *John of Gaunt*, pp. 189–90.
[65] *Early Lincoln Wills*, ed. Gibbon, p. 70; *Scrope v. Grosvenor*, I, p. 215.
[66] *CP*, XII (I), pp. 432–4; *Testamenta Vetusta*, I, pp. 114–15.
[67] Goodman, *John of Gaunt*, p. 281.
[68] *Scrope v. Grosvenor*, I, pp. 63; 67.

Earl of Warwick (1350), and Edward, the Black Prince (1355–6), prior to entering John of Gaunt's service (1359).[69] By accruing the support of gentry who had fought in these various military retinues, Scrope was naturally able to add to his witness list an eclectic mix of knights and esquires from the Midlands, the Home Counties, the West Country and East Anglia, whose testimony balanced out the northern bias of his witness list. His late brother's connections with Northampton's retinue, for example, brought to his cause such seemingly disparate witnesses as William Hesilrige of Northumberland, William Biset of Somerset, and Sir Robert Marny of Essex.[70] Similarly, his cousin Geoffrey's crusading activities with Hereford were crucial to the testimony of another Essex man, Sir Alexander Goldingham, as well as Sir William Lucy of Dorset and Sir Henry Ferrers of Leicestershire.[71] The memories of Scrope's oldest witnesses harked back to his ancestors' participation in the Scottish wars of Edward III,[72] whilst Lord Richard's own service on the Black Prince's Gascony campaign in 1355–6, and his subsequent reappearance alongside the Prince's retainers, in the Lancastrian military retinue, in Spain a decade later, explains why at least 35 former military followers of the Prince were able to provide the Court with useful testimony.[73]

So, if these were the types of connections Lord Richard utilised, how exactly was his witness list formed? We know the instructions he received to develop a body of evidence in his defence, based in part upon, 'the testimonies of lords, knights, and esquires of honour, and gentlemen having knowledge of arms'.[74] Yet, no record of the process of witness-list formation survives, whilst those who gave evidence were largely interviewed (it strongly appears for convenience sake) at Plymouth, York and London.[75] By delving into the character of Scrope's relationships with his various groups of witnesses, however, it may prove possible to uncover small hints of the precise strategies involved. In the broadest sense, it must be acknowledged that Lord Richard's entire witness list is highly unlikely to have been centrally

[69] Vale, 'The Scropes', pp. 70–8.
[70] *Scrope v. Grosvenor*, I, pp. 126–7; 125–6; 170–1.
[71] *Scrope v. Grosvenor*, I, pp. 70; 77–8; 188.
[72] *Scrope v. Grosvenor*, I, pp. 74, 76.
[73] *Scrope v. Grosvenor*; Green, 'The Household and Military Retinue of Edward the Black Prince', Appendix, pp. 1-39.
[74] Nichols, 'The Scrope and Grosvenor Controversy', pp. 389–90.
[75] Vale, 'The Scropes', pp. 98–9.

planned down to the last man. There would almost certainly have existed an element of spontaneity to its construction. This would especially have been the case when acquiring the support of lesser gentry military professionals, some of whom had never borne arms with him personally, but rather with other members of his family in far-flung military theatres. In such circumstances, Lord Richard would very likely have relied upon his friends, relatives and servants to suggest men whose military memories might prove useful. Moreover, even amongst the knightly élite, the line between the acquisition of individual witnesses with whom he was personally acquainted, and the active mining of an entire region in search of support, was far from clear cut.

An examination of Scrope's small body of 14 deponents from Norfolk and Suffolk neatly illustrates the ways in which a regional support base could develop almost incidentally.[76] Two-thirds of these Norfolk and Suffolk gentry deposed at Plymouth, prior to embarking for Spain with John of Gaunt.[77] Yet, this was no straightforward mobilisation of Lancastrian interests. Indeed, these men ranged from seasoned Lancastrians of long familiarity with Scrope, such as Sir Thomas Morieux and Sir Hugh Hastings III,[78] to younger gentry new to Gaunt's service, such as Sir John White,[79] who would barely have been acquainted with Scrope at all. At the same time, Lord Richard's close ties with the Ufford earls of Suffolk brought gentry from their orbit onto his witness list, most notably, Sir John Brewes, Sir Robert

---

[76] The fourteen Norfolk and Suffolk gentry who deposed for Scrope were: Sir John Brewes; Sir Thomas Erpingham; Robert Fitzrauf; Sir Thomas Geney; Sir Stephen Hales; Sir Hugh Hastings III; Sir John Loudham; Sir Thomas Morieux; Sir Robert Morley; Roger, Lord Scales; Sir Richard Waldegrave; Sir John White; Sir John Wilton; Sir William Wingfield. *Scrope v. Grosvenor*, I, pp. 63; 59; 52; 67; 163; 51; 150-1; 56; 60; 67; 165; 59; 71; 173-4. Additionally, Sir Miles Boys, the third son of a Yorkshire gentry family, had married into East Anglian society and had settled in Norfolk. *Scrope v. Grosvenor*, II, pp. 220-1.

[77] Sir Hugh Hastings III; Robert Fitz Rauf; Sir Thomas Morieux; Sir Thomas Erpingham; Sir John White; Sir Robert Morley; Sir John Brewes; Roger, Lord Scales; Sir Thomas Geney; Sir Miles Boys. The first seventy depositions were taken at Plymouth. *Scrope v. Grosvenor*, II, pp. 163-234.

[78] Goodman, *John of Gaunt*, pp. 214, 357-8.

[79] Walker, *The Lancastrian Affinity*, p. 284.

Morley and Sir William Wingfield.[80] Their testimony focused upon memories of Lord Richard's campaigning with the Black Prince in Gascony (1355–6) and Spain (1366–7), since all three, through the Uffords' intimate ties with the Prince, had simultaneously become members or associates of the latter's affinity during the 1350s and 1360s.[81]

Moreover, underscoring the disparate, and at times overlapping, threads that held together Scrope's Norfolk–Suffolk support base, one finds amongst this body of deponents a man like Sir Stephen Hales, whose career was shaped by his military service with the Black Prince, but who would have known Scrope primarily through his recent stint as a regular member of parliament and as a household knight at the Ricardian court.[82] Reinforcing these complexities, Sir Thomas Erpingham – notwithstanding his entry into the Lancastrian affinity – had spent much of his early career in the service of the Earl of Suffolk, and was thus tentatively connected with this circle as well.[83] Lastly, revealing just how incidental were the East Anglian origins of this body of witnesses, perhaps the most admired individual in the group, Sir Richard Waldegrave – despite his undeniably high standing in his native Suffolk – was known to Scrope through his parliamentary career and, as we have seen, was desired as a witness due to his youthful exploits, alongside Scrope's Masham cousins, in the Bohun military retinue.[84] The regional origins of these 14 Norfolk and Suffolk witnesses, in short, were purely coincidental.

Most of Lord Richard's witness list seems to have been constructed in precisely this incoherent fashion, bringing to his cause miscellaneous individuals he knew through his Lancastrian, courtly, or some other ties. Yet, this was not uniformly the case, and there were, it appears,

---

[80] Brewes was Ufford's cousin. The Morleys and Uffords, as we shall see below, had enjoyed intimate ties dating back at least two generations. Sir William Wingfield acted for the Uffords in their private business and was sufficiently close to their family that Earl William left him a life pension of £20, as well as a covered goblet to keep in his memory. *Scrope v. Grosvenor*, II, pp. 219-20; 208-10; NRO, Reg Heydon, f. 117.

[81] D. S. Green, 'Edward the Black Prince and East Anglia: An Unlikely Association?', in *Fourteenth Century England III*, ed. W. M. Ormrod (Woodbridge, 2004), p. 88.

[82] See above, pp. 49–51.

[83] Curry, 'Sir Thomas Erpingham', p. 60.

[84] Keen, *Origins of the English Gentleman*, pp. 92–3; *Scrope v. Grosvenor*, I, pp. 165–6.

at least three parts of the realm in which Lord Richard employed a calculated strategy, designed to mine the regions in question for appropriate witnesses. First and foremost, this was very obviously the case in his native Yorkshire and its surrounding counties, where the Scropes would have possessed a detailed knowledge of which gentry were best placed to provide weighty and convincing testimony.[85] A regional strategy also appears to have been employed when the commissioners journeyed to Chester, where the bulk of Sir Robert Grosvenor's witnesses were interviewed. Almost certainly by design, a series of rather reluctant Cheshire gentry, who would go on to uphold Grosvenor's claim, were called upon by the commissioners to describe their memories of Scrope possession of the disputed arms.[86] Further depositions were taken at Nottingham, where a handful of knights, including three local men long acquainted with Lord Richard through the Lancastrian affinity, were interviewed, whilst the commissioners also stopped briefly at Leicester in order to interview the elderly and militarily-distinguished Sir Ralph Ferrers.[87]

That Scrope should have been best prepared, and most systematic in his strategy, when acquiring witnesses from amongst the gentry networks of the northern shires, with which he was most familiar, is hardly surprising. That a regional approach to the formation of his witness list could flourish beyond these neighbourly surroundings is most clearly revealed in the interviewing panel's sojourn through Devonshire on their way to Chester.[88] Plymouth, York and London, as touched upon, represented the three main centres where the vast majority of Scrope's witnesses were interviewed.[89] York proved an obvious location, given

[85] See above, pp. 98–104.

[86] Sir John Massy (of Tatton); Sir John Massy (of Puddington); Robert Danyell; Sir William Lye; Sir Laurence Dutton; Sir Ralph Vernon; Sir Hugh Browe; Sir Richard Bingham; Sir William Brereton; John Leicester; Sir John Pole. *Scrope v. Grosvenor*, I, pp. 79–84. On their depositions, see below, pp. 164–71.

[87] Sir Gervase Clifton; Sir Sampson Strauley; Sir Edmund Pierrepoint. *Scrope v. Grosvenor*, II, pp. 356–9, 361–6.

[88] The first set of depositions were taken at Plymouth on 16 June 1386. The second set were taken at Dorset the following month. Chester was the commission's next stop in September 1386, before the bulk of Scrope's witnesses (153 men) were interviewed in and around York. Thereafter, the commission stopped briefly in Nottingham and Leicester, before ending their investigation with another large-scale batch of interviews in London. Vale, 'The Scropes', pp. 98–9; *Scrope v. Grosvenor*.

[89] *Scrope v. Grosvenor*.

the number of gentry from the three Ridings on Scrope's witness list; Plymouth was the embarkation point for John of Gaunt's Spanish army and thus a convenient spot for interviewing long-serving Lancastrians; and London provided a central location at which the numerous southern and East Anglian gentry, royal courtiers, and members of parliament on Scrope's witness list could provide evidence. Amongst Scrope's witnesses from Devon and Dorset, by contrast, the interviewing panel came to them, underscoring Scrope's awareness that sections of the West Country gentry possessed a body of knowledge useful to his cause.

It is highly probable that the interviewers journeyed through Devonshire specifically to take down the deposition of Sir John Sully – a Garter Knight of immense military experience, who claimed (inaccurately) to have been 105 years old, but whose military memories of multiple generations of Scropes bearing the disputed arms, combined with his Garter rank, would have made him a witness whose testimony Lord Richard was determined to secure.[90] Since Sully was unsurprisingly too infirm to travel, the interviewers came to him, and he became one of only a handful of witnesses interviewed in his own home.[91] Indeed, it strongly appears that Scrope anticipated the need to interview older witnesses in this fashion. At the very outset of the case, he specifically requested from the judges that interviews could be conducted in the homes of those too aged or infirm to travel, and thus not only was Sully's testimony taken in this fashion, but also those of three elderly Yorkshire gentry, Sir Richard Roucliffe of Pickering, Sir William Aton of Aton and John Rither of Scarborough – all men of exceptionally long military memory – who were deemed incapable of making the journey to York, where the bulk of Scrope's Yorkshire testators were interviewed. One may surmise from his request, then, that Scrope already had the likes of Sully, Roucliffe, Aton and Rither in mind as potential witnesses and was starting to contemplate the logistics involved in acquiring their depositions.[92]

---

[90] *Scrope v. Grosvenor*, I, p. 74.

[91] The young Edward Courtenay, Earl of Devon – John of Gaunt's 'very dear and well-beloved Cousin' – was interviewed at the same location, although his testimony was extremely vague, claiming to have been too young and inexperienced to know anything about the Scropes' armorial right. Goodman, *John of Gaunt*, pp. 283–4; *Scrope v. Grosvenor*, I, pp. 73–4. On the Courtenay family, see M. Cherry, 'The Courtenay Earls of Devon: Formation and Disintegration of a Late Medieval Aristocratic Affinity', *Southern History*, 1 (1979), pp. 71–99.

[92] Nichols, 'The Scrope and Grosvenor Controversy', pp. 389, 392.

More generally, an assessment of Scrope's remaining deponents from the West Country reveal how successful Lord Richard was in tapping into random knightly social networks with which he enjoyed only fleeting personal connection. Scrope very likely recommended that the interviewers take testimony from his friend and fellow courtier, the now elderly Guy, Lord Brian, and consequently Brian headed a list of five knights who testified in the refectory of the Abbey of Abbotsbury in Dorset.[93] These men essentially comprised a local knightly circle, one whose military memories were collectively of considerable use to Scrope's cause. Sir James Chuddleigh, whose daughter married Brian's son, had provided the preceding deposition at Sir John Sully's Tiverton manor.[94] Brian's own deposition was followed by that of another of his kinsmen, Sir John Chydioke, who claimed, like Sully, to have been over 100 years of age, and whose recollections stretched back as far as the battle of Stanhope Park in 1327.[95] Speaking at the same location was their mutual kinsman, Sir Robert Fitz Payne, who was Brian's son-in-law and whose daughter had wed a Chydioke.[96] Beyond direct kinship ties, others knights from within this network of esteemed Devonshire families likewise deposed at Abbotsbury. These included Sir William Bonville, a dominant figure in shire politics, who engaged in land transactions with Chydioke and was such a close friend of Lord Brian's that he was asked, in an early will, to act as guardian to Brian's daughters;[97] Sir Ralph Cheney, a cadet, who made his career in Wiltshire and Somerset, but whose son would later marry Bonville's daughter;[98] and Sir William Lucy, an illustrious member of the Bohun circle, who outlined those numerous occasions on which he had seen the Scrope arms borne in a military setting.[99] Scrope thus acquired, very likely through his friendship with Guy, Lord Brian, a significant body of testimony from distinguished West Country gentry who were Brian's intimates and knowledgeable elder statesmen in their own right.

Although Scrope and his advisors almost certainly did not plan his witness list down to the last man, it seems clear, at the very least, that

---

[93] *Scrope v. Grosvenor*, I, p. 76; II, pp. 245–55.
[94] *Scrope v. Grosvenor*, I, pp. 75–6; *Reg. Wykeham: Wykeham's Register*, ed. T. F. Kirby, 2 vols. (Hampshire Record Society, 1896–9), II, pp. 378–9.
[95] *Scrope v. Grosvenor*, I, pp. 76–7; II, pp. 255–7.
[96] *Scrope v. Grosvenor*, I, p. 77; II, pp. 256, 259.
[97] *Scrope v. Grosvenor*, I, p. 77; *HPC, 1386–1421*, II, pp. 282–4.
[98] *Scrope v. Grosvenor*, I, p. 77; *HPC, 1386–1421*, II, pp. 554–5.
[99] *Scrope v. Grosvenor*, I, pp. 77–8; Guard, *Chivalry, Kingship and Crusade*, p. 141.

amongst the knightly élite of Yorkshire, amongst his West Country supporters, and amongst the more prominent of those Cheshire men appearing for Grosvenor, Scrope targeted areas where he well knew that numerous gentry had seen him or his kinsmen bearing the disputed arms on multiple occasions. In so doing, he naturally leant, where possible, upon the testimony of older men, whose memories stretched back before his own time to encompass tales of his father's and uncle's exploits in war and tournaments. For the rest of his witness list, Lord Richard turned to a range of nobles, knights and esquires from all parts of the realm with whom he enjoyed a close connection (personal, familial, regional, Lancastrian, courtly, or otherwise). Their collective presence before the Court of Chivalry, in addition to the insights they provided in their testimony, seemingly reinforced the claim, espoused by many of his witnesses, that Scrope possession of the arms, *azure a bend or*, was 'common knowledge'. Against this array of magnates and barons, northern knights, high-ranking churchmen, impressively-credentialled career soldiers, and a host of courtiers and members of the Lancastrian affinity, Sir Robert Grosvenor – with his body of witnesses almost exclusively drawn from his native stronghold in Cheshire, Lancashire and North Wales – stood little chance of success.[100]

Finding Witnesses II: Thomas, Lord Morley

The formation of Thomas, Lord Morley's predominantly East Anglian witness list provides a natural point of comparison with Lord Scrope's, not least because both men were of the same rank and enjoyed almost identical positions at the apex of their respective county communities.[101] Yet, almost everything about Morley's native Norfolk – from its geography and demography, to its social and political structure, to its military scene – was vastly different from Scrope's Yorkshire. Norfolk was a shire isolated from the tumults of the Scottish and Welsh borderlands, and its knightly families bore arms against the Scots and Welsh almost exclusively on royal expeditions.[102] At the same time, although commissioners of array were regularly charged with

---

[100] On Grosvenor's struggles before the Court, see Nichols, 'The Scrope and Grosvenor Controversy', pp. 385–400; Stewart-Brown, 'The Scrope and Grosvenor Controversy', pp. 1–22; Morgan, 'Sir Robert Grosvenor', pp. 78–82.
[101] Vale, 'The Scropes'; Caudrey, 'War and Society in Medieval Norfolk', pp. 93–9.
[102] Caudrey, 'War and Society in Medieval Norfolk', pp. 143–5.

defending the coast, and fears of a French invasion were ever present, none eventuated and most foreign raids took place further south.[103] There was, in short, no immediate threat to Norfolk's security, and consequently it never became a deeply militarised society. Norfolk was also part of a nexus of shires – spread throughout the eastern counties – in which most of its numerous magnate landholders were absentees, thereby breeding a largely independent gentry, many of whom sought employment with several great lords simultaneously, and could pick and choose the expeditions on which they served far more easily than their northern brethren.[104] Thomas, Lord Morley's power-base, then, was located within a wide tract of territory in which no single magnate monopolised authority, in which numerous power structures intersected and learned to peacefully co-exist with one another, and in which a recruitment ground flourished that the region's various authority figures could utilise as they saw fit.[105]

The Morleys themselves were one of only three long-lasting baronial families resident in Norfolk, their core estates located west and south-west of the capital, Norwich.[106] Their principle residence was at Hingham, their two most significant outliers at Great Hallingbury in Essex and Walkern in Hertfordshire.[107] It appears to have been from the areas surrounding his private estates, primarily those in Norfolk, that Thomas, Lord Morley acquired the bulk of his 102 secular and

[103] J. R. Alban, 'English Coastal Defence: Some Fourteenth-Century Modifications to the System', in *Patronage, the Crown and the Provinces in Later Medieval England*, ed. R. A. Griffiths (Gloucester, 1981), pp. 57–9.

[104] R. Virgoe, 'The Crown and Local Government: East Anglia under Richard II', in *The Reign of Richard II*, ed. F. R. H. du Boulay and C. M. Barron (London, 1971), pp. 218–41. Certainly, the testimony of Morley's deponents reveals a tendency to find service amongst a variety of captains, e.g., C 47/6/1, nos. 6, 29, 51, 52. This aspect of the testimony has been addressed by Ayton and Keen. Ayton, 'Knights, Esquires and Military Service', p. 94; Keen, *Origins of the English Gentleman*, pp. 66–7.

[105] Caudrey, 'War and Society in Medieval Norfolk', pp. 43–8.

[106] On the Morleys, see C. Richmond, 'Thomas Lord Morley (d. 1416) and the Morleys of Hingham', *Norfolk Archaeology*, 39, pt. 1 (1984), pp. 1–12; P. Morgan, 'Going to the Wars: Thomas, Lord Morley in France, 1416', in *The Hundred Years War (Part III): Further Considerations*, ed. L. J. A. Villalon and D. J. Kagay (Leiden, 2013), pp. 285–314; A. Ayton, 'Robert, second Lord Morley (c. 1295–1360)', *ODNB*, XXXIX, pp. 236–7; *CP*, IX, pp. 209–20. The other long-lasting baronial families in Norfolk were the Lords Scales and Bardolf. Caudrey, 'War and Society in Medieval Norfolk', p. 43.

[107] *CIPM*, X, no. 634; XI, no. 365; XV, nos. 124–9; XXII, nos. 185–6.

58 ecclesiastical witnesses. Many of the former were relatively obscure middling and lesser gentry, whilst those churchmen who deposed were largely parish priests or Augustinian friars, whose Norwich friary the Morleys had long patronised.[108] The character of Lord Morley's witness list ultimately reflected the fact that his support base, notwithstanding his family's eminence, was much more localised than Lord Scrope's, containing far fewer knights, and resting heavily upon the testimony of parish level notables.[109]

A note of caution, however, ought rightly to be exercised, since the Morley testimony is clearly less complete than Scrope's. We are lacking those depositions taken between mid-April and mid-August 1386, whilst some of the witnesses named in the Court's itinerary do not appear amongst the surviving depositions.[110] Morley most assuredly possessed significantly fewer connections and markedly less personal cache than Lord Scrope. It is highly unlikely, however, that a man of his stature would have struggled to find support beyond his Norfolk–Suffolk–Essex stronghold. Indeed, there are hints that his reach was rather more extensive than this. A rare example of a non-East Anglian on his witness list was Sir Alan Heton, a Northumbrian knight who had been in arms since 1333 and attested to having fought in that year under the Percy earls of Northumberland at the battle of Halidon Hill, where he saw Robert, Lord Morley bearing the disputed arms.[111] Another testator from beyond the eastern counties was Sir Nicholas Goushill, a Nottinghamshire knight of violent disposition, who recalled seeing members of the Morley family in Scotland, Ireland and France.[112] Sir John Burgh of Cambridgeshire and Sir Thomas Mandeville of Leicestershire had both been retainers of the late Humphrey Bohun, Earl of Hereford, and they were joined on Morley's witness list by 11 other men who had borne arms beneath Hereford's banner.[113] Another Cambridgeshire knight, Sir William Papeworth, had been acquainted

---

[108] Blomefield, *History of Norfolk*, IV, pp. 86-90.
[109] C 47/6/1; Ayton, 'Knights, Esquires and Military Service', pp. 94–6; Keen, *Origins of the English Gentleman*, pp. 65–7; Caudrey, 'War, Chivalry and Regional Society', pp. 120–4.
[110] See above, pp. 4–5.
[111] C 47/6/1, no. 97.
[112] C 47/6/1, no. 29.
[113] C 47/6/1, nos. 37 (Burgh); 47 (Mandeville); 21; 25; 38; 44; 52; 55; 56; 58; 61; 67; 102. On Burgh's and Mandeville's connections with Hereford, see Holmes, *The Estates of the Higher Nobility*, p. 70.

with the Morleys for over 40 years, and was sufficiently certain of the veracity of their armorial claim that he turned out on Lord Thomas' behalf, despite the plaintiff, Lord Lovel, being his kinsman.[114] Lastly, at a more exalted level, Lord Thomas' friendship with Thomas of Woodstock, Duke of Gloucester, in all likelihood facilitated his access to at least a few of the latter's retainers.[115]

Morley's support base may have been rather wider, and his knightly contingent possibly larger, than the depositions on his behalf reveal. Regardless of such speculation, however, since Morley's surviving witnesses overwhelmingly hailed from East Anglia, it might be best to think of his 160 testators as roughly comparable to Richard, Lord Scrope's ample body of Northern witnesses.[116] Viewed in this fashion, the value of the Morley testimony lies primarily in the opportunity it presents to examine in depth the intricacies of Morley's East Anglian support base, peeling back the layers of inter-gentry solidarity that held sway in the region and which came to his aid before the Court of Chivalry. In so doing, the complexities of these networks will be revealed, not least because Morley's stepson, Sir Edward Hastings, utilised the very same network, a generation later and in vastly different circumstances, when constructing his own witness list for *Grey v. Hastings*.[117]

Thomas, Lord Morley's acquisition of testators in East Anglia comprised no straightforward galvanisation of local interests, nor did it necessarily reflect an overt exercise of Morley lordship. As we saw in the previous chapter, only a bare few of Lord Thomas' witnesses enjoyed a

---

[114] C 47/6/1, no. 28.

[115] E.g., C 47/6/1, nos. 44; 47; 67. Morley and Gloucester had served together on the Brittany expedition in 1380. Over the years, they regularly enjoyed each other's company, visiting each other's homes, exchanging gifts, and doing favours for one another. Morley may have fought alongside Gloucester in the factional battle of Radcot Bridge in 1387. Certainly, he accompanied him on his aborted Prussian Crusade in 1391. Morley's preparedness to fight a trial by combat before the Court of Chivalry in 1400, to restore Gloucester's reputation after the latter's execution by Richard II, provides the clearest indication of the genuine affection the two men shared. Goodman, *The Loyal Conspiracy*, pp. 38, 133; Guard, *Chivalry, Kingship and Crusade*, pp. 82–4; Morgan, 'Going to the Wars', pp. 289–90.

[116] This is not to imply that Morley enjoyed anywhere near the levels of support beyond his native shire that Scrope had at his disposal. It is very clear, despite the missing depositions, that we possess the bulk of the Morley testimony, and undeniably the vast majority of his witnesses hailed from East Anglia. C 47/6/1.

[117] See pp. XX–XX.

formal tie with his family. Despite this, the number of deponents who lived deep within the Morleys' territorial heartland hints at the fact that Lord Thomas' exercise of his lordship was perhaps rather more extensive than formally acknowledged in the surviving testimony. Several of those who spoke for him were his tenants, not only local families on the rise, such as the Cursons and Gerberghs, whom we have already encountered,[118] but also knights from the very front rank of Norfolk society, such as Sir John Mauteby and Sir Leonard Kerdiston.[119] Various obscure lesser gentry and churchmen, moreover, also resided on estates over which the Morleys were lord.[120] Such bonds, indeed, may well have shaped Lord Thomas' connections with at least a few of those militarily active esquires who testified to lengthy bouts of campaigning beneath his family's banner.[121] Moreover, even amongst distinguished knightly families from farther afield, the bonds of lordship could play their part. The Suttons of Suffolk and Essex, for example – three of whom provided testimony – had for generations held parcels of land from the Morleys.[122]

As heir to one of East Anglia's foremost families, there can be little doubt that the vertical ties of lordship played a significant role in the formation of Morley's witness list, even if only indirectly. Yet, there can equally be little doubt that the inner core of Lord Thomas' support base had its roots in his family's longstanding and largely horizontal ties with a host of knightly families, resident in central and southern Norfolk and northern Suffolk, who had long ruled the roost in the two shires, and whose authority, although to some degree supplanted after the Revolution of 1399, was nonetheless still considerable.[123] These families included, most prominently, the Uffords, Kerdistons, Breweses, Stranges, Wingfields, Sheltons, Geneys, Mortimers, Harsyks, Elmhams and Thorpes, and by extension the Feltons, who had recently

---

[118] See above, pp. 90–1.
[119] *CIPM*, XV, nos. 124–9.
[120] E.g., C 47/6/1, nos. 71; 109; 137; 147.
[121] E.g., C 47/6/1, no. 20 (Thomas Rose).
[122] *CIPM*, XVI, nos. 383, 389, 392, 674, 821. The three family members who deposed for Morley were Sir Richard, Sir John, and William Sutton. C 47/6/1, nos. 38, 17, 5, 166.
[123] On political change in Norfolk brought about by the fall of Richard II, see Castor, *The King, the Crown, and the Duchy of Lancaster*, pp. 53–81.

suffered extinction in the senior male line.[124] From this influential pool of Norfolk and Suffolk gentry, Thomas, Lord Morley acquired extensive support before the Court of Chivalry, whilst the wider ties enjoyed by these families opened up further linkages into the region's middling and lesser gentry, which he was additionally able to mine. Most of the above families had been members of Norfolk's and Suffolk's knightly élite since the thirteenth century. Their ancestors had been amongst the cream of gentry society, listed on the Parliamentary Roll of Arms of 1312, and summoned to attend Edward II's grand military council in 1324.[125] Given their high standing, they were naturally also fixtures in shire office, where they served in each other's company.[126] Several were of sufficient substance that they had received a personal summons to Parliament at some point during the fourteenth century,[127] although only the Morleys and Uffords, from within this circle, maintained their membership of the peerage throughout these years.[128] What one encounters, then, is a collection of families, long at the apex of Norfolk–Suffolk society, who were heavily interconnected and had been for decades.

The Morleys' most significant tie within this circle was undoubtedly with the Ufford earls of Suffolk and their numerous cadet branches. Robert, second Lord Morley (c. 1295–1360), and Robert Ufford, first Earl of Suffolk (1298–1369), were men of the same generation, who, in their early adulthood, had been drawn into the affinity of East Anglia's preeminent resident magnate of the time, Edward II's half-brother, Thomas of Brotherton, Earl of Norfolk (d. 1338).[129] By the 1330s, both men were on the rise as stalwarts of Edward III's

---

[124] The Feltons had failed in the senior male line in 1381. Their influence nonetheless remained strong through the maternal line and through their wider kinship ties within the region. *CP*, V, pp. 292–3; P. Morgan, 'Sir Thomas Felton (d. 1381)', *ODNB*, XIX, pp. 286–7.

[125] *Parl. Writs.*, I, p. 415; II (ii), pp. 641–3.

[126] E.g., *CPR, 1348–50*, p. 526; *CPR, 1350–4*, p. 89; *CPR, 1354–8*, pp. 60–1, 388; *CPR, 1361–4*, p. 285; *CPR, 1374–7*, p. 138; *CPR, 1385–9*, p. 82; H. Le Strange, *Norfolk Official Lists* (Norwich, 1890), pp. 41–5; *List of Sheriffs*, p. 87.

[127] E.g., Sir William Kerdiston, Sir John Norwich, Sir Robert Felton. The Norfolk branch of the Brewes family were baronial cadets. *CP*, VII, pp. 191–3; IX, pp. 762–6; V, pp. 289–94; II, pp. 302–10.

[128] *CP*, IX, pp. 209–20; XII (i), pp. 429–38.

[129] A. Marshall, 'An Early Fourteenth-Century Affinity: The Earl of Norfolk and his Followers', in *Fourteenth Century England V*, ed. N. Saul (Woodbridge, 2008), p. 4.

fledgling regime. Morley developed a reputation as one of the finest naval commanders of his day, whilst Ufford – a household banneret, who had participated in the ambush of Queen Isabella and Roger Mortimer in their bedchamber – remained a lifelong intimate of King Edward, reflected in his elevation to the specially-created Earldom of Suffolk in 1337.[130] The latter event had enabled Ufford to significantly expand his affinity in Suffolk and southern Norfolk, where his and Morley's lands intersected.[131] Both men, in consequence, cooperatively mined the same broad region in search of lordly influence and military support, as did a range of neighbouring bannerets, including Sir Walter Mauny, Sir John Norwich and Sir William Kerdiston II. Their collective military needs, as well as their mutual political influence over the wider region, undoubtedly helped strengthen the sense of solidarity amongst those middling and lesser gentry (and churchmen) who served their interests. Certainly, the shared military experiences of those who fought in their retinues was graphically illustrated in their recollections of past campaigns before the Court.[132]

At a personal level, the Morley–Ufford relationship was naturally about more than royal favour, public duty, and high standing in their native East Anglia. As the years rolled by, the two families consistently aided each other in their private affairs, transacting land, acting as each other's witnesses, and occasionally doing favours for one another, as when Robert, Lord Morley employed one of Ufford's younger sons, Master John, as rector of his family's church at Hingham.[133] The ongoing nature of their relationship was underscored by the level of Ufford assistance provided to Lord Thomas before the Court of Chivalry. Despite the

[130] *Chronicon Henrici Knighton*, ed. J. R. Lumby (RS, London, 1895), II, p. 10; *Political Poems and Songs relating to English History composed during the period from the Accession of Edward III to that of Richard II*, ed. T. Wright, 2 vols. (London, 1859), I, pp. 70–2; C. L. Lambert, *Shipping the Medieval Military: English Maritime Logistics in the Fourteenth Century* (Woodbridge, 2011), pp. 116, 168; E 101/384/7, m. 4; Ormrod, *Edward III*, pp. 90–1, 137–8. On the circumstances surrounding Ufford's elevation to the Earldom of Suffolk, see J. S. Bothwell, 'Edward III and the 'New Nobility': Largesse and Limitation in Fourteenth-Century England', *EHR*, 112 (1997), pp. 1111–40.

[131] On Robert Ufford's construction of his affinity in East Anglia, in the wake of his elevation to the Earldom of Suffolk, see R. Gorski, *The Fourteenth-Century Sheriff: English Local Administration in the Late Middle Ages* (Woodbridge, 2003), pp. 22–8.

[132] C 47/6/1.

[133] E.g., Blomefield, *History of Norfolk*, II, pp. 423–4; VI, p. 33.

recent extinction of the senior Ufford line with the sudden death of William, second Earl of Suffolk, in 1382,[134] William's younger brother, Sir Robert, appeared before the Court to describe his campaigning experiences with the Morleys.[135] The Uffords' maternal cousin, Sir John Brewes, likewise provided a deposition, his military memories stretching back to the days of the siege of Calais in 1347.[136] Two other knightly testators, Sir John Loudham and Sir John Lakyngheth, were the sons of close followers of Robert, first Earl of Suffolk,[137] whilst four obscure lesser gentry deponents openly described themselves as former Ufford retainers.[138] All had regularly borne arms in Earl Robert's military retinue between the 1330s and the 1350s, reminding one of just how often Robert, Lord Morley and Robert, first Earl of Suffolk, had saddled up as senior commanders on the same expeditions.[139]

These depositions, moreover, were augmented by the recollections of several other East Anglian knights and esquires, who claimed no such formal ties with the Ufford affinity, but whose descriptions of their own war records revealed that their military careers had been a least partially carved out beneath the Ufford banner.[140] Such men included Sir Ralph Bocking, who testified to having been with Earl Robert on the Rheims campaign in 1359–60 and with Earl William on John of Gaunt's *chevauchée* in 1373;[141] Sir Richard Cosyn, who was

---

[134] Castor, *The King, the Crown, and the Duchy of Lancaster*, p. 60.

[135] C 47/6/1, no. 48.

[136] C 47/6/1, no. 102.

[137] Loudham's eponymous father had served Earl Robert in war and peace, whilst the younger Loudham had borne arms beneath the Ufford banner on the Rheims expedition (1359–60), before undertaking subsequent bouts of service with Humphrey, Earl of Hereford, and Robert, Lord Scales. *CPR, 1338–40*, p. 531; C 76/14, m. 4; C 76/15, m. 32; C 47/6/1, no. 52. For Lakyngheth's deposition, see C 47/6/1, no. 45. A man of sub-knightly rank bearing the same name, probably the deponent's father, had acted as a receiver for Earl Robert in the 1350s. *CPR, 1354–8*, p. 223.

[138] C 47/6/1, nos. 13; 39; 42; 92. Multiple family members, of varying ranks, were sometimes drawn into the Ufford affinity. E.g., Sir Robert and William Erpingham. C 71/15, m. 27; *CPR, 1334–8*, p. 527; Wrottesley, *Crecy and Calais*, pp. 82, 235; *CPR, 1345–8*, p. 497.

[139] Morley and Suffolk campaigned together in Scotland in the 1330s; at the battle of Crécy and the ensuing siege of Calais (1346–7); at the sea-battle off Winchelsea (1350); and on the Rheims expedition (1359–60). C 47/6/1.

[140] C 47/6/1, nos. 14; 31; 34; 37; 48; 53.

[141] C 47/6/1, no. 101.

with Earl Robert at Poitiers (1356) and Rheims, and with Earl William at St. Malo (1378);[142] William Phelip, who fought with Earl Robert at the sea-battle off Winchelsea (1350);[143] Sir Godfrey Stratton, who bore arms with Earl Robert in the 1350s and Earl William in the 1370s;[144] and William Thweyt, who had additionally seen service with another Ufford cousin, the late banneret, Sir John Norwich.[145] Through the family ties and lordly influence of the wider Ufford clan, Thomas, Lord Morley acquired at least 20 witnesses – almost one-quarter of his militarily active testators – each of whom outlined occasions when his family had borne the disputed arms in a military setting.

The Morley–Ufford relationship, on the one hand, reflected their families' membership of the peerage and mutual standing at the absolute apex of East Anglian society. Yet, arguably of even greater significance to Lord Thomas in the formation of his witness list were the largely horizontal friendships and associations his family had forged across the generations with the knightly élite of central and southern Norfolk and northern Suffolk. Like Richard, Lord Scrope's generations-old ties with the knightly élite of the North Riding,[146] the Morleys and Uffords could move freely amongst the greater gentry of their native locality, essentially because this was the social milieu from whence their own families hailed and from which they had been elevated to national prominence.[147] The Morleys' connections with several of these families were anyway of such long duration that their appearance on Lord Thomas' behalf before the Court of Chivalry would have been entirely expected.[148]

One of the more exalted of these families, whose ongoing relationship with the Lords Morley may stand for the rest, were the Kerdistons of Claxton and Repham. They and the Morleys had been on the closest of terms for more than half a century. As far back as the

---

[142] C 47/6/1, no. 23.
[143] C 47/6/1, no. 42.
[144] C 47/6/1, no. 36.
[145] C 47/6/1, no. 92.
[146] See above, pp. 98–104.
[147] *CP*, IX, pp. 209–11; XII (i), pp. 429–30.
[148] E.g., The Cursons and Gerberghs had regularly participated in land transactions with the Morleys and other prominent families within their orbit. *CPR, 1370–4*, p. 419; *CCR, 1381–5*, p. 420; Blomefield, *History of Norfolk*, VI, p. 344; Oxford, Magdalen College, Guton Deeds 20A, no. 292; Guton Deeds 24A, no. 197; Guton Deeds 147, no. 280; *CAD*, I, C1013; *CAD*, III, D1139; TNA, E 210/6455.

1320s, Robert, second Lord Morley, had transacted land and acted as a witness alongside Sir Roger Kerdiston (1264–1337), a veteran Justice of the King's Bench, several years his senior.[149] In 1328, Lord Robert had been one of those who formally attested that Roger's heir, the future banneret, Sir William Kerdiston II (c. 1307–1361), had come of age, and nine years later, when Sir William came into his inheritance, Lord Robert provided him with assistance as he set about organising his estates.[150] As their generation gave way to the next, William Kerdiston III (c. 1325–1391) continued holding land from William, third Lord Morley (1319–1379), reminding one of the feudal element to their relationship, with the Morleys as lords and the Kerdistons, at one level, as merely one of their more important tenants.[151] Yet, the ongoing intimacy enjoyed by their families into the 1380s and beyond underscores that their relationship was far more 'affective' than 'instrumental' in character.[152] William Kerdiston III's son, Sir Leonard (c. 1368–1421), not only deposed before the Court of Chivalry as a very young man in Morley's defence, but turned out a second time in 1408–9 to testify on behalf of Lord Thomas' stepson, Sir Edward Hastings.[153] In between, he remained actively involved in the Morleys' private affairs. In 1392, for example, he joined the cadets, Sir Robert Morley and Sir Robert Ufford, in attempting to intercede on behalf

---

[149] *CPR, 1330–4*, pp. 287, 296; W. L. E. Parsons, *Salle: The Story of a Norfolk Parish. Its Churches, Manors and People* (Norwich, 1937), p. 216.

[150] *CIPM*, XI, pp. 74–5.

[151] *CIPM*, XV, pp. 47–9.

[152] The intimacy enjoyed by the shire's élite with gentry of slightly lesser rank has been explored through case studies of other Norfolk social circles. C. E. Moreton, 'A Social Gulf?', pp. 255–62; J. Hughes, 'Stephen Scrope and the Circle of Sir John Fastolf: Moral and Intellectual Outlooks', in *Medieval Knighthood IV: Papers from the fifth Strawberry Hill Conference, 1990*, ed. C. Harper-Bill and R. Harvey (Woodbridge, 1992), pp. 109–46; Castor, *The King, the Crown, and the Duchy of Lancaster*, pp. 128–55. When characterising such relationships, Maddern drew a distinction between 'instrumental' and 'affective' friendship – the former reflecting mutual association or assistance (such as two parties engaging in a business transaction), the latter reflecting genuine affection between those involved (such as the affection felt by a devoted father for a younger son or daughter, to whom he left a small parcel of land in his will). Both types of friendship, however, could reflect a level of genuine trust between the two parties. P. C. Maddern, "Best Trusted Friends': Concepts and Practices of Friendship among Fifteenth-Century Norfolk Gentry', in *England in the Fifteenth Century: Proceedings of the 1992 Harlaxton Symposium*, ed. N. Rogers (Stamford, 1994), pp. 100–17.

[153] C 47/6/1, no. 64; *PCM*, I, p. 456.

of the harried widow of their mutual friend, Edmund Clippesby, who had been murdered by servants of the Bishop of Norwich, with the result that all three men were themselves menaced by the Bishop's servants.[154] Finally, a further generation on, Lord Thomas' grandson and Sir Leonard's son – Thomas, fifth Lord Morley (1393–1435), and Sir Thomas Kerdiston (c. 1395–1446) – were still heavily involved in each other's private affairs, upholding a family tie that by this stage was more than a century old.[155] Indeed, as but one noteworthy public expression of the bonds their families shared, their arms, alongside those of Ufford, were collectively displayed above the west door of Salle Church, bordering the Kerdiston estates, of which all three families were patrons.[156]

Thomas, Lord Morley's relationship with the Uffords, and with senior knightly families like the Kerdistons, was undoubtedly crucial in the construction of his witness list, not least because such ties enhanced his access to the wider body of knights and esquires who resided in the region and who were themselves heavily interconnected. The ongoing private interactions of a small subset of these families may serve to illustrate the levels of personal trust they enjoyed. To cite but a few noteworthy examples, Sir William Elmham acted regularly in his private affairs with at least two of his fellow Morley deponents, Sir William Wingfield and Sir Thomas Gerbergh.[157] Wingfield, Sir John Strange and Sir Robert Ufford were similarly reliant upon one another in their land transactions. Ufford employed Wingfield as his feoffee, whilst Strange and Ufford became trustees of each other's estates. Indeed, such was their intimacy that Ufford, on his deathbed, chose to impart only to Strange explicit instructions regarding the inheritance of his youngest daughter.[158] Strange was also involved in

---

[154] R. Virgoe, 'The Murder of Edmund Clippesby', *Norfolk Archaeology*, 35 (1972), p. 303.

[155] *CAD*, III, D 433, D 426; TNA, E 210/10839.

[156] C. Pamela-Graves, *The Form and Fabric of Belief: An Archaeology of the Lay Experience of Religion in Medieval Norfolk and Devon* (British Archaeological Reports cccxi, Oxford, 2000), p. 85; Parsons, *Salle*, pp. 216-18.

[157] *CCR, 1377–81*, p. 193; *CCR, 1385–9*, p. 139; *CCR, 1392–6*, p. 236; *CPR, 1385–9*, p. 176; *CCR, 1381–5*, p. 595; *HPC, 1386–1421*, III, p. 179.

[158] NRO, Reg. Heydon, f. 117; *CPR, 1381–5*, pp. 83, 133; *CCR, 1413–19*, p. 447; *CCR, 1422–9*, pp. 72, 126–7; *HPC, 1386–1421*, IV, p. 501.

private business with Sir John White, as well as the lawyer-families, the Berneys and Winters, all of whom testified on Morley's behalf.[159]

Moreover, as has long been recognised, the knightly élite of East Anglia enjoyed a marked propensity for intermarrying, and such bonds proved crucial in binding together the Morley–Ufford circle.[160] Sir Leonard Kerdiston and Sir John Strange were cousins;[161] Sir John Brewes was Kerdiston's uncle and cousin both to Strange and Sir Robert Ufford;[162] Sir William Kerdiston II married Sir John Norwich's sister, whilst Norwich, in turn, wed the sister of Robert Ufford, Earl of Suffolk;[163] and, as perhaps the finest illustration of the breadth of kinship ties that arose from this high degree of intermarriage, the three surviving daughters of the late Garter Knight, Sir Thomas Felton (d. 1381), another central figure in this circle, took as their respective husbands, Sir John Curson, Sir Robert Ufford, and the cadet, Sir Thomas Morley.[164]

Something else most of these families shared was an attachment to the affinity of Edward, the Black Prince. This connection has traditionally been viewed from a top-down perspective as the East Anglian contingent to the Prince's affinity.[165] Yet, rather as mutual service to John of Gaunt merely reinforced pre-existing bonds between Lord Scrope and the knightly élite of the North Riding, so the Prince's East Anglian following may at least partially be understood as an offshoot of his friendship with Robert Ufford, first Earl of Suffolk, through whom he gained access to the knightly élite of the Ufford–Morley circle. Suffolk had been one of several of Edward III's intimates who had actively mentored the young Prince, in which capacity he was appointed titular head of the Prince's council and became one of his closest military allies, accompanying him to Gascony in the

---

[159] Magdalen College, Guton Deeds 23A, 1566; NRO, Le Strange MSS., A16; NRO Phi/23; BL, Add. Ch. 14128; *CCR, 1399–1402*, pp. 305, 392; *CCR, 1405–9*, pp. 279, 385, 462–3, 524; C 47/6/1, nos. 46, 65, 75, 76, 80.

[160] E.g., Walker, *The Lancastrian Affinity*, pp. 193–4.

[161] Green, 'Edward the Black Prince and East Anglia', p. 92.

[162] Parsons, *Salle*, pp. 216–18; Green, 'Edward the Black Prince and East Anglia', p. 92; *Scrope v. Grosvenor*, II, pp. 208–10.

[163] Parsons, *Salle*, pp. 216–18; *CP*, IX, p. 764.

[164] *HPC, 1386–1421*, II, p. 719; *CP*, V, p. 294.

[165] Green, 'Edward the Black Prince and East Anglia', pp. 83–98.

mid-1350s.¹⁶⁶ William, third Lord Morley, had cut his military teeth as a teenager on this expedition, fighting in Suffolk's retinue at the battle of Poitiers (1356),¹⁶⁷ but it was chiefly Morley's and Ufford's gentry friends and associates who gradually moved into the Prince's employ, either on a formal or *ad hoc* basis, becoming the lynchpins of his East Anglian affinity. Sir William Kerdiston II – grandfather of Morley's deponent – was retained as a banneret of the Prince's household in the mid 1340s and fought in his retinue at the battle of Crécy (1346);¹⁶⁸ two other Morley witnesses, Sir William Elmham and Sir William Wingfield, were amongst the Prince's retainers and annuitants;¹⁶⁹ the father of a fourth, the lawyer John Berney, was steward of the Prince's Norfolk estates;¹⁷⁰ Sir Richard Walkefare, late father-in-law of the deponent, Sir John Strange, had been the Prince's bachelor and the surveyor of his game at his Norfolk manor of Castle Rising;¹⁷¹ another of Walkefare's sons-in-law, the late Sir Thomas Felton, had held the illustrious posts of steward of the Prince's household, chamberlain of Chester, and seneschal of Aquitaine;¹⁷² and, perhaps most impressively, the late Sir John Wingfield, two of whose immediate family spoke for Morley, had risen, before his premature death, to become steward of the Prince's estates and 'governor of his business'.¹⁷³

Overall though – notwithstanding the various ties his witnesses enjoyed with members of the higher nobility – the Morley circle remained an essentially horizontal network, whose leading figures survived both the collapse of the Ufford affinity in 1382, and, more seriously, the rise of the Erpingham clique after 1399, whose coterie of native-born Lancastrian gentry to some degree supplanted them as

---

¹⁶⁶ R. Virgoe, 'The Government and Society of Suffolk in the Later Middle Ages', *Lowestoft Archaeology and Local History Society* (1967–8), pp. 29–30; *BPReg*, IV, p. 144.
¹⁶⁷ *Foedera*, III (i), p. 325.
¹⁶⁸ *BPReg*, I, p. 80; A. Ayton, 'The English Army at Crécy', in *The Battle of Crécy, 1346*, ed. A. Ayton and P. Preston (Woodbridge, 2005), p. 242.
¹⁶⁹ C 47/6/1, nos. 8, 62, 149, 150; Green, 'Edward the Black Prince and East Anglia', p. 88; *BPReg*, IV, p. 603.
¹⁷⁰ C 47/6/1, no. 80; *BPReg*, IV, pp. 261, 263.
¹⁷¹ *BPReg*, IV, p. 470. For Strange's deposition, see C 47/6/1, no. 46.
¹⁷² Green, 'Edward the Black Prince and East Anglia', p. 88.
¹⁷³ C 47/6/1, no. 53; *BPReg*, IV, pp. 167, 191, 326, 350–1, 380. His brother, Sir William, and cousin, Sir John, both testified for Morley. C 47/6/1, nos. 8, 53, 149.

Norfolk's new governing élite under Henry IV.[174] Any sense of division between these two groups, however, proved only temporary. Indeed, by sheer coincidence, one encounters members of the Morley circle a second time before the Court of Chivalry in *Grey v. Hastings*, now in their new fifteenth-century incarnation.[175] By 1407, when the case came before the Court, Erpingham and his colleagues were actively working to develop a broader, non-Lancastrian legitimacy to their rule, and they achieved this by forging increasingly strong ties with Norfolk's leading fourteenth-century families.[176] Their efforts achieved incidental expression through Sir Edward Hastings' witness list, whose deponents included a number of senior members of the Erpingham circle, as well as several gentry hailing from families who had been part of the Morley–Ufford orbit for well over three generations.[177]

This situation essentially arose from Hastings' privileged position within Norfolk society. On the one hand, as we have seen, he was the heir to a strongly Lancastrian family, resident in the heartland of John of Gaunt's estates in northeast Norfolk.[178] He thus grew to adulthood surrounded by gentry tied to varying degrees to Gaunt, who were his father, Sir Hugh Hastings III's, friends, associates and former wartime comrades in the Lancastrian military retinue.[179] At the same time, Hastings' distinguished ancestry – as a cadet of the earls of Pembroke and heir to three consecutive generations of bannerets – enabled him to walk comfortably amongst the shire's long-established élite: something Erpingham and his cohorts, whose ancestors had merely been the retainers of these great families, simply could not

---

[174] Virgoe, 'The Crown and Local Government', pp. 218–41; Castor, *The King, the Crown, and the Duchy of Lancaster*, pp. 59–81.

[175] *PCM*.

[176] Caudrey, 'War and Society in Medieval Norfolk', pp. 84–6, 98–9.

[177] The Erpingham Circle: Edmund Barry; Sir Simon Felbrigg; John Reymes; Sir Robert Berney; John Payn; and Sir Thomas Erpingham. *PCM*, I, pp. 393, 443, 444, 474, 502, 439. The Morley Circle: Sir Robert Morley; Sir Ralph Shelton; Sir John Geney; Sir Leonard Kerdiston; Sir Thomas Gerbergh; Constantine Mortimer; and Thomas, Lord Morley. *PCM*, I, pp. 421, 423, 425, 456, 496, 509, 435.

[178] Goodman, *John of Gaunt*, p. 214.

[179] On Gaunt's recruitment drive in northeast Norfolk, see Walker, *The Lancastrian Affinity*, pp.183–94.

do.¹⁸⁰ These weighty ties of Hastings', moreover, had been reinforced by his widowed mother's recent marriage to Thomas, Lord Morley, who undeniably leapt to his new stepson's defence in the face of Lord Grey's challenge.¹⁸¹ Consequently, as we shall see in the next chapter, the Hastings testimony was largely divided between memories of his father's exploits in Lancastrian service, provided by members of the Erpingham circle and lesser gentry who had served in the Hastings' own retinue, combined with detailed recollections of his family's ancient armorial right, revealed through anecdotal evidence garnered, amongst others, from members of the wider Morley circle, who cited the views of such luminaries as the Duke of York and the Countesses of Pembroke and Norfolk in Hastings' defence.¹⁸²

What is also apparent, when one considers the backgrounds of Hastings' witnesses, is the extent to which, by 1407, the Morley and Erpingham circles – representatives of the shire's long-established and newly-risen élite – had become increasingly interconnected. Given the relative independence of Norfolk's gentry, some of these relationships had already developed of their own accord before 1399. Sir Ralph Shelton II, to cite a prime example, enjoyed traditional family ties with several members of the Morley circle, yet spent significant time in John of Gaunt's service.¹⁸³ Shelton became exceptionally close to Erpingham and several of his oldest friends, including Sir Simon Felbrigg, Sir Robert Berney and John Reymes. He engaged with all four in land transactions, dating back to the early 1390s, and had even acted as a trustee of Erpingham's estates when the latter went into exile with Henry of Bolingbroke in 1398.¹⁸⁴ Other members of the Morley circle, however, merely saw which way the winds were blowing after the Lancastrian usurpation and responded accordingly:

---

¹⁸⁰ E.g., Sir Thomas Erpingham's grandfather and uncle had been retainers of the Ufford earls of Suffolk, whilst Sir Thomas himself had cut his military teeth in their retinue alongside his father. C 71/15, m. 27; *CPR, 1334–8*, p. 527; *CPR, 1345–8*, p. 497; C 47/6/1, no. 39; Curry, 'Sir Thomas Erpingham', p. 60. Sir Robert Berney's father had been a lawyer in the pay of Edward, the Black Prince. *BPReg*, IV, pp. 261, 263. John Reymes had twice served as a member of Sir Hugh Hastings III's military retinue during the 1380s. *PCM*, I, p. 444.

¹⁸¹ *CP*, IX, p. 217; *PCM*, I, p. 435.

¹⁸² See below, pp. 154–6, pp. 174–7.

¹⁸³ *HPC, 1386–1421*, IV, pp. 355–7; *PCM*, I, pp. 423–4.

¹⁸⁴ NRO, (Phillips) Phi32078, no. 61; *CFR, 1422–30*, p. 130; C 139/23/31; NRO, Reg. Harsyk, f. 240.

Sir John Curson acquired Erpingham's services as a feoffee, whilst his son would go on to fight in Erpingham's retinue on the Agincourt expedition;[185] Sir Thomas Kerdiston transacted land with Erpingham and witnessed his will;[186] Sir Miles Stapleton likewise engaged members of the Erpingham circle in his private affairs and married Sir Simon Felbrigg's daughter;[187] Sir Thomas Gerbergh wed his only daughter to the Lancastrian esquire, Edmund Barry;[188] and, as perhaps the clearest indication of how well-integrated the two circles had become, the year after Thomas, Lord Morley's sudden death in 1416, Erpingham headed a list of 19 gentry who witnessed a complicated land transaction undertaken by the recently widowed Lady Morley. Most of her more distinguished witnesses were longstanding members of the Morley circle, but their number included Erpingham, his nephew, Sir William Phelip, and the leading Lancastrian bureaucrat, Edmund Oldhall.[189] The Morley circle's surviving members thus continued assisting one another in their private business well into the fifteenth century, whilst increasingly developing close ties with the shire's newly prominent families, few of whom had been their equals a generation earlier.

Although Thomas, Lord Morley acquired the support of dozens of lesser gentry, who were his family's tenants, servants and associates, it was the knightly élite of the Morley–Ufford circle that proved of greatest practical value in the construction of his witness list. Collectively, they comprised a group of more than a dozen knightly families, who had assisted each other in their private affairs, were often interconnected by marriage, and who had fought alongside each other in the Hundred Years War for at least three generations.[190] These families memorialised

[185] *CPR, 1396–9*, p. 586; E 101/44/30, no3 m. 3.
[186] E 326/13549; NRO, (Phillips) Phi65/576/9 (single parchment); *Reg. Chichele*, II, p. 381.
[187] Oxford, Magdalen College, Hickling 109, no. 238; Castor, *The King, the Crown, and the Duchy of Lancaster*, p. 76n.
[188] *The Paston Letters*, ed. Davis, I, pp. cliii, liii, 49.
[189] NRO, (Phillips) Phi65/576/9 (single parchment). On Phelip's and Oldhall's careers, see *HPC, 1386–1421*, IV, pp. 71–4; III, pp. 870–1.
[190] In sum, knightly testators from this broadly-defined network included: Sir William and Sir John Wingfield; Sir Thomas Gerbergh; Sir John Strange; Sir Robert Ufford; Sir William Elmham; Sir John Harsyk; Sir Leonard Kerdeston; Sir John White; Sir John Brewes; Sir Edmund Thorpe. C 47/6/1, nos. 8; 149; 53; 40; 46; 48; 62; 150; 63; 64; 65; 102; 104. Additionally, at least ten largely obscure lesser gentry testified to regular bouts of military service in the Morley or Ufford retinues. C 47/6/1, nos. 5; 10; 11; 13; 20; 26; 39; 42; 59; 92.

their bonds, and celebrated their dominant position at the forefront of fourteenth-century Norfolk and Suffolk society, by displaying their arms in parish churches and religious houses throughout the region.[191] It was the galvanisation of this knightly circle, with their wider ties to lesser gentry soldiers of immense military experience, and with their long memories of Morley possession of the disputed arms, that represented the cornerstone of Thomas, Lord Morley's defence before the Court of Chivalry.

Yet, it is equally clear that these patterns of inter-gentry solidarity were ultimately rooted in the propitious circumstances of the high Edwardian age, which enabled these families to simultaneously enjoy the fruits of political stability at home and military triumph abroad.[192] When these pillars of their longstanding prosperity were shaken by the changing political climate that followed the Revolution of 1399, these great local families smoothly adapted themselves to the new status quo, developing friendships, associations, and marriage ties with Norfolk's new governing élite, thus maintaining their long-established positions at the forefront of East Anglian society.[193] Through *Lovel v. Morley* (1386–7) and *Grey v. Hastings* (1407–10), one may chart the evolution of this powerful network of East Anglian gentry, from their Edwardian heyday to their successful accommodation with the altered political realities of Lancastrian England.

Conclusion

Undoubtedly the least explored aspects of the *Scrope v. Grosvenor* and *Lovel v. Morley* testimony are the insights they provide into the vertical and horizontal ties of their protagonists. The investigation of inter-gentry solidarities has long proven a staple of county histories, yet the Scrope and Morley witness lists, which reveal respectively the

---

[191] The earlier example of Morley–Kerdiston–Ufford commemoration of their shared bonds in Salle Church (Pamela-Graves, *The Form and Fabric of Belief*, p. 85) can be replicated many times over. The arms of Morley and Ufford, and the rest of the knightly families in their orbit, festooned the churches of central and southern Norfolk, celebrating the innumerable bonds they shared. E.g., Blomefield, *History of Norfolk*, III, pp. 355–7; 417-19; IV, pp. 522–8.

[192] Ormrod, *Edward III*, pp. 446–97.

[193] Virgoe, 'The Crown and Local Government', pp. 218–41; Castor, *The King, the Crown, and the Duchy of Lancaster*, pp. 59–81.

depth of Scrope's reach within Yorkshire and the breadth of his reach beyond it, as well as the intricacies of Morley's position in his native East Anglia, have been largely ignored in the existing scholarship on the two cases. By focusing directly upon these types of relationships, one may discern some of the specific networks into which Scrope and Morley tapped in search of support, as well as how these, in their turn, opened wider linkages into other networks that were farther removed from the protagonists' own personal centres of authority.

Through Scrope's surviving testimony, one is reminded, on the one hand, of how far the baronage's horizons stretched beyond their native localities, and, on the other, of how deeply rooted their power bases were in their native shires. Scrope was a man of the North Riding, yet simultaneously a figure of national renown with connections to the royal court, the Lancastrian affinity, to other members of the peerage, and to a range of gentry from all parts of the realm who were acquainted, directly or indirectly, with his wider family. If Morley's witness list reveals the importance of the locality, even to a figure of national standing, Scrope's underscores how the line between region, county and locality – so often differentiated from one another in studies of individual shires[194] – inevitably blurred. Through these two witness lists, the fluidity of gentry society is reinforced.

---

[194] For examples, of studies that stress the intersection between region, county and locality, see esp. Bennett, *Community, Class and Careerism*; Pollard, *North-Eastern England*; Carpenter, *Locality and Polity*.

4

Soldiers, Civilians and Chivalric Memory

Long before historians began appraising the Court of Chivalry's testimony for insights into patterns of military service and retinue formation, or evidence of inter-gentry solidarities, it was above all the impressive chivalric flavour of the depositions that caught the eye of early scholars. From Sir Harris Nicolas' effusive claims about the reign of Edward III representing 'the brightest page in the annals of British chivalry',[1] to Maurice Keen's suggestion that members of the Scrope family would have provided fine models for Chaucer's Knight,[2] to Keen's later assertion that the Hastings testimony lacked the chivalrous gloss found in the depositions of the 1380s,[3] there has been widespread acknowledgement amongst historians that the Scrope and Morley testimony in particular provided vivid insights into the world of English chivalric culture in the fourteenth century.[4] In essence, what we possess in the surviving Scrope, Morley (and, indeed, Hastings) depositions is an eclectic body of chivalric memories, expressed through an intricate and interlocking combination of war recollections, family and regional history, and popular hearsay, augmented by a combination of written and iconographic material. The concept of 'chivalric memory' has been aptly defined as 'a form of family memory, part of the stock of myths and narratives passed down over the generations, which brought lustre to a family's name', but which 'also belonged to the chivalric class as a whole'.[5] As we shall see, when that chivalric class came before the Court of Chivalry, their testimony revealed not merely partisan

---

[1] *Scrope v. Grosvenor*, I, p. 14.
[2] Keen, 'Chaucer's Knight', pp. 108–10.
[3] Keen, 'Grey v. Hastings', p. 182.
[4] Ayton, 'Knights, Esquires and Military Service', p. 87; Keen, *Origins of the English Gentleman*, pp. 48–58; Rosenthal, *Telling Tales*, pp. 79–84; Caudrey, 'War, Chivalry and Regional Society', pp. 132–4.
[5] Saul, *Chivalry in Medieval England*, p. 283.

support for their protagonist, but more broadly laid bare the extent to which chivalric memory, beneath its national façade, had taken deep root within the localities, acting as a source of cultural cohesion for the realm's regional military communities.[6]

This chapter explores the character of English chivalry between the reigns of Edward III and Henry IV by engaging with the testimony provided in all three armorial cases and relating the deponents' various strands of tale-telling, hearsay, war memories and iconographic evidence to the wider chivalric culture of the age. Its purpose is to tease out – through the words of those who deposed before the Court – the everyday impact of the Hundred Years War, and the chivalric ethos it spawned, upon genteel society at a national, regional, and intensely local, level. In so doing – following on from Chapter 1 – it will be posited that the continuities in English chivalric culture between the battles of Crécy (1346) and Agincourt (1415) were considerable. This chapter is sub-divided into two parts: the first examines, on its own terms, the military testimony imparted before the Court; the second expands upon this body of evidence to consider the practical impact of chivalric culture upon regional society, with a predominant focus upon the military communities of Yorkshire, Cheshire and Norfolk.

Chivalric Memory I: The Recollections of War Veterans

The relationship between memory and wartime experience enjoys an incredibly rich historiography. Almost everything that has been written on the subject as concerns English soldiering, however, has derived from recent military history, where private letters, diaries, memoirs, and a mass of interviews with ex-soldiers, have granted specialists access to an incredibly diverse range of military experiences.[7] Historians of medieval England are sadly prevented, by the absence of such material, from engaging in the same fashion with the military

---

[6] On the concept of the 'military community' and its various forms, see Ayton, 'Armies and Military Communities', pp. 215–39.

[7] The ground-breaking study of the British experience of modern warfare, galvanising historians to explore the everyday experiences of soldiers in the two World Wars, was J. Keegan, *The Face of Battle* (London, 1976). For a thought-provoking survey of the British experience of the First World War, addressing the long-term impact of Keegan's study upon the existing scholarship, see Reynolds, *The Long Shadow*.

experiences of veterans of the Hundred Years War.[8] Yet, it would not be unreasonable to claim that the testimony proffered by war veterans before the Court of Chivalry provides as close an approximation to this type of evidence as can be found. The witnesses for each protagonist were answering a coherent set of questions, and the focus, of the judges and those who deposed, was on establishing the validity of the protagonist's claim to the arms under dispute. Without ever losing sight of the limited purpose of the testimony, then, this section seeks to deduce how England's fourteenth-century gentry thought about war; how they wove their own personal military experiences, and those of their protagonist's family, into their wartime recollections; and whether their attitudes towards military service and the chivalric ethos began to shift as the triumphs of the Hundred Years War's first phase (1337–60) gave way to the military failures of its second (1369–89).

A good place to start might be with a pair of depositions from *Scrope v. Grosvenor*, provided by aged testators, hailing respectively from Northumberland and Yorkshire, who could recall extensive careers in arms and who had plenty to say about the Scrope family's heraldic identity. The men in question – both of whom we have already encountered – were a pair of esquires of incredible military experience, Nicholas Sabraham and John Rither.[9] Sabraham estimated that he was over 60 years of age. He had probably first borne arms in Brittany in the retinue of the Earl of Northampton in 1345. Having served at the battle of Crécy (1346) and the siege of Calais (1347), he subsequently took his martial talents to Scotland, participating in Edward Balliol's summer campaign of 1347, marching, once again in Northampton's retinue, from Lochmaben to Peebles in the autumn of 1350, before undertaking a spell of garrison service at Roxburgh Castle. Sabraham later participated on the Rheims expedition of 1359–60 and fought variously in Normandy, Brittany, Gascony and Spain during the 1350s and 1360s, seeing on a number of occasions the plaintiff, Richard, Lord Scrope, and his Masham cousins, Henry, William and Stephen, each bearing the disputed arms in full or with a difference. More impressively still, soldiering on his own account, Sabraham described crusading with the Teutonic Knights in Prussia (1362–3) and with King

[8] Keegan sought to do just that in *The Face of Battle*, though, hampered by the relative limitations of the medieval sources, his case study of the battle of Agincourt (1415) proved rather less convincing than his seminal study of the battle of the Somme (1916). Keegan, *The Face of Battle*.

[9] *Scrope v. Grosvenor*, I, pp. 124–5; 144–50.

Peter of Cyprus at the siege of Alexandria (1365). Rounding out his remarkable military career, he additionally crusaded in Hungary, on the Bosphorus, and at Nessebar on the Black Sea coast of Bulgaria, served in the defence of Constantinople against the Turks, and campaigned in Italy as a mercenary in the retinue of the legendary English condottiere, Sir John Hawkwood.[10]

John Rither's war record, as we saw in Chapter 1, was of similar duration and intensity to Sabraham's. Rither began his deposition by recounting tales of the tourneying exploits of the plaintiff's father, Henry, and uncle, Geoffrey. He then moved on to describe those numerous occasions when he had fought in the company of various members of the Scrope family. He had seen Geoffrey Scrope bearing the arms with a difference at the battle of Buirenfosse (1339) and the siege of Tournai (1340); he had seen the plaintiff's elder brother, William, and cousin, Henry, at the siege of Vannes (1342); he recalled William, once again, bearing the arms at the siege and battle of Morlaix (1342); and he had additionally fought alongside various cadets of the Scropes of Masham at the battles of Sluys (1340) and Crécy (1346) and the sieges of Calais (1347), Berwick (1355–6) and Rennes (1356–7); towards the end of his career, he journeyed to Wellon in Lithuania with the young Geoffrey Scrope (1362), fought with the plaintiff at the battle of Nájera (1367), and saw the Scrope arms borne on campaign one last time in Gascony and Normandy (1369).[11]

Even as a mere register of military service, there is – as numerous scholars have noted – more than a hint of glamour to Sabraham's and Rither's accounts, their memories stretching from campaign to siege and battle, across land and sea, and even encompassing martial exploits as local as domestic tournaments and as international as the Crusade against the heathen.[12] Obviously, since both men were answering direct questions about the Scrope family's heraldic identity, their enticing recollections arose purely because the Scropes of Bolton and Masham between them happened to have borne arms on a quite breathtaking

---

[10] *Scrope v. Grosvenor*, I, pp. 124–5; Keen, 'Chaucer's Knight', p. 110; Keen, *Origins of the English Gentleman*, pp. 63–4; Sumption, *The Hundred Years War III*, p. 736; Bell et al., *The Soldier*, p. 118. For a complete reconstruction of Sabraham's service record, in so far as the military sources allow, see Ayton, 'Nicholas Sabraham', pp. 99–112, 115–16.

[11] *Scrope v. Grosvenor*, I, pp. 144–50; Keen, 'Chaucer's Knight', p. 110.

[12] See above, nn. 9–10.

array of expeditions.[13] Of greater significance than the range of wartime memories on offer, however, is the style in which they were packaged. Most noticeably, the fuller responses before the Court tended to focus upon specific military actions rather than the wider outcome of the expedition. A classic example is the way in which the Rheims campaign of 1359–60 was invariably described as the occasion when the late King Edward had stood before the gates of Paris. Here we see a fine instance of oral tradition at work. It was this single chivalrous moment, in which the English army had made their stand before the French capital, which was evidently the highpoint of the expedition as far as its gentry participants were concerned: the most memorable event of a large-scale enterprise which had witnessed no set-piece battle or successful siege.[14]

This preoccupation with individual chivalrous moments, moreover, very much mirrored the style of war chronicling pioneered by Jean Le Bel and Jean Froissart, and, in fragmented, oral form, was not entirely dissimilar to the glowing catalogues of feats of arms expounded in medieval knightly biographies.[15] Le Bel and Froissart told the history of the Hundred Years War as a series of 'notable perilous adventures and battles, feats of arms and prowess', and Froissart, in particular, incorporated a range of oral testimony into his chronicle.[16] Their heroes were the great knights of the age, first and foremost, Edward

[13] For an overview of the Scrope family's military record, see Keen, 'Chivalrous Culture', pp. 15–17.
[14] *Scrope v. Grosvenor*, C 47/6/1; Caudrey, 'War, Chivalry and Regional Society', p. 136; Ayton, 'English Armies in the Fourteenth Century', pp. 303–4.
[15] Jean Le Bel, *Chronique*, ed. J. Viard and E. Deprez, 2 vols. (Paris, 1904–5); Jean Le Bel, *The True Chronicles of Jean Le Bel 1290–1360*, trans. N. Bryant (Woodbridge, 2011); Froissart, *Oeuvres*, ed. Lettenhove; Froissart, *Chroniques*, ed. Luce; Jean Froissart, *Sir John Froissart's Chronicles of England, France, Spain, and the Adjoining Countries, from the Latter Part of the Reign of Edward II to the Coronation of Henry IV*, ed. and trans. T. Johnes, 5 vols. (London, 1803–10); *The Online Froissart*, ed. P. Ainsworth and G. Croenen (Sheffield, 2013). The two principle English knightly biographies were *L'Histoire de Guillaume le Maréchal*, ed. P. Meyers, 2 vols. (Paris, 1891); Chandos Herald, *The Life of the Black Prince*, ed. and trans. E. Lodge and M. K. Pope (Oxford, 1910); Chandos Herald, *La Vie du Prince Noir*, ed. D. B. Tyson (Tübingen, 1975). See also, D. Crouch, *William Marshal: Court, Career and Chivalry in the Angevin Empire 1147–1219* (Harlow, 1990); R. Barber, *The Life and Campaigns of the Black Prince from contemporary letters, diaries and chronicles, including Chandos Herald's Life of the Black Prince* (Woodbridge, 1979).
[16] Le Bel, *The True Chronicles*, pp. 21–2; Saul, *Chivalry in Medieval England*, p. 320.

III, and his son, Edward, the Black Prince, and the wider purpose of these works was to ensure that

> the honourable enterprises, noble adventures, and deeds of arms, performed in the wars between England and France, may be properly related, and held in perpetual remembrance – to the end that brave men, taking example from them, may be encouraged in their own well-doing.[17]

Knightly biographies were written with essentially the same goals in mind. In Chandos Herald's *The Life of the Black Prince*, nothing was said of the Prince's questionable political and administrative career, and the chief aim of its author was to portray him as the epitome of knightly virtue.[18] Authors like Froissart, Le Bel and the Chandos Herald were, at one level, simply tapping into a ready-made pool of genteel military knowledge on both sides of the Channel, reinforcing the fact that although the visual horizons of a soldier on the battlefield were naturally limited to his immediate surroundings, heroic (or tragic) moments nonetheless remained deeply imbedded in the memory bank of those who had witnessed them, or even just those who had been present. Before the Court of Chivalry, with their narrow focus upon the protagonists' armorial claim, this emphasis upon individual acts of heroism, which implicitly brought honour to the arms in question, came to stand at the heart of Scrope's and Morley's more detailed depositions.

Nicholas Sabraham's testimony is entirely indicative of this style. When recalling his campaigning days in Scotland, his outstanding memory was of participating in the Earl of Northampton's nighttime *chevauchée* towards Peebles via torchlight, whilst his chief recollection of the siege of Alexandria was of the knighting, immediately upon landing, of Stephen Scrope, and other young men, by King Peter of Cyprus. In similar vein, John Rither outlined the tourneying triumphs and knighting of Geoffrey Scrope and other young Yorkshiremen at the Northampton tournament of Edward II's reign. In Sabraham's

---

[17] Froissart, *Chronicles of England*, I, p. 1.
[18] Chandos Herald, *The Life of the Black Prince*. Although the Black Prince's is the only surviving fourteenth-century English knightly biography, it seems likely that others were produced. Saul, *Chivalry in Medieval England*, pp. 323–4. On the Black Prince's mixed reputation as a politician and administrator, see, Morgan, *War and Society in Medieval Cheshire*, pp. 97–148; R. Barber, *The Black Prince* (London, 1978), pp. 170–91.

recollections, his service on the Black Sea coast was remembered for his discovery of a Scrope buried in the church at Nessebar. Along the same lines, Rither recalled his crusading experiences in Lithuania in terms of the death there of the young Geoffrey Scrope of Masham. That Rither was almost certainly in Scrope service at the time is reinforced by his description of Geoffrey's burial in Königsberg Cathedral and of how he had personally organised the painting of the Scrope arms in the cathedral window, using as a guide the blazon Geoffrey had upon his person at the time of his death. Finally, Rither could also recall, when Edward III assembled his force in full array before the gates of Paris, precisely which Scropes were present, and in whose company they had served, underscoring just how awe-inspiring a sight this grand muster of a 10,000-strong English army must have appeared.[19]

Turning toward the Scrope and Morley testimony at large, precisely the same pattern of wartime recollection emerges. Each military deponent's defence of the Scropes' and Morleys' armorial right was built upon a series of stock recollections about the relevant family's recent military past, augmented by hearsay about their good name and the validity of their heraldic identity. These recollections essentially focused upon five central themes: (1) participation at famous battles and sieges; (2) crusading exploits; (3) death on campaign; (4) tourneying prowess; and (5) anecdotal evidence of individual feats of heroism.[20] Shared memories of battlefield triumphs were common. Fifteen Morley deponents recounted the leadership of the defendant's grandfather, Robert, Lord Morley, at the battle of Sluys (1340), whilst twenty described his participation a decade later at the battle of Winchelsea (1350).[21] Those who could recall multiple battles at which the protagonist's family had been present would naturally have made excellent witnesses. The aged Garter Knight, Sir John Sully, for example, had seen various Scropes fighting at the battles of Halidon Hill (1333), Crécy (1346), Winchelsea (1350), Poitiers (1356) and Nájera (1367)

---

[19] *Scrope v. Grosvenor*, I, pp. 124–5; 144–50.
[20] A similar division of the martial arts, ranking feats of arms according to their perceived worthiness, had been composed at the height of the English triumphs of the mid fourteenth century by the distinguished French knight, Geoffroi de Charny. *The Book of Chivalry of Geoffroi de Charny: Text, Context, and Translation*, eds. R. W. Kaeuper and E. Kennedy (Philadelphia, 1996). On the significance of Charny's book as an expression of contemporary secular views on chivalry, shared by French and English armigerous society, see Keen, *Chivalry*, pp. 1–17.
[21] C 47/6/1; Ayton, 'Knights, Esquires and Military Service', p. 91.

during his long and distinguished career in arms.[22] Sieges, meanwhile – often long and drawn-out affairs – provided ample opportunity for young soldiers to gaze upon the heraldic splendour of their own army, identifying the banners and pennons of the realm's greatest families.[23] Amongst Scrope's testators, Sir Brian Stapleton, Sir William Aton and Sir Ralph Ferrers recalled Geoffrey Scrope parading his banner at the siege of Tournai (1340),[24] whilst 41 of Morley's deponents, and more than 50 of Scrope's, recalled the presence of each family before Paris in 1359–60.[25] Beyond such matter-of-fact statements about the Scropes' and Morleys' war records, death on campaign undeniably stood out as an exemplary act of self-sacrifice in a noble cause. Sir Walter Urswick, Sir Thomas Beauchamp and William Hesilrigge – like John Rither – recounted William Scrope's death from his wounds after the battle of Morlaix (1342).[26] Similarly, reflecting the very highest cause in which a knight could perish, Sir Thomas Boynton, Sir Thomas Fitz Henry and Sir Henry Ferrers supported Rither in outlining the death on Crusade of Geoffrey Scrope and his subsequent burial in Königsberg Cathedral (1362).[27] Amongst Morley's testators, too, much was made of Robert, Lord Morley's passing on the Rheims expedition in early 1360, at which point his arms – according to his grandson's supporters – passed directly and without complaint to his heir, William.[28]

Not all feats of arms, of course, were performed in time of war and several elderly deponents could caste their minds back at least two generations to the tourneying exploits of the Scropes and Morleys in the 1320s and 1330s. John Rither was not the only witness to recount the knighting of the plaintiff's uncle, Geoffrey, at the Northampton tournament of Edward II's reign. Sir William Aton likewise recalled this event, whilst also stressing the tourneying prowess of the plaintiff's father, Henry.[29] Sir Gerveys Clifton and Sir Ralph Ferrers provided similar evidence, emphasising the role of the tournament

---

[22] *Scrope v. Grosvenor*, I, p. 74.
[23] Jones, *Bloodied Banners*, pp. 11–56.
[24] *Scrope v. Grosvenor*, I, pp. 104–5; 142–3; 155–60.
[25] *Scrope v. Grosvenor*, C 47/6/1.
[26] *Scrope v. Grosvenor*, I, pp. 51; 198; 126–7.
[27] *Scrope v. Grosvenor*, I, pp. 117; 123; 188.
[28] Forty-one Morley supporters recalled this expedition in their testimony. C 47/6/1.
[29] *Scrope v. Grosvenor*, I, pp. 142–3.

as a genuine 'school of arms'.[30] Henry and Geoffrey's reputations as master tourneyers was clearly common knowledge amongst the gentry of their generation, particularly in the northern shires. The Norfolk knight, Sir Stephen Hales, for instance, asserted that he had learned that Henry and Geoffrey Scrope had been the finest tourneyers in the North of England from an old Yorkshire man.[31] Such tales were worth spotlighting since Henry and Geoffrey had made their names in the legal profession: a fact that appears to have caused a level of unease amongst one or two testators, who took the trouble of highlighting the brothers' martial talents as something of an antidote to their civilian occupations.[32] Perhaps most evocatively, seeking to circumvent the issue entirely, Sir Thomas Roos turned to the memory of his late ancestors, who had told him that Henry and Geoffrey's father, William Scrope, had been 'the most noble tourneyer of his time that one could find in any country', making clear that he had risen into the knightly class by virtue of his skill in arms.[33] Moreover, if the Scrope testimony hints at the celebrity-status champion tourneyers could acquire, the Morley testimony reinforces just how common a pastime the tournament became during the early years of Edward III's reign. Nine witnesses, including three clergymen, described Robert, Lord Morley's participation at seven different tournaments, held over a dozen years, most memorably his last, at Smithfield in June 1343, when Morley had competed dressed as the Pope, accompanied by twelve companions dressed as Cardinals.[34]

For all the blandness of the vast majority of depositions, it was occasional anecdotes like this last one that are primarily responsible for providing the Scrope and Morley testimony with the kind of overt chivalric flavour that so enthralled Sir Harris Nicolas.[35] These more effusive depositions vividly evoked valorous moments when individual members of the protagonist's family had honoured the disputed arms through their courage and martial talent. Sir Thomas Roos, for example, recalled Henry Scrope of Masham '[receiving] great applause from the late Noble King [Edward III]' at the Dunstable Tournament

---

[30] *Scrope v. Grosvenor*, I, pp. 152; 155–60.
[31] *Scrope v. Grosvenor*, I, p. 163.
[32] Vale, 'The Scropes', pp. 22–37.
[33] *Scrope v. Grosvenor*, I, pp. 132–4.
[34] C 47/6/1, nos. 2, 7, 14, 15, 19, 71, 72, 73, 92.
[35] See above, p. 1.

in 1332.³⁶ Sir Henry Ferrers described how Geoffrey Scrope had died in Lithuania 'before a castle called Piskre',³⁷ whilst Sir Thomas Peteyven recalled the fame achieved by the Masham cadet, William Scrope, in the Black Prince's retinue, before describing his death in Spain in the Vale of Zorie in 1367.³⁸ The Morleys were remembered in similar fashion. It was related how Sir Thomas Bolyngton had erected banners in several East Anglian churches to commemorate Robert, Lord Morley, after the latter's death on the Rheims expedition in 1360.³⁹ Another witness described William Morley gifting his coat-armour to the parish church at Somerton,⁴⁰ whilst others referred to a statuette in Reydon church, celebrating the spot where the heart of a thirteenth-century crusader Morley was buried.⁴¹ And those who survived naturally stood to reap the rewards of their heroism, returning home, at the very least, with their military reputations enhanced. Perhaps most evocatively, Sir William Moigne related how, at the siege of Calais, 'when the French attempted to victual the town…by night… Sir William Scrope conducted himself in those arms so gallantly in capturing the said supplies, and the French at the Water Gate…that every Englishman spoke of him with great honour'.⁴² Small wonder the Suffolk knight, Sir John Brewes, should have recounted, from the same siege, the reaction of his esteemed uncle, Robert Ufford, Earl of Suffolk, who purportedly marvelled, upon hearing that the Scrope's high birth had been questioned, that a family of such ancient gentility should have been so challenged.⁴³

In the context of the cases themselves, this type of chivalric testimony served a dual purpose. On the one hand, it represented a matter-of-fact statement of occasions when the deponent had seen members of the protagonist's family bearing the disputed arms in a military setting. Yet, it is surely no coincidence that the moments selected were quite often ones when these families had distinguished themselves militarily. Martial prowess, after all, traditionally legitimised genteel status and armigerous rank, demonstrating, in this instance, that the Scropes and

---

³⁶ *Scrope v. Grosvenor*, I, pp. 132–4.
³⁷ *Scrope v. Grosvenor*, I, p. 188.
³⁸ *Scrope v. Grosvenor*, I, pp. 185–6.
³⁹ C 47/6/1, nos. 158–64.
⁴⁰ C 47/6/1, no. 82.
⁴¹ C 47/6/1, nos. 151–7.
⁴² *Scrope v. Grosvenor*, I, p. 165.
⁴³ *Scrope v. Grosvenor*, I, p. 63.

Morleys had not only borne the disputed arms, but had honoured them through their deeds with the sword.[44] At the same time, however, if one moves beyond the specific purpose of the testimony, what one encounters – especially in the depositions of those overlapping generations of gentry who had borne arms during the high Edwardian age – is a deeply interwoven pattern of remembrance, containing more than a hint of nostalgia, which provided a common language through which their wartime experiences could be expressed.

Scrope's and Morley's middle-aged and elderly testators had forged their careers in arms during a long period of sustained English triumph between the 1330s and the 1360s. As such, despite the hardships of campaigning and the losses – material and in human terms – that individual gentry soldiers would have suffered, the overall experience of most would have been largely positive. Many, after all, as their own depositions indirectly reveal, had participated in two or three, and sometimes in more than half-a-dozen, victorious sieges and battles.[45] Success undoubtedly bred success, with younger gentry over these decades consistently taking up the baton of their celebrated forebears. The considerable generational overlap within English armies, moreover, enabling veteran and novice soldiers to serve side by side, not only would have provided a steadying influence in the field, but would have helped to preserve the winning culture forged during the 1330s and 1340s.[46]

The Scropes and Morleys themselves provide a fine example of how family military traditions developed across the middle-third of the fourteenth century. Henry and Geoffrey Scrope – already middle-aged men – had served in Scotland during the 1330s and in France during the early campaigns of the Hundred Years War; their sons became prominent members of the Crécy-Poitiers generation; and their grandsons upheld this proud military tradition into the 1360s and 1370s: the family's unusual enthusiasm for fighting abroad as knights errant serving to augment the Scropes' already impressive reputation in the world of English chivalry.[47] The Morleys, if less militarily active, were perhaps more indicative of the average genteel experience: Robert, Lord Morley had acquired his esteemed reputation

---

[44] Jones, *Bloodied Banners*, pp. 20–1; Keen, *Origins of the English Gentleman*, p. 51; Caudrey, 'War, Chivalry and Regional Society', p. 137.
[45] See above, pp. 23–4.
[46] Ayton, 'English Armies in the Fourteenth Century', pp. 303–19.
[47] Keen, 'Chivalrous Culture', pp. 14–15.

fighting at the battles of Halidon Hill (1333), Sluys (1340), Crécy (1346) and Winchelsea (1350). His heir, William, cut his military teeth at the battle of Poitiers (1356), and his younger sons, Robert and John, both served under the Black Prince in Spain and likely participated in the last great English battlefield triumph of the age at Nájera (1367).[48] The overwhelming majority of knightly testators in both disputes, as we saw in Chapter 1, could point to similar family military traditions, extending into the 1370s and beyond, and dating back, at the very least, to the early years of Edward III's reign.[49]

Amidst this wealth of military experience, war stories would undoubtedly have been passed down from father to son (or even simply from older soldiers to younger ones), with the result that, by the 1380s, gentry of all ages, especially elderly veterans of the Hundred Years War's first phase, had at their disposal a stock of tales of the wars of the three Edwards to which they could readily turn. Some of these tales were even outlined before the Court. The Scrope witness, John Thirlewalle, for example, described how his aged, bedridden father – at the time the oldest esquire in the North, armed for 69 years – had gathered his sons around his bed to refute the rumour that Henry Scrope was no gentleman, relating how Henry's own father, William, had been knighted by Longshanks (Edward I) at the battle of Falkirk in 1298.[50] Sir John Mauleverer based his knowledge of the Scropes' armorial right upon what 'He had heard from his father and valiant knights and esquires now deceased'.[51] This chain of memory extended even more clearly in the deposition of Sir Hugh Hastings III, who told the Court that he 'had heard his father state that his grandfather and Sir Geoffrey Scrope were companions in divers battles and journeys'.[52] And, suggesting that some retired soldiers grappled with their military memories in more tangible fashion than mere table-talk, Sir Robert Laton related how his father, in his old age, had set about the task of drawing up the arms of the great families with whom he had served, constructing what was essentially a commemorative roll of arms of an entirely personal nature.[53]

[48] *CP*, IX, pp. 209–15; *Scrope v. Grosvenor*, II, pp. 202–3; C 47/6/1, no. 32.
[49] See above, pp. 42–3.
[50] *Scrope v. Grosvenor*, I, pp. 181–3.
[51] *Scrope v. Grosvenor*, I, pp. 109–10.
[52] *Scrope v. Grosvenor*, I, p. 51.
[53] *Scrope v. Grosvenor*, I, pp. 110–11.

Given the direct correlation, in the fourteenth century, between a family's martial prowess and their heraldic identity, it makes perfect sense that so many veterans of the high Edwardian age should have viewed their military experiences through the prism of individual feats of arms and chivalrous moments. Before the Court of Chivalry, we are privy to very specific examples of how old war stories were spread at an everyday level. Those gentry who deposed were essentially being asked to delve into their fount of wartime recollections and pull out every memory of the Scrope or Morley family that they could. If they had witnessed a Scrope or Morley performing a valorous deed (or if one of their kinsmen had furnished them with a worthy tale of this nature), then it would undoubtedly have been worth mentioning. If not, as most of the shorter depositions reveal, a simple catalogue of occasions when they had seen a Scrope or Morley bearing the arms in a military setting would have sufficed. Moreover, most deponents appear to have been scrupulously honest about the limits of their memory, even if their answers were decidedly partisan.[54] Several witnesses were quite prepared to admit that although they had seen a Scrope or Morley at a certain siege or battle, they could no longer recall precisely which family member it was.[55] In the more expansive depositions provided before the Court, numerous witnesses retrieved shared memories of the same chivalrous act or sacrificial demise. Five elderly veterans, for example, recalled Robert, Lord Morley's participation at the battle of Halidon Hill (1333);[56] Geoffrey Scrope's burial in Königsberg Cathedral was clearly a pivotal event on the Baltic Crusade of 1362 for the English contingent involved, described by a range of deponents;[57] and a coterie

---

[54] On conflicting memories of the same event, usually dependent upon whose side the witness in question was on, see below, pp. 172–7.

[55] E.g., The Essex knight, Sir Robert Marny, recalled numerous occasions when he had borne arms with members of the Scrope family. He was, however, at times rather hazy on the details. He asserted that when the Earl of Derby first went into Gascony, he had in his company one of the Scropes, but could not remember his name. He also saw a different Scrope bearing the arms in Tournai, but was similarly unsure of his identity. Marny's memory lapses were clearly not due to his age, for he was only 52 at the time he deposed before the Court. *Scrope v. Grosvenor*, I, pp. 170–1.

[56] C 47/6/1, nos. 10, 29, 92, 97, 106.

[57] E.g., Sir Thomas Boynton; Sir Thomas Fitz Henry; Sir Henry Ferrers; Sir Alexander Goldingham; Sir Richard Waldegrave; John Rither. *Scrope v. Grosvenor*, I, pp. 117; 123; 188; 70; 165–6; 144–50. For the events surrounding Geoffrey Scrope's death and burial, see Guard, *Chivalry, Kingship and Crusade*, pp. 88–9.

of gentry, largely from the Earl of Northampton's retinue, attested to the wounding and subsequent death of the young William Scrope at the battle of Morlaix (1342).[58]

Since the military witnesses in each case were essentially being asked simply to recount occasions when they had seen their protagonist's family bearing the disputed arms, we are consequently getting in their depositions nothing more than a well-organised fragment of their wartime memories. This is made abundantly clear in the testimony of those few witnesses who spoke, months apart, for both Scrope and Morley.[59] Three aspects of their depositions stand out. Firstly, as alluded to, only relevant campaigns and battles were considered worth mentioning. Hence, Sir John Brewes and Sir John Lakynghethe, to cite a popular example, each touched upon their participation at the battle of Mauron (1352) in *Scrope v. Grosvenor*, but made no mention of it in *Lovel v. Morley*, since no Morley had been present.[60] Secondly, it is apparent that a noteworthy event on campaign enjoyed a much wider resonance in the memory bank of an individual witness than they cared to reveal before the Court. So, for instance, Sir William Wingfield recalled in both disputes his presence in the 10,000-strong English army gathered under the command of Edward III before the gates of Paris in 1359–60.[61] Yet, whilst in his first deposition, he described the presence of Richard, Lord Scrope and his cousin, Henry, with their banners prominently displayed, in his second, having set an essentially identical scene, he instead described the Morley banner in the same fashion. Presumably, he could have recounted the presence before Paris of numerous other distinguished families, had he been so required, and what he revealed before the Court comprised merely the Scrope- and Morley-related fragments of his memories of that

---

[58] E.g., Sir Walter Urswick; Sir Thomas Beauchamp; William Hesilrigg; John Rither. *Scrope v. Grosvenor*, I, pp. 51; 198; 126–7; 144–50.

[59] Eight testators deposed for Scrope and Morley. Sir John Brewes; Sir Thomas Geney; Sir Stephen Hales; Sir John Lakyngheth; Sir Robert Marny; Sir Richard Sutton; Sir John White; Sir William Wingfield; One deposed for Scrope and Lovel. Sir Maurice de Bruyn. Two deposed for Scrope and Hastings. Sir Thomas Erpingham; Sir Robert Morley; Three deposed for Morley and Hastings. Sir William Berdewell; Sir Thomas Gerbergh; Sir Leonard Kerdiston. *Scrope v. Grosvenor*; C 47/6/1; PRO30/26/69; *PCM*.

[60] *Scrope v. Grosvenor*, I, pp. 63, 208–9; C 47/6/1, nos. 102, 45. This difference between the two sets of testimony has not gone unnoticed. Ayton, 'Knights, Esquires and Military Service', p. 91; Keen, *Origins of the English Gentleman*, p. 60.

[61] *Scrope v. Grosvenor*, I, pp. 173–4; C 47/6/1, nos. 8, 149.

significant day. Finally, along similar lines, one is reminded that even the experience of a single expedition would have left an indelible mark upon its participants, who would have returned home imbued with a range of military memories, many of which would have been entirely unrelated to one another. Sir John Brewes' recollections of the siege of Calais (1347) provide a perfect case in point. Appearing first for Scrope and later for Morley, he recalled before the Court two entirely separate incidents: for Scrope, it was his uncle, Robert Ufford, Earl of Suffolk's, fit of pique upon hearing that someone had dared question the Scropes' ancient gentility; for Morley, his focus shifted to Robert, Lord Morley's victory before the Court of Chivalry in the *Burnell v. Morley* case, adjudicated whilst the siege was in progress.[62] Like Sir William Wingfield's recollections of English sabre rattling before Paris, we are being provided, through his separate depositions, with only the narrowest window into Sir John Brewes' eclectic experiences at the siege of Calais.

These rare examples of gentry deposing in two different causes underscore that the overwhelming majority of Scrope's and Morley's deponents – men who had borne arms regularly and with considerable success between the 1330s and the 1360s – were very neatly tailoring their tales to suit the case at hand. At home in their native localities, by contrast, unfettered by the constraints of the Court, they were free to roam in any given direction with their war stories and would doubtless have proven entirely capable of conjuring up similarly cherished war memories about their own, and numerous other, gentry families. Through such tale-telling, the martial exploits of the Hundred Years War's first phase rapidly became legend, representing a high watermark of military achievement for the next generation to emulate.

From the standpoint of the cases themselves, Richard, Lord Scrope and Thomas, Lord Morley brought together approximately 300 gentry soldiers, capable of providing a deep well of individual memories of their families' contribution to the Hundred Years War. Because clutches of gentry shared the same military experiences, at a macro-level, fighting the same battles and besieging the same towns, and, at a micro-level, serving alongside each other in the same retinues, many of these personal memories simultaneously became shared 'small-group' memories, sometimes evolving further still and developing into

---

[62] *Scrope v. Grosvenor*, I, p. 63; C 47/6/1, no. 102.

something resembling the institutional memory of the retinue itself.[63] It was these shared everyday experiences of the Hundred Years War that united distinguished war captains, like Sir William and Sir Geoffrey Scrope, with obscure lesser gentry who had served alongside them, like Nicholas Sabraham and John Rither. Yet, one ought to bear in mind that these personal and shared military experiences, expressed through a combination of tale-telling, hearsay, family history and heraldic display, were articulated against the backdrop of a national chivalric revival, orchestrated by Edward III, which in various ways provided a singular 'national memory' of the first phase of the Hundred Years War that overlaid the personal military experiences, and coloured the subsequent recollections, of its gentry participants.

From his adolescent enthusiasm for the tournament, to his interest in Arthurian themes, to his cultivation of the Order of the Garter, Edward III brilliantly constructed a reputation for himself as a model king, part lawmaker and part warrior, whilst simultaneously developing a strong sense of chivalric *esprit de corps* amongst his nobility and gentry. His unexpected triumph at the battle of Crécy legitimised his chivalric credentials and provided a springboard for the growing international reputation of English arms.[64] Before the Court of Chivalry, Edward himself, his late heir, the Black Prince, as well as numerous magnates, barons and bannerets of Edward's own generation, were spoken of reverentially, often with more than a hint of name-dropping.[65] Two factors were at play here. Firstly, in attempting to illustrate before the Court that the Scropes and Morleys were worthy bearers of the disputed arms, not only was their prowess at a string of English victories emphasised, but by implication so was their place in the vanguard of the English war effort, their senior kinsmen of baronial rank portrayed as members of an exclusive band of war

[63] Caudrey, 'War, Chivalry and Regional Society', pp. 135–6.
[64] J. Vale, *Edward III and Chivalry: Chivalric Society and its Context 1270–1350* (Woodbridge, 1983); Barber, *Edward III and the Triumph of England*; Saul, *Chivalry in Medieval England*, pp. 93–114; Ormrod, *Edward III*, pp. 299–321.
[65] E.g., References linking the Scropes with Edward, the Black Prince at the scenes of his greatest triumphs. Sir John Sully recalled Sir William Scrope 'armed in the same arms with the Prince at the battle of Poitiers'; Sir Ralph Hastings noted that he had seen Richard, Lord Scrope fighting in the Lancastrian military retinue at the battle of Nájera (1367) 'in the presence of the Prince'; and Sir Thomas Reresby touched upon Scrope participation 'when the Prince of Wales first went into Guyenne'. *Scrope v. Grosvenor*, I, pp. 74; 103–4; 114–16. See also, Rosenthal, *Telling Tales*, pp. 85–6.

captains who had repeatedly carried the day in the service of 'the late noble King Edward III'.⁶⁶ What appears also to have been happening was that the testators themselves, ranging from nobles and greater knights to lesser gentry, were indirectly celebrating their own small contribution to the triumphs of the age. The fact that great men like Richard, Lord Scrope and Thomas, Lord Morley should have delved so deeply into the militarily active squirearchy when constructing their witness lists reinforces just how successful Edward III had been in developing a sense of solidarity amongst genteel military society at large.⁶⁷ From the battle of Halidon Hill (1333) to the battle of Najéra (1367), with the battles of Crécy (1346) and Poitiers (1356) placed on a pedestal, those who had forged England's international martial reputation between the 1330s and the 1360s could look back upon their achievements from the vantage point of the mid 1380s and proudly perceive themselves, with more than a hint of collective nostalgia, as members of a 'greatest generation'.⁶⁸

The pride of Scrope's and Morley's older deponents in the triumphs of their youth, moreover, may well have swollen considerably by the time they deposed before the Court of Chivalry, due to the relative failure of the younger gentry of the Hundred Years War's second phase to defend their military achievements. By the spring and summer of 1386, when the vast majority of testators were interviewed, not only had almost all the gains acquired by Edward III from the Treaty of Brétigny (1360) been lost, but England itself was facing the threat of invasion, the French raiding the southern coast with impunity.⁶⁹ The *Scrope v. Grosvenor* and *Lovel v. Morley* testimony consequently provides a fascinating insight into the shifting character of English military society during the reign of Richard II, because the martial

⁶⁶ *Scrope v. Grosvenor*, C 47/6/1.
⁶⁷ See above, n. 64.
⁶⁸ Although far removed from the Middle Ages, the First World War (1914–1918) provides the classic modern British example of generational shared military memories, solidified (and, to some extent, distorted) by the passage of time. Neatly articulating this enduring sense of shared generational solidarity – albeit with a focus upon the tragedy, rather than the triumph, of war – Sir Charles Carrington, a veteran of the battles of the Somme (1916) and Passchendaele (1917), wrote reflectively in 1968, 'Twenty million of us…shared the experience with one another but with no one else, and are what we are because, in that war, we were soldiers'. Cited in J. M. Winter, *The Great War and the British People* (London, 1985), p. 293.
⁶⁹ Sumption, *The Hundred Years War III*, pp. 511–57.

heyday of the mid fourteenth century was being fondly recalled at a distance, largely by older men whose time had almost passed, and was being expressed against the backdrop of a widely perceived crisis in English chivalry that was supposedly infecting the realm.

As far as this crisis was concerned, there were two chief causes of complaint amongst contemporary commentators. On the one hand, there was widespread horror at the atrocities perpetrated throughout Continental Europe (especially in France and Italy) by mercenary companies, many stocked with English soldiers who had found themselves unemployed after the Treaty of Brétigny.[70] Chroniclers' accounts of the period are full of gruesome descriptions of pillage, rape and murder, capped off by savage acts of torture designed to wring the whereabouts of the last scrap of wealth from helpless prisoners.[71] As this unscrupulous type of military professional gained notoriety, and as the English cause in France deteriorated, some of the most celebrated literary figures of the Ricardian age, most famously Geoffrey Chaucer and John Gower, began openly criticising the current state of English chivalry. In *The Knight's Tale* and several of his other writings, Chaucer critiqued the knightly ideal and prompted questions about the degeneration of the chivalric ethos, whilst Gower, who likewise wrote at length on the subject, provided perhaps the pithiest statement of how English chivalric culture had supposedly declined, lamenting, 'I see that honour is now neglected for gold.'[72]

---

[70] For an overview of the complaints-literature of the 1380s, see D. Grummitt, 'Changing Perceptions of the Soldier in Late Medieval England', in *The Fifteenth Century X: Parliament, Personalities and Power. Papers Presented to Linda S. Clark*, ed. H. Kleineke (Woodbridge, 2011), pp. 189–202.

[71] For numerous examples of atrocities perpetrated against the French peasantry, see N. Wright, *Knights and Peasants: The Hundred Years War in the French Countryside* (Woodbridge, 1998). For examples of the ruthlessness of English condottiere, see Fowler, *Medieval Mercenaries*; W. Caffero, *John Hawkwood: An English Mercenary in Fourteenth-Century Italy* (Baltimore, 2006); S. Cooper, *Sir John Hawkwood: Chivalry and the Art of War* (Barnsley, 2008).

[72] Geoffrey Chaucer, *The Canterbury Tales*, ed. and intro. D. Wright (Oxford, 1998), pp. 2–3, 23–79; John Gower, *The Major Latin Works of John Gower*, ed. E. W. Stockton (Seattle, 1962), p. 207; V. J. Scattergood, 'Chaucer and the French War: *Sir Thopas* and *Melibee*', in *Court and Poet: Select Proceedings of the Third Congress of the International Courtly Literature Society*, ed. G. S. Burgess (Liverpool, 1981), pp. 287–96; R. F. Yeager, '*Pax poetica*: On the Pacifism of Chaucer and Gower', *Studies in the Age of Chaucer*, 9 (1987), pp. 97–121; N. Saul, 'A Farewell to Arms? Criticism of Warfare in Late Fourteenth-Century England', in *Fourteenth Century England II*, ed. C. Given-Wilson (Woodbridge, 2002), pp. 131–46.

Condemnation of the avarice and violence of English soldiers was paralleled by a second, starkly different, cause of complaint, which insinuated that knights were turning away from their martial responsibilities and becoming soft. This accusation was, to a significant degree, a conservative backlash against the direction in which contemporary gentry society was evolving. Lesser gentry were increasingly becoming armigerous and, troublingly for some, these included not just men who had forged military reputations in the war with France, but also those whose claims to gentility rested upon their royal and magnate affiliations, and upon their professional standing as lawyers, bureaucrats and urban officials.[73] Simultaneously, for a variety of reasons, the Crown began dubbing fewer knights at the same time as fewer gentry were choosing to accept the burdens of knighthood, with the result that many men whose ancestors, in recent generations, had been 'fighting knights' were now living quite comfortably as landed and armigerous esquires: a trend that would only grow during the truce years of the 1390s and 1400s.[74]

The gentry were also becoming more politically active than ever before. The reign of Edward III had witnessed the growth of Parliament as a political forum, whilst Edward's judicial reforms had accelerated what was already a long-term trend of the county gentry filling the senior posts in shire administration.[75] At the highest levels of government, similarly – especially from the 1370s onwards, as Edward descended into dotage and was succeeded by the boy-king Richard II – the knights of the royal household began evolving away from their original purpose as a household in arms, and were starting to serve their sovereign more as policy advisors and diplomats. Indeed, by the mid 1380s, the peace-minded King Richard was surrounded by a coterie of household knights who were as firmly committed to the peace process as he was.[76] For those who favoured a continuation of the war with France, and who looked upon the conflict as a Just War, the military failures of the 1370s and 1380s rested squarely upon the shoulders of the young knights and esquires currently prosecuting the

---

[73] Keen, *Origins of the English Gentleman*, pp. 71–86.
[74] Bell et al., *The Soldier*, pp. 54–94.
[75] A. Musson and W. M. Ormrod, *The Evolution of English Justice: Law, Politics and Society in the Fourteenth Century* (London, 1998), pp. 1–11, 68–73.
[76] J. O. Prestwich, 'The Military Household of the Norman Kings', *EHR*, 96 (1981), pp. 1–35; Given-Wilson, *The Royal Household*, pp. 142–202; Harriss, *Shaping the Nation*, pp. 419–24; Saul, *Chivalry in Medieval England*, pp. 133–4.

war effort, who had so signally failed to uphold the military legacy of the heroes of Crécy and Poitiers. As Thomas Walsingham famously claimed in his chronicle, when denouncing the lack of martial spirit amongst Richard II's knights, they

> were more knights of Venus than of Bellona, more valorous in the bedchamber than on the field of battle, defending themselves rather with their tongues than with their spears, being alert in speech, but asleep when martial deeds were required.[77]

This chivalric crisis is worth spotlighting in the context of the Court of Chivalry for two reasons. Firstly, as alluded to, it helps to explain the nostalgic tone of those older knights and esquires in *Scrope v. Grosvenor* and *Lovel v. Morley*, who recalled their youthful exploits in their testimony. Secondly, and more significantly, the hypothesis that there was something seriously amiss with contemporary English chivalry can quite explicitly be tested, by comparing the military depositions of veterans of the Hundred Years War's first phase, cited above, with those of younger testators, who bore arms primarily during the war's second phase during the 1370s and 1380s. Maurice Keen long ago addressed this very issue, finding, in his view, more than a few hints in the Hastings testimony (1407–10) that chivalric attitudes were changing. In Keen's words, 'the Hastings testimony has not quite the full flavour that makes the evidence of the Scrope and Grosvenor witnesses such a marvelous companion piece…to set alongside the stories of Froissart'.[78] Keen continued, 'All these campaigns and expeditions of the 1370s and 80s were in their own way important…but none of them could be called glorious.'[79] And, whilst accepting that the defendant's father, Sir Hugh Hastings III, had 'clearly made his mark' and was undoubtedly 'a chivalrous man', Keen nonetheless concluded that the chivalric testimony on behalf of Hastings 'had not…the kind of resonance in recall that the great campaigns of the 1340s and 50s had had'.[80] This last point is hardly in doubt. Yet, the balance of the testimony does suggest that the contrasts drawn between the Hastings and Scrope/Morley

---

[77] Thomas Walsingham, *The Chronica Maiora of Thomas Walsingham*, trans. D. Preest and ed. J. G. Clark (Woodbridge, 2005), p. 248. On the political context behind Walsingham's complaint, see W. M. Ormrod, 'Knights of Venus', *Medium Aevum*, 73 (2004), pp. 290–305.

[78] Keen, 'Grey v. Hastings', p. 181.

[79] Keen, 'Grey v. Hastings', p. 182.

[80] Keen, 'Grey v. Hastings', p. 182.

depositions have been rather oversold and that the noticeable shift in tone between the two sets of witness statements, although very real, was not in fact symptomatic of 'a distinct cooling of bellicose ardour' amongst Hastings' testators.[81]

The first point to be made is that the military credentials of the Hastings of Elsing were almost as impressive as the Scropes', and probably more impressive than the Morleys'. Sir Hugh Hastings I had indeed – as his grandson attested in *Scrope v. Grosvenor* – fought in 'divers journeys and battles' during the early stages of the Hundred Years War, most famously leading the English diversionary expedition through Flanders in 1346 and dying at the siege of Calais the following year.[82] Sir Hugh Hastings II had actively participated in the campaigns of the 1350s, spent the early 1360s crusading in the Eastern Mediterranean, fought at the battle of Nájera in 1367, and died two years later, on the Gascony expedition of 1369. Sir Hugh Hastings III was in the Earl of Pembroke's fleet destroyed off La Rochelle in 1372; undertook John of Gaunt's grand *chevauchée* in 1373; was present at the siege of St. Malo in 1378; survived the sinking of Sir John Arundel's fleet in 1379; accompanied the Earl of Buckingham to Brittany in 1380; and rounded out his military career in Scotland in 1385 and Spain in 1386, succumbing to disease on the latter expedition. Even the defendant, Sir Edward Hastings, though barely out of his teens, had maintained his family's military traditions to the best of his ability. He became a household knight of Henry IV and served on the Scottish expedition of 1400, on which occasion his arms had been challenged by his cousin, Lord Grey of Ruthin.[83] As we saw in Chapter 1, a significant body of Sir Edward's witnesses, deposing before the Court of Chivalry in 1408–9, were middle-aged gentry who described the campaigning days of their youth with the defendant's father, Sir Hugh Hastings III, in the 1370s and 1380s,[84] although a few older deponents could cast their minds back a little further to the expeditions undertaken by Sir Hugh Hastings II in the 1360s.[85] Only two military witnesses were old

---

[81] Keen, 'Grey v. Hastings', p. 182

[82] *Scrope v. Grosvenor*, I, p. 51; Ayton, 'The Crécy Campaign', p. 42; Sumption, *The Hundred Years War II*, p. 585.

[83] The war records of Sir Hugh Hastings II and Sir Hugh Hastings III are obviously described at length by Sir Edward Hastings' deponents. *PCM*, I, pp. 390–544.

[84] See above, pp. 29–30.

[85] Robert Fishlake; Alexander Denton; Sir Thomas Gerbergh. *PCM*, I, pp. 429–35; 453–5; 496–7.

enough to recall the campaigns of the 1350s,[86] and only one – a veteran of the Crécy-Calais expedition – had any personal memory of Sir Hugh Hastings I.[87]

Yet, even though the bulk of Hastings' witnesses were focusing upon a period of consistent military failure, in which the gains of the Treaty of Brétigny (1360) were systematically lost, and in which English armies enjoyed not a single major battlefield triumph, there appears at first glance precious little difference between the style in which they, and the veterans of the high Edwardian age in *Scrope v. Grosvenor* and *Lovel v. Morley*, framed their depositions. Just like this earlier generation of witnesses, there was a marked propensity to focus upon individual acts of heroism. Robert Fishlake and Alexander Denton recalled Sir Hugh Hastings II's participation on Crusades to the East and his presentation of an escutcheon of his arms to the Knights Hospitaller at Rhodes, and in other places in the Eastern Mediterranean;[88] Sir Thomas Erpingham related how he had seen the Hastings arms displayed in the church window of Marienburg Cathedral;[89] Robert Lymworth and Nicholas Braynton described Sir Hugh Hastings III being knighted in the field during the *chevauchée* of 1373;[90] Thomas Pickworth recalled how the same Sir Hugh, having got safely to land after surviving the storm that sank Sir John Arundel's fleet, had hung a banner bearing his arms in the church at Falmouth in thanksgiving for his deliverance from the sea;[91] Erpingham, Sir John Wiltshire and Thomas Lucas made great play of Sir Hugh III's bravery in the skirmishing at Brest on the way to Castile;[92] and, perhaps most evocatively, David Hemenhale recounted how Sir Hugh III had led the assault on St. Malo by ladder, whereupon Lord Fitzwalter reportedly exclaimed, 'Here's one of the finest knights of the kingdom'.[93]

The preparedness of these gentry in 1408–9 to recall, long after the fact, the Hastings family's chivalrous exploits is especially interesting because it stands in stark contrast to the testimony provided by other men of the same generation, who testified in their youth for Scrope

[86] John Bere; John Parker. *PCM*, I, pp. 426–7; 533.
[87] Sir William Hoo. *PCM*, I, p. 544.
[88] *PCM*, I, pp. 429–35; 453–5.
[89] *PCM*, I, pp. 439–42.
[90] *PCM*, I, pp. 413–21; 529.
[91] *PCM*, I, pp. 404–5.
[92] *PCM*, I, pp. 439–42; 401–4; 445–51.
[93] *PCM*, I, pp. 458–64.

and Morley in the mid 1380s, and who adopted a much blander and less celebratory tone in their depositions. Most of Scrope's and Morley's younger witnesses simply proffered straightforward statements, touching upon a range of military theatres in which they had seen the protagonist's family bearing the disputed arms, without necessarily specifying the expeditions in question, or polishing their statements with chivalrous tales of how younger Scropes and Morleys had recently brought honour to the arms through their martial deeds.[94] The only two veterans of the Hundred Years War's second phase to provide depositions in any way comparable to those of the war's first phase, were the Scrope witnesses, John Charnels and Sir John Godard. Charnels recalled an incident in France when he and 40 companions had been operating from a castle called Quarranteau,[95] whilst Godard alluded to his service with the plaintiff's son, William, 'in the company of the Duke of Duras beyond Venice'.[96] The absence of overtly chivalrous anecdotes amongst the young witnesses of the mid 1380s is telling. They may perhaps have felt a sense that whatever heroic deeds the current crop of Scropes and Morleys had performed in recent years would have appeared rather small beer compared to the heroism of their grandfathers, fathers and uncles at the famous tournaments, sieges and battles of the high Edwardian age. Consequently, most of their depositions remained firmly rooted in the mid-fourteenth-century past. Having glossed over recent occasions when they had seen a Scrope or Morley in arms, they hurried along to describe the hearsay of their ancestors regarding the families' martial exploits in an earlier and more successful era, or to provide iconographic evidence of the longstanding display of the disputed arms in their native shires.[97]

Sir Edward Hastings' witnesses, by contrast – likewise recalling the 1370s and 1380s – focused extensively upon the Hastings family's chivalrous deeds, much more in the style of those veterans of the Hundred Years War's first phase who supported Scrope and Morley. So, how is this difference to be explained? By 1408–9, the passage of time had allowed the campaigns of the Hundred Years War's second phase to recede into long-term memory, to a significant degree

---

[94] E.g., Sir Ralph Ipre; Sir John Loudham 'the son'; Sir Nicholas Grey; Sir Geoffrey St. Quintin; Sir David Roucliffe. *Scrope v. Grosvenor*, I, pp. 52; 53; 59–60; 62–3; 65.

[95] *Scrope v. Grosvenor*, I, pp. 171–2.

[96] *Scrope v. Grosvenor*, I, pp. 211–12.

[97] See above, nn. 94–6.

overtaken as a source of popular lamentation by more recent political events at home.[98] Just as older gentry, speaking for Scrope and Morley, had by the mid 1380s packaged their experiences of fighting between the 1330s and the 1360s into a series of war stories and chivalrous anecdotes, so, one may surmise, with the failure of the Hundred Years War's second phase less fresh, it no longer felt inappropriate to celebrate what little had gone right. More importantly, by focusing upon individual acts of bravery at the expense of the wider outcome of the expedition, these middle-aged Hastings deponents in 1408–9 were highlighting the ongoing martial prowess of the Hastings family (and implicitly that of their own generation), whilst distracting from the overall failures of the campaigns in question.[99] For older Scrope and Morley witnesses, simply by mentioning their presence at the battles of Halidon Hill (1333), Sluys (1340), Crécy (1346), Poitiers (1356) or Nájera (1367), there was an implicit acknowledgement that they had been part of what must have been a heroic endeavour. For Hastings' witnesses, the reverse was true. Better to describe the knighting of Sir Hugh Hastings III in 1373 than question the overall strategic worth of Gaunt's *chevauchée*.[100] Better to focus upon the same Sir Hugh hanging his banner in Falmouth Church in thanksgiving for his deliverance from the sea than emphasise his participation in a horrendous naval disaster in which a grand fleet, with considerable loss of life, had failed even to reach its destination.[101] Better to focus upon Sir Hugh's courage in skirmishing off Brest on the way to Spain than relate how signally John of Gaunt had failed to capture the Castilian throne, losing Sir Hugh and a number of distinguished Lancastrian captains to disease in the process.[102] Perhaps most pertinently, better to focus upon Sir Hugh scaling the walls of St. Malo, reinforcing his reputation as one of the finest knights in the kingdom, than recall the young Earl of Arundel failing to fortify the besiegers' position, thus allowing the town's

---

[98] Bennett, *Richard II and the Revolution of 1399*; C. Given-Wilson, *Henry IV* (New Haven, 2016). For a succinct summary, see Harriss, *Shaping the Nation*, pp. 491–501.

[99] Such attitudes are, again, comparable to the writing style of the great fourteenth-century chroniclers, Jean Le Bel and Jean Froissart, who were not backward in celebrating the self-sacrificial courage of the vanquished in the same breath as they praised the martial prowess of the victors. Le Bel, *Chronique*; Froissart, *Chroniques*.

[100] *PCM*, I, pp. 413–21; 529; Sumption, *The Hundred Years War III*, pp. 171–211.

[101] *PCM*, I, pp. 404–5; Froissart, *Chroniques*, IX, pp. 209–11.

[102] *PCM*, I, pp. 439–42; 401–4; 445–51; Goodman, *John of Gaunt*, pp. 118–28.

defenders to destroy the English earthworks – an amateur mistake, which saw Arundel reprimanded by Gaunt, and which helped facilitate the failure of the expedition.[103]

The Hastings testimony, in short, shows little sign that those who deposed were any less martially inclined, or any more detached from the chivalric ethos, that their immediate forebears.[104] If anything, the chivalric flavour of the Hastings depositions was rather more overt than in those depositions provided much closer to the time, by men of the same generation, speaking in their youths for Scrope and Morley. On the other hand, the broader claim of a clear shift in tone between the depositions of the mid 1380s and those of 1408–9 is undeniable. Those young gentry speaking for Scrope and Morley appear to have been uneasily seeking to place their very recent military experiences in the 1370s and 1380s into a continuum with those of their immediate ancestors during the Hundred Years War's first phase. By the time of *Grey v. Hastings*, however, the impression one is left with is that the young gentry of the 1370s and 1380s – now mostly middle-aged men of relative influence – had worked out how to appropriately package the military memories of their youth to best affect. In the Hastings testimony, the overall outcome of individual expeditions was silently ignored, since their failure stood in damning contrast to the victories of the high Edwardian age. Yet, at an individual level, tales such as those surrounding Sir Hugh Hastings III proved indisputably that he had spent the second phase of the Hundred Years War successfully maintaining the military legacy of his esteemed father and grandfather. The fact that he did so in a period of military failure was hardly his fault.

Hastings' deponents, moreover – many of them distinguished gentry in their own right, whose fathers and grandfathers had likewise fought with distinction in the Crécy-Poitiers era[105] – could equally apply this logic to themselves. In the world of the localities, unconstrained by

---

[103] *PCM*, I, pp. 458–64; Froissart, *Oeuvres*, IX, pp. 79–83, 89–93.

[104] Keen, 'Grey v. Hastings', pp. 182–5.

[105] E.g., Sir Ralph Shelton II; Sir Miles Stapleton; Sir Simon Felbrigg; Sir Thomas Erpingham. *CPR, 1345–8*, p. 481; *HPC, 1386–1421*, IV, p. 356; J. Lee-Warner, 'The Stapeltons of Ingham', *Norfolk Archaeology*, 8 (1879), p. 200; Blomefield, *History of Norfolk*, VIII, pp. 108–9; *CPR, 1354–8*, p. 67; *CPR, 1367–70*, p. 18; *BPReg*, IV, p. 445; Curry, 'Sir Thomas Erpingham', pp. 55–60. On the standing of Hastings' leading witnesses at the time they deposed, see Castor, *The King, the Crown, and the Duchy of Lancaster*, pp. 59–81.

the judges' line of questioning, they could place the military failures of their generation to one side and focus instead upon defending and celebrating their own small contributions to their family's military traditions through a combination of public acts of commemoration and the oral transmission of old war stories. The world of the localities, indeed, lay behind much of the chivalric testimony outlined before the Court. It was in the protagonists' native shires, more than anywhere else, that popular opinion valued their chivalric reputations and fiercely upheld their long-established right to the arms under dispute. Consequently, having traced the wider relationship between chivalry and the English gentry through the military testimony provided before the Court, the next step is to ask how English chivalric culture achieved popular expression at an everyday level within the localities, where a range of military communities co-existed and where military and county society intersected.

Chivalric Memory II: Regional Military Communities

England's national 'military community' – cultivated with such success by Edward III – has been aptly defined as 'first and foremost a community of the mind and of function, of shared mentality, skills and perhaps focus: of shared identity'.[106] Yet, as has been long established, English military society during the fourteenth century, in structural terms, was composed of a series of smaller military communities, based upon bonds of affinity, social rank, specialist military activity, and regional origin.[107] Most gentry soldiers belonged to more than one of these communities and shared multiple military identities. Moreover, it is abundantly clear that heraldic and chivalric knowledge was far from the preserve of those possessing military experience, and was simultaneously essential to gentry culture at large, as a marker of social rank and as an ongoing reminder of the historic relationship between gentility and military service. Chivalry thus remained a core cultural component of gentry life, even for those who had no intention, nor were necessarily expected, ever to bear arms.[108]

---

[106] Ayton, 'Armies and Military Communities', p. 216.
[107] Ayton, 'Armies and Military Communities', pp. 216–17; Morgan, *War and Society in Medieval Cheshire*.
[108] Keen, *Origins of the English Gentleman*.

Before the Court of Chivalry, each protagonists' witness list contained a wide cross-section of gentry society: soldiers and civilians; laymen and churchmen; occasional, intermittent and full-time military participants; shire élites, parish-level notables, and men of such obscurity that nothing about them, beyond their depositions, appears to have survived. A common thread amidst all this diversity, however, as we saw in Chapter 3, was the recruitment of vast numbers of testators from the protagonists' county of birth. This eclectic mix of gentry – with a strong regional component focused upon Richard, Lord Scrope's Yorkshire, Sir Robert Grosvenor's Cheshire, and Thomas, Lord Morley's and Sir Edward Hastings' Norfolk – makes it possible to investigate the nuances of regional chivalric culture, as expressed through a combination of tale-telling, hearsay, local history, iconographic display and written evidence. The value of this body of testimony, in a purely cultural context, lies in the fact that the parallel chivalric traditions of different regional military communities collided before the Court, reinforcing just how fragmented English military society was, away from the battlefields of the Hundred Years War, and how deeply parochial chivalric culture, at an everyday level, could become.

What is especially striking about the testimony across all three disputes is the extent to which the long-cultivated reputations of the protagonists' families in their native shires facilitated the situation in which their possession of the disputed arms had quite simply become a known fact, one so entrenched in the shared historic memory of the region that the requirement of hard evidence to support their armorial right was almost deemed insulting. The Scrope depositions, the most detailed of the four, provide a perfect case in point: time and again, Scrope possession of the disputed arms, *azure a bend or*, was described as 'common knowledge', a claim often associated with what the deponent had been told by his ancestors, or by other older men. John of Gaunt initiated this line of defence with the very first deposition, telling the Court, 'We have seen and known that Sir Richard hath borne his arms...[and] we have heard from many nobles and valiant men, since deceased, that the said arms were of right the arms of his ancestors'.[109] There was a vagueness to Gaunt's testimony that would prove common to most Scrope supporters from beyond the North. The Suffolk knight, Sir Thomas Morieux, for instance, claimed

---

[109] *Scrope v. Grosvenor*, II, p. 164.

'that the arms belonged to Scrope from time beyond the memory of man',[110] whilst his contemporary, Sir Richard Waldegrave, seemingly succumbing to the popular opinion of his fellow Scrope adherents, stated that he 'could not say which of the ancestors of Sir Richard first bore the arms, but since this dispute he had heard that his ancestors came direct from the Conquest'.[111]

Yet, if one turns to the testimony provided by Scrope's Yorkshire, and especially his North Riding, deponents – those whose families had interacted with his own in a public and private capacity for generations[112] – a very clear narrative of the Scrope's heraldic identity and accompanying ancient gentility arises. Sir John Mauleverer knew of the Scropes' armorial right 'from his father, and valiant knights and esquires now no more, and never to the contrary'.[113] Sir Robert Conyers was aware of the Scrope's ancient gentility because 'in his youth he often heard from his ancestors and valiant men of arms now no more, that those arms had descended to the said Sir Richard from his ancestors, who came in with the Conqueror, and that they had always peaceable possessed the said arms from beyond the time of memory'.[114] Variations upon this theme persisted amongst other Yorkshiremen, usually grounded in the tale-telling of their own family, or else acquired more broadly through the transmission of local history and hearsay from the old to the young. Sir Randolf Pygot, for instance, 'had heard from his ancestors, and they from their ancestors, that the said arms had descended to Sir Richard by descent from the time of memory',[115] whilst Sir Walter Atte Lee 'had frequently heard very old people say that they [the Scropes] had continually used those arms'.[116] Local churchmen learned of the Scrope's armorial right in the same fashion. The Abbot of Selby acquired his information through 'old monks who were in the said abbey in the time of his youth';[117] the Abbot of Rievelaux was enlightened in almost identical style;[118] whilst the Prior of Lanercost explained very precisely that he 'had heard the

[110] *Scrope v. Grosvenor*, II, pp. 186–7.
[111] *Scrope v. Grosvenor*, II, pp. 377–8.
[112] See above, pp. 99–104.
[113] *Scrope v. Grosvenor*, II, p. 299.
[114] *Scrope v. Grosvenor*, II, p. 318.
[115] *Scrope v. Grosvenor*, II, p. 314.
[116] *Scrope v. Grosvenor*, II, p. 391.
[117] *Scrope v. Grosvenor*, II, p. 271.
[118] *Scrope v. Grosvenor*, II, p. 272.

prior his predecessor who was an old man say that he had heard from… the prior who preceded him…that they [the Scropes] were cousin to one Gant', who had come to England with William the Conqueror.[119]

Finally, reinforcing just how seamlessly 'facts' learned from the tales of older men melded with 'facts' widely acknowledged as true by the community at large, numerous Yorkshire gentry defended the Scropes in the language of regional collective memory. The Prior of Newburgh claimed that the information he provided was known by 'common report throughout the country [i.e. the North Riding] where he resides';[120] Waryn Eyrdale knew the arms were Scrope's 'as the public voice and common fame testified';[121] the Prior of Lanercost asserted that his Gant tale of Scrope ancestry dating back to the Conquest 'was known by common report in all parts of the North';[122] Thomas Saltmersshe declared 'that throughout his country [i.e. Richmond] the common fame was that they [the disputed arms] had lineally descended to Sir Richard Scrope';[123] and Sir John Bosville told the Court quite explicitly that 'the Scropes were reputed throughout the counties of York and Richmond to have descended from an ancient line of ancestors'.[124]

Even when deponents turned to the raft of available written and iconographic evidence that supported the Scrope's armorial claim, and which was liberally spread throughout the North Riding, such documents and artifacts often served merely to compliment the tale-telling and hearsay cited above.[125] The Prior of Guisborough, for example, told the Court of a glass window within his priory containing the disputed arms, which he swore 'was granted to one of the Scropes by the Earl of Lincoln', claiming that he knew this to be true 'from tradition, and the information of old friars then deceased'.[126] Most of the time, however, documentary and iconographic evidence was

[119] *Scrope v. Grosvenor*, II, p. 280.
[120] *Scrope v. Grosvenor*, II, p. 280.
[121] *Scrope v. Grosvenor*, II, p. 217.
[122] *Scrope v. Grosvenor*, II, p. 280.
[123] *Scrope v. Grosvenor*, II, p. 342.
[124] *Scrope v. Grosvenor*, II, p. 296.
[125] On the ways in which this type of material culture was viewed before the Court, see J. Luxford, 'Art, Objects and Ideas in the Records of the Medieval Court of Chivalry', in *Courts of Chivalry and Admiralty in Late Medieval Europe*, ed. A. Musson and N. Ramsay (Woodbridge, 2018), pp. 47–74.
[126] *Scrope v. Grosvenor*, II, pp. 277–8.

used, in the opposite direction, to legitimise the more romantic claims associated with the Scropes' ancient gentility. William Holme, canon and celerer of Watton Priory, spoke of monks who 'have in their house a chronicle from the time of the Conquest, with the names of the lords who came over...[and] amongst them is the name of one of the Scropes'.[127] John Yeversley and John Queldrike, canons of Bridlington, pointed towards a seal on a charter that showed knights with swords 'like those used at the time of the Conquest' and that contained the name of one William Scrope as a witness, implying that the family had, indeed, entered England around 1066.[128] Perhaps most evocatively, the Abbot of Selby knew of an old book, 'illuminated in colours, full of escocheons [sic.] of the arms of kings, princes, earls, barons, bannerets, knights, and esquires...amongst which are found the arms of Scrope'.[129]

Augmenting such seemingly compelling evidence, the presence of the Scrope arms publicly displayed throughout the abbeys, priories and parish churches of the three Ridings served to reinforce the commonly-held belief that their right to the arms extended back 'from time beyond the memory of man'.[130] The Abbot of Jervaulx, for example, said the Scrope arms were to be found 'in divers places in his Abbey, in glass windows and painting, entire and with differences',[131] whilst the Prior of Lanercost described how 'at the west end of his church are the arms of Scrope...the same arms are placed in the refectory'.[132] The Scrope arms were naturally also sculpted upon their funeral monuments. The Abbot of Coverham told of 'one Sir Geoffrey Scrope...interred in the body of his church before the high cross, in a lofty tomb, with the effigy of a knight armed in those arms', together with 'his son, who lies below under a flat stone, with a shield of arms differenced... and another of his line and name on the other side below ground';[133] Wensley Church contained the remains of a Simon Scrope, two Henrys and a William, 'all resting in tombs with

---

[127] *Scrope v. Grosvenor*, II, pp. 282–3.
[128] *Scrope v. Grosvenor*, II, p. 281.
[129] *Scrope v. Grosvenor*, II, p. 271.
[130] On the turns of phrase employed by Scrope's witnesses, see Rosenthal, *Telling Tales*, pp. 63–94.
[131] *Scrope v. Grosvenor*, II, p. 273.
[132] *Scrope v. Grosvenor*, II, p. 279.
[133] *Scrope v. Grosvenor*, II, p, 277.

appropriate markings and symbols';[134] and St. Agatha's – the Scropes' foundation abbey near their Richmond home – provided the resting place for Lord Richard's father and elder brother.[135]

Thanks to Scrope's marshalling of Yorkshire's ecclesiastical community, the senior churchmen of his native shire spoke at length before the Court about his family's heraldic identity. Yet, expert though such men undoubtedly were in the iconography of their own abbeys, priories and parish churches, such evidence was equally familiar to the region's secular gentry. Plenty of laymen, often associated with the same religious houses, buttressed their military testimony with similar descriptions of local heraldic display. Richard Beaulieu referred to Henry Scrope's arms in the window of Weatherall Church;[136] Richard Hampton declared that he had seen the arms 'in churches on windows, and they were always called the arms of Scrope';[137] even some of the greatest men in the North could provide such evidence: Lord Dacre described the Scrope arms painted upon glass in Lanercost Priory;[138] and Scrope's North Riding neighbour, Sir Randolf Pygot, more effusively related having 'seen monuments of the ancestors of the said Sir Richard in abbeys painted as knights with these arms, and also paintings in glass in the windows of abbeys, priories, cathedrals, and other churches throughout his country [i.e., Richmond]',[139] indirectly reminding one of just how commonplace such acts of public commemoration and display were, and how familiar passers-by would have become with nearby architectural memorials that they encountered on a daily basis.

Ultimately though, as we saw in the previous chapter, what Richard, Lord Scrope most required were witnesses who could provide the Court with the widest possible range of evidence, touching upon Scrope heraldic display, addressing the facts of his family's ancestry through documentary evidence, whilst also having seen him and his ancestors honouring the disputed arms on campaign. A noteworthy example of just such a witness was another of Scrope's lesser neighbours from the North Riding, the esquire, Thomas Saltmersshe. Saltmersshe began his

---

[134] *Scrope v. Grosvenor*, II, pp. 329–30.
[135] *Scrope v. Grosvenor*, II, p. 274.
[136] *Scrope v. Grosvenor*, II, p. 441.
[137] *Scrope v. Grosvenor*, II, p. 453.
[138] *Scrope v. Grosvenor*, II, p. 413.
[139] *Scrope v. Grosvenor*, II, p. 314.

testimony by providing military evidence of having seen Lord Richard and his cousin, Henry, with the Earl of Warwick in Scotland and before the gates of Paris with Edward III. Like so many Yorkshire-born witnesses, Saltmersshe, as we have seen, additionally proved himself thoroughly immersed in the popular history of the Scrope family, as related through local oral traditions, telling the Court he

> had heard from his ancestors, and many valiant soldiers then deceased, that Sir Richard and his ancestors had borne these arms from the time of the Conquest, and that throughout his country [i.e., Richmond] the common fame was that they had lineally descended to Sir Richard Scrope.

Yet, unlike so many others who described variations on this well-worn tale, Saltmersshe came armed with an offer of more tangible evidence to support his claim, for he further related

> that he possessed a charter made by one of the name of Scrope, ancestor of the said Sir Richard, by which charter [he] held a parcel of the manor of Appelby of the said Sir Richard Scrope; and the said charter bore date eight score years and upwards ago; and he had also divers ancient muniments to which persons of the name of Scrope were witnesses.[140]

This extensive body of Yorkshire-based evidence – its potential breadth neatly encapsulated in Saltmersshe's wide-ranging testimony – underscores just how deeply entrenched the Scropes' heraldic identity and feats of arms had become in the public consciousness of the gentry of the North Riding, and in the popular history of the wider region. Yet, before the Court of Chivalry one is essentially encountering a battle of memory, since the claims of Sir Robert Grosvenor's witnesses provided a competing tradition of the history of the disputed arms that was common to the gentry of the Cheshire–Lancashire borderlands. According to this tradition, the arms, *azure a bend or*, had indeed descended from the time of the Conquest, though not from a certain Gant down to the Scropes, but rather from a Sir Gilbert Grosvenor, nephew of the first Earl of Chester. This version of the arms' descent was supported by the provision of documentary evidence by Grosvenor's deponents, and by reference to the public display of the

---

[140] *Scrope v. Grosvenor*, II, p. 342.

disputed arms in various manors and religious houses throughout Cheshire and Lancashire.[141]

Owain Glyn Dwr – the future leader of the Welsh revolt against Henry IV – succinctly captured the vibrancy of these competing oral traditions, informing the Court that in Cheshire, Flintshire and the districts abounding it, the arms, *azure a bend or*, were indisputably considered those of Grosvenor. Glyn Dwr further claimed to have seen various charters, bearing the arms of Grosvenor on their seals, which, from the look of the parchment, appeared to have been very old.[142] Other Grosvenor witnesses picked up on this theme with even greater precision. The Abbot of Chester told the Court that he had seen the names of some of Grosvenor's ancestors as witnesses to charters and letters in the treasury of his abbey.[143] Sir Laurence Dutton asserted that he had in his possession several documents sealed with the Grosvenor arms.[144] John Eton declared that he held an old charter, conveying land from an earlier Sir Robert Grosvenor to William Cotton, sealed in wax with the disputed arms.[145] Sir John Massy of Puddington and Sir Hugh Browe referred to the same charter,[146] whilst Hugh Cotton, a descendant of the above William, could produce documentary evidence of a range of other transactions between his family and the Grosvenors.[147] Finally, providing the hardest-hitting available evidence from a pro-Grosvenor perspective, the Abbot of Vale Royal set out a detailed pedigree of the Grosvenor family, from Sir Gilbert Grosvenor down to the present defendant, claiming to have constructed it with the aid of relevant chronicles, old writings, and muniments housed within his abbey.[148] The veracity of this pedigree, moreover, was seemingly verified by William Praers, who produced muniments from his grandfather's time which outlined essentially the same descent.[149]

Detailed iconographic evidence, to which dozens of Grosvenor witnesses subscribed, further reinforces that their family's historic

[141] Stewart-Browne, 'The Scrope and Grosvenor Controversy', pp. 10–18; Morgan, 'Sir Robert Grosvenor', p. 91.
[142] *Scrope v. Grosvenor*, I, pp. 254–5.
[143] *Scrope v. Grosvenor*, I, pp. 253–4.
[144] *Scrope v. Grosvenor*, I, pp. 255–6.
[145] *Scrope v. Grosvenor*, I, p. 316.
[146] *Scrope v. Grosvenor*, I, pp. 255; 256–7.
[147] *Scrope v. Grosvenor*, I, pp. 316; 320–1.
[148] *Scrope v. Grosvenor*, I, pp. 253–4.
[149] *Scrope v. Grosvenor*, I, pp. 314–15.

claim to the disputed arms was taken for granted in Cheshire and parts of Lancashire and North Wales. Four of Grosvenor's most distinguished deponents – Sir Laurence Dutton, Sir William Brereton, Thomas Davenport, and the Abbot of Vale Royal – each attested that there was a shield, painted with the disputed arms, hanging by the tomb of the defendant's eponymous grandfather, who had been buried 'before the great pestilence' of 1349.[150] Dutton and William Danyell told of how the arms were painted on an altar-piece in the Church of the Friars Minors in Chester, where the defendant's great-grandfather had long ago been buried.[151] John Holcroft described seeing the arms displayed in Grosvenor's private chapel and embroidered upon a tunic in the time of his grandmother.[152] Elsewhere, the arms appeared in glass in Mobberley, Davenham and Waverton churches;[153] on a cross on the grave of Grosvenor's father;[154] in the great hall of William Praers' manor house;[155] in the chamber of Sir Thomas Dutton;[156] and on the church wall of Vale Royal Abbey.[157]

Against such claims, Richard, Lord Scrope essentially adopted three tactics. Most straightforwardly, he cried foul over aspects of Grosvenor's more compelling testimony. In particular, he complained that the Abbot of Vale Royal had fabricated the Grosvenor pedigree he presented before the Court.[158] For the most part, however, Scrope's adherents largely took the high road, ignoring the claims of Grosvenor's supporters and seeking to portray Grosvenor himself as nothing more than an obscure upstart, unjustly bearing the arms of a true gentleman of ancient ancestry. This approach is made abundantly clear in the surviving testimony. Deponent after deponent echoed Sir Walter Urswick's early statement that 'Of Sir Robert Grosvenor, or of his arms, he never had knowledge until the last expedition into Scotland with our Lord the King'.[159] A few testators adopted an even harsher tone. Sir Thomas Morieux declared that 'He had never heard of the

[150] *Scrope v. Grosvenor*, I, pp. 255–6; 262–3; 263; 253–4.
[151] *Scrope v. Grosvenor*, I, pp. 255–6; 318.
[152] *Scrope v. Grosvenor*, I, p. 295.
[153] *Scrope v. Grosvenor*, I, pp. 255; 270–1; 275; 282; 313; 316.
[154] *Scrope v. Grosvenor*, I, pp. 266; 267–8; 270–1.
[155] *Scrope v. Grosvenor*, I, pp. 314–15.
[156] *Scrope v. Grosvenor*, I, p. 290.
[157] *Scrope v. Grosvenor*, I, p. 312.
[158] Stewart-Browne, 'The Scrope and Grosvenor Controversy', p. 11.
[159] *Scrope v. Grosvenor*, II, p. 170.

said Sir Robert Grosvenor or of his ancestry, whence he was, or whence he came';[160] Sir John Gybbethorpe was even clearer on this point, stating that, 'As to Sir Robert Grosvenor, he had no knowledge of him, nor ever heard any one speak of him or of his ancestors before the dispute arose';[161] and Sir John Brewes emphasised Grosvenor's implied obscurity by alluding to how well-connected he himself was, telling the Court, 'As to Sir Robert Grosvenor, in all the places where he the said Sir John had been armed, he never saw him armed, nor any of his name, until the last expedition in Scotland'.[162]

Scrope's witnesses additionally sought to infer that not only was Scrope possession of the disputed arms common knowledge in Yorkshire and beyond, but that even in Grosvenor's native locality, the Cheshire and Lancashire gentry were far from united in acknowledging the veracity of his claim. This argument was perhaps most forthrightly expressed by Sir Ralph Cheney of Dorset, who emphasised that, when on campaign with Richard and Henry Scrope during the reign of Edward III, both cousins had prominently displayed the disputed arms in full and with a difference, yet, he added 'there were many gentlemen...from the counties of Chester and Lancaster, and...no one from either of these counties said anything', nor challenged their right to the arms.[163] Such specific claims, by individual witnesses like Cheney, were reinforced by the military memories of those numerous Scrope supporters who had been longtime members of the Black Prince's military retinue. The deposition of the Prince's annuitant, Sir Stephen Hales, may stand for the rest. Hales asserted that 'during all his time Sir Richard Scrope was in company of the Prince wherever he was armed, on which occasions he had with him knights and esquires from Cheshire, who were armed in their proper arms; but he never saw any knight or esquire armed Azure, a bend or, excepting of the name of Scrope, or ever heard of any other until the last expedition in Scotland. He had never heard of Sir Robert Grosvenor, or of his ancestors, until the commencement of this dispute'.[164]

Scrope plainly sought to convince the judges that Cheshire and Lancashire society was heavily divided over Grosvenor's claim, thus

---

[160] *Scrope v. Grosvenor*, II, p. 187.
[161] *Scrope v. Grosvenor*, II, p. 225.
[162] *Scrope v. Grosvenor*, II, pp. 209–10.
[163] *Scrope v. Grosvenor*, II, pp. 260–1.
[164] *Scrope v. Grosvenor*, II, pp. 369–70.

making the solidarity of his own large body of witnesses appear all the more compelling. Scrope, moreover, enjoyed a distinct advantage over Grosvenor as a figure of national repute in the spheres of both war and politics. Consequently, as witnesses like Cheney and Hales implied, he must have been aware that many of Grosvenor's more martially-inclined supporters would likely have seen him or his kinsmen bearing the disputed arms on the larger expeditions of the age, and could thus hope to pin at least a few of them into a corner, making it difficult for them to provide their own man with a full-throated defence. It appears to have been with this strategy in mind that Scrope utilised, for his own ends, the gathering at Chester of the bulk of Grosvenor's witnesses to provide their depositions, sending his own proctors to acquire testimony from several of their number.[165]

Unfortunately for Scrope, the dozen Cheshire men, whose interviews with his proctors survive, proved entirely united in their support of Sir Robert Grosvenor (to whom they were almost all related by blood or marriage).[166] Eleven of the 12 claimed to know nothing of Scrope's possession of the arms, or by what right he claimed to bear them. Even those who had served regularly in the king's wars, and whom Lord Richard would probably have hoped would have had no choice but to acknowledge having seen his family bearing the arms, found loopholes to get around such an admission. Sir Richard Bingham appealed to failing memory, telling the Court he had seen the arms, *azure a bend or*, borne during the Rheims expedition of 1359–60, but declared himself unable to remember to whom they belonged, or the names of any who had borne them.[167] Sir Hugh Browe claimed never to have seen a Scrope bearing the arms because he had spent his entire military career in garrison service and had never participated in any campaigns or *chevauchées*: a statement we now know to have been, at best, misleading.[168] Others proved even less cooperative. John Leycestre, who provided a detailed deposition in defence of Grosvenor, replied to every question from Scrope's proctors by asserting that he knew nothing on the subject;[169] Sir John Pole, similarly, responded to each question by claiming 'he knew not how to answer such

[165] *Scrope v. Grosvenor*, II, p. 262.
[166] *Scrope v. Grosvenor*, II, pp. 262–9.
[167] *Scrope v. Grosvenor*, II, pp. 267–8.
[168] *Scrope v. Grosvenor*, II, p. 266; Bell, 'The Soldier '"hadde he riden, no man ferre"', pp. 214–15.
[169] *Scrope v. Grosvenor*, I, pp. 263–4; II, p. 268.

inquiries';[170] and Sir William Brereton even took the drastic measure of repeatedly refusing to appear before the Court, receiving a £20 fine for his stubborn contumacy.[171]

These Grosvenor witnesses, moreover, not only avoided saying anything that might have damaged their man's cause, they also found opportunities to subtly critique Scrope's armorial right in the same breath. Sir John Massy of Tatton, when questioned about the Scrope's ancestral possession of the arms, deposed that, 'Sir Richard Scrope had a man of the law for his father, and that another man of law was father of Sir Henry Scrope, the which were the first men of the Scropes who had used the said arms',[172] whilst Sir Laurence Dutton, echoing Massy, declared that, 'He had not heard who was the first of Sir Richard's ancestors that had borne these arms, but had heard that he was a man of the law'.[173] Massy and Dutton were tapping into a theme commonly exploited by Grosvenor's witnesses in their attacks upon the Scrope family's ancient gentility, setting the scene for the battle of memory alluded to above, in which older Scrope witnesses, like Sir Peter Roos and John Thirlwalle, recalled the career in arms of the plaintiff's grandfather, William Scrope, with the aim of demonstrating that Lord Richard was by no means merely the descendant of lawyers.[174] The fact that the legal backgrounds of Henry and Geoffrey Scrope should have been held against Lord Richard by his opponents, and was treated as a claim worth countering by his own supporters, serves to underscore the radical shift occurring in the relationship between heraldry and gentility at the time *Scrope v. Grosvenor* was in session. In *Grey v. Hastings*, a generation later, a number of Lord Grey's civilian witnesses openly claimed membership of armigerous society, whilst being equally

---

[170] *Scrope v. Grosvenor*, II, p. 269.
[171] *Scrope v. Grosvenor*, II, p. 268.
[172] *Scrope v. Grosvenor*, II, p. 264.
[173] *Scrope v. Grosvenor*, II, pp. 265–6.
[174] Perhaps the most forthright defence of the Scropes' ancient gentility came from Armand Monceaux, who detailed, in a laborious anecdote, how Sir Richard Hilton, after Richard, Lord Scrope rejected a marriage alliance between their families, claimed cattily that he was glad his daughter had not married into their family, since they were not of ancient lineage, to which Sir John Hasethorpe supposedly responded, 'Oh, Sir! Say not so, for of certainty, and upon my soul, he is come of 'grand gentilshommes [sic]' from the time of the Conquest'. *Scrope v. Grosvenor*, II, pp. 336–7.

clear about never having served in war.[175] If lawyers, bureaucrats and wealthy merchants and townsmen were largely accepted within the ranks of the armigerous by the early fifteenth century, in the mid 1380s, such claims were, in some quarters, still very much open to debate.[176]

The other point that derives from these competing claims regarding the ancient gentility of the Scropes is that with hundreds of gentry scattered throughout the realm, and with the ranks of the armigerous swelling during the final third of the fourteenth century, it would have been only natural for men from far-flung regions to have accidentally come to bear the same arms. National military expeditions provided one of the few occasions when the paths of such men might cross and hence it is no surprise that we possess ample scraps of evidence inferring that the Court of Chivalry was kept extremely busy with armorial cases during these years.[177] Indeed, from *Scrope v. Grosvenor* itself, we know that Richard, Lord Scrope and Sir Robert Grosvenor's father-in-law, John Danyell, had both challenged the armorial right of a Cornish esquire, Thomas Carminowe, whom they had separately encountered, bearing *azure a bend or*, on the Rheims expedition in 1359–60. In the former case, it was decided that both plaintiff and defendant should be allowed to keep their arms, on the dubious grounds that Cornwall had once been a separate kingdom, whilst in the latter, although no record of the verdict survives, Danyell clearly either prevailed or achieved the same result as Scrope, for his son-in-law's deponents placed great stock in this event in their depositions.[178]

More broadly, what this potential proliferation of armorial cases reveal is the extent to which competing oral and iconographic traditions over the armorial right of individual families persisted in their native regions, reinforcing the influence of chivalric culture as a source of local, as much as national, identity. Simply put, the Scropes' high standing within chivalric society, given teeth by their impressive military records and their numerous feats of arms in war and tournaments, represented a source of patriotic pride for Yorkshire (and especially North Riding) society. Similarly, as obscure as Sir Robert Grosvenor may have appeared to those gentry from far

---

[175] E.g., John Henry, John Lee, John Styrecle, Robert Baa, John Enderby. *PCM*, I, pp. 176; 198; 243; 284; 290.
[176] Keen, *Origins of the English Gentleman*, pp. 64–5.
[177] Keen, *Origins of the English Gentleman*, pp. 43–4.
[178] Vale, 'The Scropes', p. 95; Stewart-Browne, 'The Scrope and Grosvenor Controversy', pp. 15–16.

off parts of the realm, within the ranks of Cheshire and Lancashire society he was evidently a man of considerable respect whose family was known to have long borne and displayed the disputed arms. Due to the extreme localism of English society in the fourteenth century, it became possible for these competing oral and iconographic traditions to thrive in parallel. This reality is reflected in the surviving testimony, where men from different regions articulated contrasting (and incredibly detailed) histories of the descent of the *azure a bend or* arms. Yet, in a very small number of depositions, these competing traditions collided, forcing testators to acknowledge their familiarity with multiple versions of the disputed arms' descent.

The Scrope testimony provides three classic examples of this phenomenon. Adam Neusom – a Cheshire-born life retainer of John of Gaunt – who had seen various Scropes bearing the arms in France, Scotland and Spain, admitted before the Court that he knew of Sir Robert Grosvenor and outlined how Grosvenor's ancestors were interred in the Abbey of Chester, with the disputed arms painted in bright colours in glass on the windows of the abbey.[179] A similar deposition was provided for Scrope by Hugh Calveley, another Cheshire man with Lancastrian connections, and the nephew of the famous career soldier of the same name. Calveley deposed that he had regularly seen members of the Scrope family bearing the disputed arms in war, yet added that 'he had heard that Sir Robert Grosvenor had greater right to the said arms than Sir Richard Scrope'. Thus, before the Court of Chivalry, Neusom's and Calveley's childhood experiences, absorbing the hearsay, tale-telling and surrounding iconography of their native Cheshire, which reinforced the Grosvenors' heraldic identity as the legitimate claimants to the arms, *azure a bend or*, rested uneasily against their adult experiences in the Lancastrian military retinue of having regularly seen Richard, Lord Scrope bearing the same arms and being widely acknowledged as their rightful possessor.[180] Lastly, Geoffrey Chaucer – providing what has now become a justly famous deposition – showed quite explicitly how competing heraldic traditions could collide in those national enclaves where gentry from different parts of the realm interacted. Having recounted his youthful exploits on the Rheims expedition of 1359–60, when he had seen Richard and Henry Scrope bearing the arms, Chaucer related that he

---

[179] *Scrope v. Grosvenor*, II, pp. 222–3.
[180] *Scrope v. Grosvenor*, II, p. 227.

had heard of the Scrope family's ancient possession of the said arms from old knights and esquires, adding for good measure that he had seen them 'displayed on banners, glass, paintings, and vestments, and commonly called the arms of Scrope'. This is hardly surprising since Richard, Lord Scrope, as a leading figure in the Ricardian royal government, would have spent a great deal of time in London during Chaucer's literary heyday.[181] Yet, in a colourful aside, Chaucer added that whilst walking in Friday Street (London) he had encountered the Scrope arms hanging above an inn, and upon inquiring 'what inn that was that had hung out these arms of Scrope?', he was informed 'That they were not hung out…for the arms of Scrope…but they are painted and put there by a Knight of the county of Chester, called Sir Robert Grosvenor', which, Chaucer told the Court, was the first occasion he had ever heard of Grosvenor or anyone bearing that name.[182] For all their differences of opinion regarding the history of the arms, *azure a bend or*, the narratives put forward by both parties in *Scrope v. Grosvenor* were essentially positive in nature. Both families had clearly borne the disputed arms in good faith for generations, so each was essentially making the same case: that they enjoyed a historic right to the arms, as architectural display, documentary evidence, and the memories of those who had seen them bearing them, collectively illustrated.

In *Lovel v. Morley* and *Grey v. Hastings*, the issues at stake and the arguments mounted were rather more complicated. John, Lord Lovel had never personally borne the disputed arms, *argent a lion rampant sable crowned and armed or*, and his claim, as we have seen, rested upon his descent from the Burnell family, to whom the arms in his view rightfully belonged. Thus, matters of lineage trumped military testimony. Thomas, Lord Morley, by contrast, sought to prove that his family had long borne and displayed the said arms, whilst also seeking to demonstrate that his grandfather, Robert, had successfully defended them against the challenge of Nicholas, Lord Burnell before the Court of Chivalry outside Calais in 1347.[183] In *Grey v. Hastings*, both parties claimed to be the rightful heir to the arms of the last Earl of Pembroke, who had been killed in a jousting accident in 1389. Reginald, Lord Grey was in a similar position to Lovel, in so far as he

---

[181] Vale, 'The Scropes', pp. 81–5.
[182] *Scrope v. Grosvenor*, II, pp. 411–12.
[183] Ayton, 'Knights, Esquires and Military Service', pp. 84, 89–90.

had never publicly borne the disputed arms. He was, however, clearly Pembroke's legitimate successor, with the result that his deponents likewise focused largely upon relevant matters of lineage. Sir Edward Hastings, meanwhile, as a cadet of the Pembroke Earls, sought to demonstrate that his family had long borne the Pembroke arms, *or a manche gules*, with a difference and that his father, Sir Hugh Hastings III, had been permitted, during the last Earl's childhood, to bear the Pembroke arms in full: hence, Hastings' heavy reliance upon military testimony cataloguing occasions when this had occurred.[184] Morley's and Hastings' battles of memory with Lovel and Grey were thus of a rather different temper to the *Scrope v. Grosvenor* controversy. The deep-rooted oral traditions of the East Anglian gentry came to the fore on their behalf and, unlike the often-vague assertions of 'ancient ancestry' outlined by Scrope's and Grosvenor's witnesses, both parties in *Lovel v. Morley* and *Grey v. Hastings* homed in upon specific past events within living memory, in the process indirectly revealing how competing oral traditions could develop, and how rapidly partisan interpretations of their details could become 'common knowledge'.

Since matters surrounding the earlier *Burnell v. Morley* case lay at the heart of Lovel's claim, it is unsurprising that a great many of his surviving 62 witnesses focused upon this dispute in some fashion. In response, Morley acquired his own support from dozens of veterans of the siege of Calais, who could likewise speak convincingly about the verdict. The battle of memory that ensued took on wide-ranging form. Morley's witnesses naturally claimed that his grandfather, Robert, had won the case without qualification. William Kyng evocatively described the judgment being proclaimed aloud in English by Henry of Grosmont;[185] Kyng and Henry Hoo suggested that Burnell had been allowed to bear the arms, but only with a difference;[186] and Sir John Brewes, casting further aspersions upon Lovel's claim, declared that he had seen Burnell bearing an entirely different coat-of-arms.[187] Lovel's witnesses produced a contrasting version of events. William Moreys recalled the opposite verdict to William Kyng;[188] Sir Thomas Blount, in a delightfully colourful deposition, revealed he had missed the

---

[184] Keen, 'Grey v. Hastings', pp. 172–6.
[185] C 47/6/1, no. 96.
[186] C 47/6/1, nos. 96; 10.
[187] C 47/6/1, no. 102.
[188] PRO30/26/69, no. 167.

announcement because he was resting in his tent after being wounded in the leg by a forcelet, but assured the Court that Sir Thomas West had come and informed him of the result;[189] and John Broyn, perhaps fence-sitting, claimed that the crush of people in the church had made it difficult to hear the verdict.[190] Even those Lovel witnesses who accepted Morley's victory over Burnell portrayed the outcome as unjust. Several argued, for instance, that Morley had pressured Edward III to see that he received a favourable verdict.[191] Adopting a rather different approach, William Moreys and Hildebrand Barre disparaged the Morleys' ancestral claim to the arms by suggesting that Robert, Lord Morley had been the first of his family to bear them.[192] It was also alleged that Edward III had ordered that the arms should be awarded to Lord Robert, but only as a reward for his distinguished military record and only for the duration of his life. Thereafter, the arms were to have reverted to the Burnells.[193]

This last allegation opened a further avenue for debate between the two sets of witnesses. On Lovel's side, Sir Maurice de Bruyn recalled that, on the point of death on the Rheims expedition in 1360, Robert, Lord Morley had ordered that the disputed arms should be returned without delay to Lord Burnell.[194] In direct contrast, the Morley witness, Henry Hoo, declared that Morley's dying wish had been that his son and heir, William (the defendant's father), should inherit the arms.[195] Additionally, by leaving the verdict of *Burnell v. Morley* as open as possible, Lovel's deponents were able to broaden their defence by focusing upon the Burnell's historic use and public display of the arms. Consequently, those depositions provided by Morley testators, outlining the burial of the heart of a thirteenth-century crusader Morley in Reydon Church, describing the banners erected in Robert, Lord Morley's memory by Sir Thomas Bolyngton, or detailing the public display of the Morley arms in various religious houses throughout East Anglia, were countered with equally elaborate recollections of the Burnell family adopting the disputed arms in their own iconography

---

[189] PRO30/26/69, no. 176.
[190] PRO30/26/69, no. 175.
[191] PRO30/26/69, nos. 169; 186; 204.
[192] PRO30/26/69, nos. 175; 227.
[193] Ayton, 'Knights, Esquires and Military Service', p. 99.
[194] PRO30/26/69, no. 221.
[195] C 47/6/1, no. 10.

in Oxfordshire and Wiltshire. Three witnesses, for instance, described how the arms were painted upon a chasuble, an amice and other vestments within the Burnell household;[196] William Wollaston – a deponent old enough to have fought at the battle of Bannockburn (1314) – was one of several Lovel supporters who described seeing the arms embroidered upon tapestries, carved upon furniture, and painted upon vessels and various utensils;[197] and, as a pertinent example of the interplay between heraldic display and oral tradition, Lovel brought the judges to the church of Stratfield Mortimer to view a *table*, on which were depicted the images of Philip, Lord Burnell and his wife, at which point two knowledgeable testators described the object's history in minute detail.[198] The extensive engagement of the *Lovel v. Morley* witnesses with the Burnell's historic claim to the disputed arms provides an excellent illustration of how competing oral and iconographic traditions persisted, even when seemingly faced with an unequivocal historical moment like *Burnell v. Morley*, in which one side was clearly the winner. At a distance of forty years, what should have been the straightforward recollection of a precise verdict before the Court of Chivalry was transformed, by the extreme partisanship of those who had witnessed it (and by the apparent loss of its records!), into a matter of opinion and a battle of regional memory.

A generation later, Sir Edward Hastings' testators defended his claim of being the legitimate heir to the Pembroke arms with equal vigour. They did so by advocating a purely local narrative, enjoying virtually no support beyond Norfolk's borders, according to which the Hastings of Elsing were widely acknowledged as the rightful heirs of the Pembroke Earls.[199] The crux of Sir Edward's defence was the argument – substantiated largely by hearsay and anecdotal evidence – that the last Earl's mother and aunt, the Countesses of Pembroke and Norfolk, had favoured the inheritance claims of his father, Sir Hugh Hastings III, during the 1380s, granting him the right to bear the Pembroke arms in full whilst the last Earl was still underage.[200]

[196] PRO30/26/69, nos. 218; 219; 220.
[197] PRO30/26/69, nos. 186; 210; 223.
[198] PRO30/26/69, nos. 216; 217.
[199] Norfolk was the only shire whose inquisitions post mortem adjudged Hastings, and not Grey, as heir to the last Earl of Pembroke. Caudrey, 'War, Chivalry and Regional Society', p. 131.
[200] On the inheritance issues surrounding the *Grey v. Hastings* case, see Jack, 'Entail and Descent', pp. 1–19.

Numerous witnesses from Norfolk and Suffolk supported this version of events. Sir Robert Berney claimed that Sir Hugh Hastings III had long borne the Pembroke arms with a label and that the Countess of Norfolk had prayed him to bear the arms in full.[201] William Plumstead and John Burlingham agreed, telling the Court that Sir Hugh III had borne the arms in full on John of Gaunt's Spanish expedition in 1386 specifically at the Countesses' request.[202] And, seeking to undermine any hint of the uncertainty surrounding this particular narrative, William Calthorpe, David Hemenhale and Hamo Claxton declared it 'common knowledge' that the Countesses of Pembroke and Norfolk had desired the Hastings of Elsing as the Pembroke's heirs, should their senior line falter.[203] Several witnesses spoke openly about where they had acquired their knowledge. Hemenhale knew the truth of it because he had heard the Countess of Norfolk herself say so, whilst John Reymes and Alexander Denton claimed Sir Hugh Hastings III had personally told them that he was Pembroke's heir.[204] Sir Miles Stapleton said he had been so advised by the Bishop of Norwich.[205] Sir Thomas Gerbergh, the former steward of Edward III's fourth son, Edmund of Langley, Duke of York, turned to even higher authority, claiming that his late royal employer had expressed surprise at the initial challenge to Hastings' arms nearly 20 years earlier and had told Gerbergh that his own father, King Edward, and other learned men, had commonly accepted that if the Earls of Pembroke died without issue, the Hastings of Elsing were their rightful heirs.[206] Moving seamlessly from general hearsay to specific anecdotal evidence, William Plumstead recalled how, on the Gascony expedition in 1369, the question was raised as to why the defendant's grandfather, Sir Hugh Hastings II, was bearing the Pembroke arms with a label when he was not Pembroke's son, and it was reportedly judged acceptable because he was the Earl's next heir, if Pembroke died without issue.[207] Lastly, tapping even deeper into the well of chivalric memory, Robert Lymworth provided a richly detailed account, describing how the Earl of Salisbury, upon landing in France,

---

[201] *PCM*, I, pp. 474–6.
[202] *PCM*, I, pp. 478–80; 469–72.
[203] *PCM*, I, pp. 456–7; 458–64; 467–9.
[204] *PCM*, I, pp. 458–64; 444–5; 453–5.
[205] *PCM*, I, pp. 442–3.
[206] *PCM*, I, pp. 496–7.
[207] *PCM*, I, pp. 478–80.

had knighted the young Hugh Hastings III, ritually returning his banner to him with the command, 'Hold this banner and God give you Grace to do as much Honour to these armes [sic] as your ancestors have done, for if the Earl of Pembroke dies without heir to his body, you shall be his next heir'.[208]

Such claims proved more than a matter of popular sentiment and were supported by a significant body of what, at the time, would have been considered 'hard evidence'. Sir John Wiltshire told the Court that before departing for Spain, Sir Hugh Hastings III had shown him the Pembroke coat-of-arms, as it was to be displayed on the banners, pennons, and on a short sword, that he had ordered for the voyage.[209] It appears that Sir Hugh was especially proud of this short sword, for he later showed it off to John Spekkesworth during the expedition.[210] Other witnesses, adopting a slightly different approach, focused upon verifying that the Countesses of Pembroke and Norfolk had, indeed, granted Sir Hugh their blessing to bear the arms in full. Spekkesworth and Thomas Lucas declared that they had been present at an inquisition taken at Norwich, upon the Countess of Pembroke's death, at which the defendant's late elder brother, Hugh IV, had been adjudged the Pembroke's rightful heir.[211] John Bryston reinforced this view, adding that two other Hastings deponents, William Plumstead and John Payn, had been jurors on this occasion, which both men acknowledged in their own depositions.[212] More broadly, Bryston and David Hemenhale attested that they had been shown a pedigree by the Bishop of Norwich which proved the Hastings' claim, whilst Thomas, Lord Morley, who had also seen the pedigree in the Bishop's possession, went a step further, accusing Grey's party of burning the Hastings' entails and bribing the Sheriff of Nottingham for a favourable inquisition.[213] Other witnesses picked up on Morley's theme. Most scandalously, Thomas Stanton claimed that Sir Hugh Hastings II's sister had begged his forgiveness after accepting a bribe to bear false witness against him to his disinheritance.[214] Lastly, there evolved a line

---

[208] *PCM*, I, pp. 413–21.
[209] *PCM*, I, pp. 401–4.
[210] *PCM*, I, pp. 395–7.
[211] *PCM*, I, pp. 395–7; 445–51.
[212] *PCM*, I, pp. 464–7; 478–80; 502–3.
[213] *PCM*, I, pp. 464–7; 458–64; 435–9.
[214] *PCM*, I, pp. 486–7.

of defence arguing that Hugh Hastings IV (the defendant's late elder brother), having been adjudged the Pembroke's rightful heir as a boy, would have entered into his inheritance had his guardian, John of Gaunt, bothered to prosecute his claim. Sir Ralph Shelton II stated unequivocally that it was common knowledge that if Gaunt had done so, Hugh IV would have been the next Earl of Pembroke: a view supported by Sir John Geney, John Bere and William Wheteley.[215] The above version of events, flying in the face of popular opinion from elsewhere, was widely accepted by the Norfolk gentry, for whom the military achievements and noble blood ties of the three Sir Hugh Hastings resonated deeply as a source of regional pride.

Across all three armorial cases, it is abundantly clear that the oral traditions of individual localities, often comprising nothing more than a combination of hearsay, tale-telling and iconographic display, carried far greater weight than popular opinion from elsewhere, no matter how extensive or compelling.[216] In *Scrope v. Grosvenor*, both protagonists had borne the arms, *azure a bend or*, for generations, and provided the Court with ample evidence from their native localities to support their claim. In *Lovel v. Morley*, Lovel's supporters upheld their man's armorial right despite Robert, Lord Morley having very obviously won his case before the Court of Chivalry against Nicholas, Lord Burnell 40 years earlier. In *Grey v. Hastings*, Sir Edward Hastings' entire line of defence essentially rested upon a hotbed of poorly-substantiated rumour, perpetuated by the Hastings themselves, and taken as fact by large sections of Norfolk's gentry. The pride in English arms that developed over the middle-third of the fourteenth century and that found national expression in the exploits of Edward III, the Black Prince, and their leading lieutenants, simultaneously took root within regional society, whose own heroes, like Sir Geoffrey Scrope, Robert, Lord Morley and Sir Hugh Hastings I, became unimpeachable figures of local legend. The vibrancy of these competing oral and iconographic traditions, and the strength of the regional solidarities upon which they rested, was laid bare when they collided before the Court of Chivalry.

---

[215] *PCM*, I, pp. 423–4; 425; 426–7; 504–6.
[216] Sir William Berdewell, for example, dubiously claimed, in the face of overwhelming evidence to the contrary, that the Hastings of Elsing's right to the Pembroke arms 'was common knowledge to all the gentry of England'. *PCM*, I, pp. 390–2.

Conclusion

One of the most enticing features of the Court of Chivalry's testimony is its overt chivalric flavour, focusing upon individual acts of valour, in many ways reminiscent of the style of tale-telling found in chivalric biographies and the leading chronicles of the Hundred Years War. These captivating vignettes, of course, were articulated before the Court for the narrowly specific purpose of aiding the relevant protagonist, demonstrating to the judges that not only had the Scropes, Morleys and Hastings long borne the disputed arms, but, through their deeds with the sword, they had undeniably brought honour to them as well. A closer reading of the depositions, however, more broadly reveals the cultural context that lay behind this body of chivalric testimony. 'Chivalry memory' – that 'form of family memory, part of the stock of myths and narratives passed down over the generations, which brought lustre to a family's name [and] also belonged to the chivalric class as a whole'[217] – was on full display before the Court, providing a source of communal solidarity that bound each set of witnesses to their protagonist. From a purely military perspective, it has been illustrated that no 'distinct cooling of bellicose ardour' differentiated Sir Edward Hastings' military deponents, testifying in 1408–9, from those who spoke for Scrope and Morley in the mid 1380s. Individual feats of heroism and tragic acts of self-sacrifice – always the bedrock of the chronicling of war in the Middle Ages – remained to the fore. Hastings' witnesses, in fact, had far more to say about the valorous deeds of the 1370s and 1380s than Scrope and Morley veterans of this epoch, who, in stark contrast to those older men who recalled the 1340s and 1350s, largely shied away from relating chivalrous tales of the Hundred Years War's second phase. This attitudinal shift, observable only a handful of years before Henry V reignited the war with France, may imply that the chivalric crisis of the late fourteenth century had passed and that a more positive attitude towards the campaigns of the 1370s and 1380s was starting to emerge. These shifting attitudes, indeed, may partly explain the enthusiasm with which the gentry – and certainly the sons and nephews of Hastings' deponents – returned to arms in 1415.

At the same time, one also encounters in the surviving testimony some of the ways in which 'regional chivalric memory' – perhaps

---

[217] Saul, *Chivalry in Medieval England*, p. 283.

best-defined as a defiant sense of parochialism that expressed itself as a body of 'common knowledge' about the military achievements and ancient gentility of the region's greatest families – was brought to bear in each dispute. Tales of the Scropes' martial prowess were central to the identity of Richmondshire's (and, more broadly, Yorkshire's) military communities, whilst the same applied to the Morleys and Hastings in Norfolk (and, more broadly, East Anglia). This strong level of regional support highlights the entrenched localism of English chivalry, beneath the national façade of the Edwardian chivalric revival of the mid fourteenth century. The gentry of Yorkshire and Cheshire were each familiar with contrasting tales of the descent of the arms, a*zure a bend or*, and neither community was in any doubt about the veracity of their man's claim. In those rare instances where Cheshire men had fought extensively in the company of Richard, Lord Scrope, they found themselves in the uneasy position of being acquainted with two contrasting versions of the disputed arms' descent, and their very obvious uncertainty about whom to believe reinforces how fully tales of the Scropes' and Grosvenors' armorial right had flourished unimpeded for generations, their roots growing ever stronger within their respective military communities. The strength of such localism is further underscored by the situation in Norfolk, where the outcome of *Burnell v. Morley* (1347) was disputed largely along regional lines, and where, even more starkly – through an elaborate combination of local tale-telling, history, hearsay, and iconographic and written evidence – Sir Edward Hastings' Norfolk supporters remained quite convinced that the Hastings of Elsing were the rightful heirs to the Pembroke arms, despite a vast body of evidence to the contrary, and the fact that virtually no-one beyond the shire's borders shared their view. This was medieval parochialism at its most stubborn. It also may have portended the future, for, as we shall see, this type of local chivalric sentiment remained significant within genteel society well into the fifteenth century, notwithstanding declining rates of gentry participation in the third phase of the Hundred Years War (1415–53), or the ultimate failure of the war effort itself.

Conclusion

This book has adopted the *Scrope v. Grosvenor* (1385–90), *Lovel v. Morley* (1386–7) and *Grey v. Hastings* (1407–10) armorial cases before the Court of Chivalry as a means of investigating the military, social and cultural history of the late medieval English gentry. Two interrelated subjects have dominated the existing scholarship on the Court: firstly, the deponents' patterns of military service, and secondly, evidence, through the surviving testimony, of the vibrancy of Edwardian chivalric culture.[1] These factors have been addressed almost exclusively in a mid-to-late fourteenth-century context, emphasising the continuities in military service and martial attitudes apparent within genteel society between the 1330s and the 1370s,[2] with minimal attention paid to the testimony centring upon the second phase of the Hundred Years War (1369–89), other than to suggest that these depositions lacked 'the kind of resonance in recall that the great campaigns of the 1340s and 50s had had'.[3] This book has argued that, when taken collectively, the value of the Court of Chivalry material lies in the fact that it cuts across a range of historiographical boundaries, making it possible to examine afresh a host of themes central to gentry studies, whilst simultaneously touching upon unexplored aspects of the cases themselves.

The first of these themes has been to test whether continuities of personnel and family traditions of military service – so apparent amongst Court of Chivalry witnesses between the Hundred Years War's first and second phases – were maintained into the early years of the War's third phase under Henry V. It was concluded,

---

[1] Keen, 'Chaucer's Knight', pp. 106–12; Keen, 'Grey v. Hastings', pp. 178–82; Ayton, 'Knights, Esquires and Military Service', pp. 81–104; Keen, *Origins of the English Gentleman*, pp. 25–70; Bell, *War and the English Soldier*, pp. 140–50; Sumption, *The Hundred Years War III*, pp. 735–7; Ayton, 'Military Service and the Dynamics of Recruitment', pp. 45-57; Bell, 'The Soldier "hadde he ridden no man ferre"', pp. 209–18; Bell et al., *The Soldier*, pp. 167–70.

[2] Ayton, 'Military Service and the Dynamics of Recruitment', pp. 45–57.

[3] Keen, 'Grey v. Hastings', pp. 182–5.

from an examination of the hitherto largely neglected Grosvenor and Hastings military testimony,[4] that although the lengthy Truce of Leulinghem (1389–1415) brought the military careers of almost every single deponent to a close, their immediate descendants, to an impressive degree, upheld their family's military traditions, sometimes to the extent that as many as five consecutive generations participated regularly in the Hundred Years War between its onset in the late 1330s and the Agincourt campaign of 1415. Given these enduring military traditions, it seems highly unlikely that the depositions of younger witnesses before the Court lacked the chivalrous gloss found in the testimony of veterans of the war's first phase.

A second equally important theme to emerge from this book is the interplay between England's regional military and county communities. An analysis of the composition of each witness list brings one face to face with an intricate web of gentry social networks, which linked together region, county and locality, and which were only partially military in character. These witness lists reveal the reliance of each protagonist upon their kinsmen, neighbours, friends, servants and associates, but also hint at how such relationships were formed. The Lancastrian affinity provided a framework within which the horizontal ties between groups of Scrope and Hastings witnesses could flourish. In the North Riding of Yorkshire, where John of Gaunt had actively recruited amongst the local élite, witnesses' mutual Lancastrian affiliations were but one of innumerable personal bonds they shared with the Scropes, many of which predated Gaunt's entry into the region. Shire borders, moreover, proved no object for a man of Richard, Lord Scrope's standing. Having spent a lifetime networking amongst the upper reaches of English gentry society, he was able to tap into a diffuse array of social circles beyond his Yorkshire heartland, utilising his brother's and cousin's service in the Bohun military retinue, his own wide-ranging Lancastrian ties, and his eclectic friendships at the Ricardian Court, to bring together witnesses from the Midlands, the West Country and East Anglia, whose private networks were largely peripheral to his own, but with whom he shared friends in common, who likely helped encourage these blocs of witnesses to speak on his behalf.

[4] Bennett, *Community, Class and Careerism*, pp. 14–16, 82–3, 166; Morgan, *War and Society in Medieval Cheshire*, pp. 129–42; Keen, 'Grey v. Hastings', pp. 167–85; Caudrey, 'War, Chivalry and Regional Society', pp. 119–45; Morgan, 'Sir Robert Grosvenor', pp. 75–94.

This intersection between vertical and horizontal ties may be considered an important sub-theme of this study. Like Scrope in Yorkshire, Thomas, Lord Morley made positive use of his position at the apex of an East Anglian network, in which the recently extinct Ufford earls of Suffolk had featured prominently alongside his own ancestors, and which had strengthened his bonds with the knightly élite of Norfolk and Suffolk at large. In similar vein, Sir Robert Grosvenor – little known outside of the Northwest – relied extensively upon personal ties of kinship, friendship and association when garnering support, yet was sufficiently well-connected in his native shire that he succeeded in galvanising a significant sector of Cheshire's élite to speak on his behalf. Sir Edward Hastings, in similar fashion, constructed his witness list essentially by turning to the gentry of his immediate locality in northeast Norfolk, many of whom had borne arms regularly in the Lancastrian military retinue with his father during the 1370s and 1380s. Hastings' support base, coming before the Court of Chivalry a near decade after John of Gaunt's death, provides a pertinent illustration of how mutual service to the same magnate affinity, on the one hand, tended to unite gentry from a particular region who were already closely aligned, and, on the other, reinforces how inter-gentry relationships, formed or solidified beneath the umbrella of magnate service, could thrive well beyond the lifetime of their lord.

If the formation of each witness list and the ties between those who testified has represented a largely neglected topic, this has been because the military-chivalric aspects of the testimony have proven so understandably compelling, and this is undeniably where the Court's material is at its most useful. Consequently, a third overarching theme of this book has been to contextualise, where possible, the military careers of individual witnesses in the broader context of the lives they led within county society. In the existing scholarship, witnesses' military records have largely been adopted either as exemplars of different types of soldiering, or as useful additional material for the historian seeking to reconstruct the personnel of English armies.[5] Scholars of the Crusade, for example, can make the most of the fact that numerous deponents explicitly described their participation on such enterprises,[6] whilst the incredibly detailed testimony of various obscure lesser gentry has shed considerable light upon the service

---

[5] See above, n. 1.
[6] Guard, *Chivalry, Kingship and Crusade*, pp. 217–40.

patterns of military careerists who never reached the front rank of English chivalric society.[7]

Yet, whilst invaluable in several respects, such an approach risks turning careers into typologies and can blind one to the motives and constraints that drove individual gentry to bear arms. By examining the wider careers of greater (and, where possible, lesser) gentry testators, the Court of Chivalry material may effectively act as a starting point for illustrating just how personal was the military journey of each participant, underscoring that superficially similar war records may have arisen from markedly different origins. The issues surrounding personal decision-making over whether to bear arms, raised by Malcolm Mercer in the context of the Wars of the Roses,[8] remain just as pertinent when considering why gentry fought in the Hundred Years War, and why some chose to keep fighting with varying degrees of consistency, whilst others hung up their swords.

One motive that naturally springs to mind is chivalric enthusiasm. The valorous tales, heraldic knowledge and impressive catalogues of battles fought and feats of arms witnessed – especially for those testators whose military careers coincided with the halcyon years of Edward III's reign between the victories at Halidon Hill (1333) and Nájera (1367) – have laid bare just what a golden age this was for English chivalry. However, since the 1830s, when Sir Harris Nicolas first enthused over the subject,[9] the actual details of the chivalric testimony, other than in a purely heraldic context,[10] have been no more than glanced over. Maurice Keen illustrated that some of the more active and glamorous careers outlined before the Court in *Scrope v. Grosvenor* would have been worthy of Chaucer's Knight, whilst Andrew Ayton emphasised how vividly the chivalric culture of the age was evoked in the 'intricate word pictures' of numerous Morley witnesses.[11] Yet, the chivalric testimony has rarely been related to the motives of those who deposed, and the assumption seems to have been that these enticing vignettes

---

[7] Keen, 'Chaucer's Knight', pp. 106-12; Ayton, 'Knights, Esquires and Military Service', pp. 89–95; Sumption, *The Hundred Years War III*, pp. 735–7; Bell et al., *The Soldier*, pp. 167–70.

[8] M. Mercer, *The Medieval Gentry: Power, Leadership and Choice during the Wars of the Roses* (London, 2010).

[9] *Scrope v. Grosvenor*, I, p. 14.

[10] Keen, *Origins of the English Gentleman*, pp. 25–70.

[11] Keen, 'Chaucer's Knight', pp. 106–12; Ayton, 'Knights, Esquires and Military Service', p. 87.

essentially reflected the chivalric culture of the Edwardian Court as expressed by everyday gentry in a narrow setting. At the same time, the claim that the testimony on behalf of Sir Edward Hastings lacked the 'resonance in recall' found amongst Scrope's and Morley's older witnesses has cultural, as well as purely military, implications.[12]

As such, a fourth overarching theme of this book has been to argue that the above claims upon the Hastings chivalric testimony do not stand up to closer scrutiny and, more generally, that the role of 'chivalric memory' before the Court, in a specifically regional context, has been rather underappreciated. Acts of heroism and self-sacrifice, combined with a deep heraldic knowledge, and an appreciation of lineage and family history, remained prominent features of the Hastings depositions. Indeed, Sir Edward's militarily active witnesses appeared rather more inclined to savour the martial deeds of the 1370s and 1380s than their contemporaries who had testified, much closer to the time, as young men for Scrope and Morley.

More broadly, one encounters in the surviving depositions across all three cases some of the ways in which chivalric memory was expressed at a regional level, as a body of 'common knowledge' about the deeds in arms and ancient gentility of the protagonists' families. The military community of the North Riding (and Yorkshire at large) was heavily invested in the Scropes' martial prowess and heraldic identity, as were Norfolk's gentry in those of the Lords Morley and the Hastings of Elsing. The entrenched localism of English chivalry was on full display before the Court. This was most forthrightly expressed in *Scrope v. Grosvenor*, where the gentry of Yorkshire and Cheshire were each familiar with contrasting tales of the descent of the arms, a*zure a bend or*, and neither community was in any doubt about the veracity of their man's claim, leaving those few witnesses familiar with both versions of its descent unsure of whom to believe. The strength of such localism is further revealed by the situation in Norfolk, where the outcome of *Burnell v. Morley* (1347) was disputed largely along regional lines, and where Sir Edward Hastings' Norfolk supporters remained quite convinced that his family were the rightful heirs to the Pembroke arms, despite overwhelming evidence to the contrary. These divisions, however, were in some ways only skin deep. What was essentially being expressed by Yorkshire's, Cheshire's and Norfolk's military communities in these cases was a sense of parochial pride

---

[12] Keen, 'Grey v. Hastings', pp. 175–82; Keen, *Origins of the English Gentleman*, pp. 71–120.

in their locality's contribution to the English cause in France. This was, moreover, a sentiment not limited to those possessing military experience, but one that encompassed churchmen and civilian gentry as well, who proved, through their knowledge of heraldry and local oral traditions, as deeply immersed in the chivalric culture of their native shire as those knights and esquires who actually went to war.

What the above evidence underscores, as the fifth and final overarching theme of this study, is that martial attitudes and the performance of military service in the later Middle Ages did not necessarily always go hand in hand. These findings have implications for our understanding of gentry military society in the fifteenth century. Recent scholarship has cautioned against the assumption that the gentry turned their backs upon the martial vocation by the close of the Hundred Years War,[13] and such views are, to some extent, borne out by the subsequent war records of our Court of Chivalry families. A noteworthy minority of our deponents' grandsons and great-grandsons remained in arms long after the death of Henry V, both in English-occupied Normandy,[14] and later, in the campaigns and battles of the

---

[13] E.g., Mercer, *The Medieval Gentry*; D. Grummitt, *A Short History of the Wars of the Roses* (London, 2013), pp. 133–55.

[14] E.g., Identifiable descendants of Yorkshire and Norfolk deponents who participated in the conquest/defence of Normandy (1417–49) included: (Yorks.) John, Lord Neville; William Neville, Lord Fauconberg; Sir Robert Roos; Sir Brian Stapleton; Sir Halnath Mauleverer; Sir Thomas Rokeby; Sir Robert Plumpton; John and Robert Swillington; Sir John Everyngham. Thomas Everyngham the elder; Thomas Everyngham the younger; Sir Robert Conyers; William Constable; George Swillington; Sir John Salvin. E 101/5/1/2, m. 44; E 101/51/2, m. 9; C 76/101, m. 4; E 101/51/2, m. 3; E 101/51/2, m. 25; C 76/101, m. 10; E 101/51/2, m. 16. BNF, MS. Fr. 25767, no. 49; BL, Add. Ch. 1419; AN, K. 62/11/19; BNF, MS. Fr. 25769, no. 465; BNF, MS. Fr. 25772, no. 1036; E 101/53/33, m. 5; E 101/48/17; E 101/48/19; BNF, MS. Fr. 25767, no. 41; BNF, MS. Fr. 25770, no. 614; BNF, MS. Fr. 25771, no. 814; BNF, MS. Fr. 25771, no. 872; E 101/53/22, m. 6; BNF, MS. Fr. 25772, no. 963; AN, K. 64/1/32; E 191/53/22, m. 1; Curry, 'Military Organization in Lancastrian Normandy', App. VII, p. cxxvii; E 101/51/2, m. 3; C 76/105, m. 2; BNF, MS. Fr. 25771, no. 826; BNF, MS. Fr. 25771, no. 843; AN, K. 66/1/50; AN, K. 67/1/34; Pollard, *North-Eastern England*, p. 212. (Norf.) Thomas, fifth Lord Morley; Thomas, seventh Lord Scales; Sir Edmund Thorpe II; Sir William Oldhall; Sir Henry Inglose; Sir Robert Harling; Sir John Radcliffe; Sir William Chamberlain; Leonard Strange; Robert Shelton; Richard Calthorpe Thomas Hengrave; Brian Harsyk; John Fishlake; William Curson; Robert Brewes; John Lampete; John Geney; William Clifton; William Witchingham. C 76/101, m. 11; C 76/104, m. 18; E 101/51/2, m. 30; J. S. Roskell, 'Sir William Oldhall: Speaker in the Parliament of 1450–1', *Nottingham Medieval Studies*, 5 (1961), p. 92; William Worcester, *Itineraries*, ed. J. H. Harvey (Oxford, 1969), pp. 359–61; Caudrey,

Wars of the Roses.[15] In overall terms, however, it is undoubtedly true that a process of relative demilitarisation was taking place.[16] Indeed, following the English expulsion from France, our deponents' families would not again enjoy the opportunity of regularly bearing arms *en masse* in a national military enterprise until the large-scale French and Scottish expeditions of the young Henry VIII.[17] By the time the military reforms of the Tudor Age were complete, the structure, composition and character of England's regional military communities had altered substantially.[18] By contrast, the martial culture that had

---

'War and Society in Medieval Norfolk', pp. 267, 277–8, 280–1, 283–4; Bell et al., *The Soldier*, pp. 61, 91; E 101/51/2, m. 30; E 101/51/2, m. 14; E 101/48/17; E 101/51/2, m. 27; E 101/51/2, m. 18; BNF, MS. Fr. 25772, no. 954; AN, K. 64/1/31; ADSM, 100J/33/16; E 101/51/2 m. 29; ADSM, 100J/33/7; BNF, MS. Fr. 25772, no. 973; BNF, MS. Fr. 25766, no. 809; BNF, MS. Fr. 25775, no. 1406; BNF, MS. Fr. 25776, no. 1603; BNF, MS. Fr. 25777, no. 1650; BNF, NAF 8606, no. 96; BNF, MS. Fr. 25777, no. 1678; BNF, MS. Fr. 25769, no. 533; BNF, MS. Fr. 25769, no. 579; BNF, MS. Fr. 25772, no. 987; BNF, MS. Fr. 25773, no. 1141; AN, K 64/1/9.

[15] E.g., Sir John Stapleton, Avery Mauleverer and William Curwen died at St. Albans (1455); Sir Ralph Eure and William Plumpton at Towton (1461); Thomas, Lord Roos in the aftermath of Hexham (1464); John Conyers and another Mauleverer at Edgecote (1469); and William Conyers at Bosworth Field (1485). Sir John Middleton, Richard Conyers, Ralph Rokeby and Richard Scrope of Bolton received pardons after Ludlow (1459); Sir Richard Tempest, Sir Thomas Everyngham, Sir William Eure and Sir William Plumpton were attainted after Towton (1461); and, if the 'Ballad of Bosworth' is to be believed, Sir Marmaduke Constable, Sir William and Sir Richard Conyers, Sir Thomas Markenfield, Sir Thomas Mauleverer, Sir Robert Middleton, and the Scropes of Bolton and Masham, all fought on the losing side at Bosworth Field (1485). C. A. J. Armstrong, 'Politics and the Battle of St. Albans', *BIHR*, 33 (1960), pp. 48, 57, 71; R. A. Griffiths, 'Local Rivalries and National Politics: The Percies, the Nevilles and the Duke of Exeter, 1452-1455', *Speculum*, 43 (1968), p. 629; Pollard, *North-Eastern England*, pp. 293, 363; M. A. Hicks, *The Wars of the Roses* (New Haven, 2010), pp. 178–9; K. R. Dockray, 'The Yorkshire Rebellion of 1469', *The Ricardian*, 83 (1983), pp. 254-5; *CPR, 1452-61*, pp. 545, 549, 577, 581, 591–2; *Rot. Parl.*, V, pp. 476–83; *CPR, 1461–7*, pp. 39, 177; *Bishop Percy's Folio Manuscript*, ed. J. W. Hales and F. J. Furnivall (London, 1868), III, pp. 233–59. On the question of the 'Ballad of Bosworth's' reliability, see C. D. Ross, *Richard III* (London, 1981), pp. 235–7; C. Richmond, '1485 and All That, or what was going on at the Battle of Bosworth', in *Richard III: Lordship, Loyalty and Law*, ed. P. W. Hammond (Gloucester, 1986), pp. 172–3, 207–8.

[16] For an overview, see Bell et al., *The Soldier*, pp. 74–94, 125–38, 171–7.

[17] S. J. Gunn, *The English People at War in the Reign of Henry VIII* (Oxford, 2018).

[18] For a national overview, see S. J. Gunn, D. Grummitt and H. Cools, *War, State and Society in England and the Netherlands, 1477–1559* (Oxford, 2007).

provided these communities with a sense of cohesion and identity appears to have survived well into the sixteenth century.[19]

Let us bring matters to a close, then, with a pertinent anecdote, a century removed from *Grey v. Hastings*. The tale in question revolves around a rather bizarre confrontation which arose in the Norwich household of Sir Philip Calthorpe – a descendant of one of our Court of Chivalry deponents.[20] Calthorpe, one presumes, returned home one evening in the summer of 1514 to find his employees literally at each other's throats. The man responsible for the fracas was the newest member of Calthorpe's household, a Lancashire priest, named Adelston Attylsey. Attylsey had come across a book in Calthorpe's library that chronicled Thomas Howard, Earl of Surrey (and Duke of Norfolk's) recent battlefield victory over the Scots at Flodden.[21] The author – the king's printer, Richard Pynson – evidently sought to magnify Howard's role in the battle, and that of his companies from Norfolk and Suffolk, at the expense of the Cheshire and Lancashire contingents led by Sir Edward Stanley. Outraged at this slight upon his native shire, Attylsey defiantly scratched out the word 'honourable' in the title, and changed it to read, 'the horrorable Erle of Surrey'. When Calthorpe's East Anglian household servants discovered this, they fell into such heated argument with Attylsey over which region's soldiers had better distinguished themselves on the day of the battle that the matter ended up before the Mayor of Norwich. Had a man from foreign parts come to Norfolk at the time of *Lovel v. Morley* or *Grey v. Hastings* and defaced the Morley family's statuette in Reydon Church

---

[19] The reading patterns of the fifteenth-century gentry, for example, suggest a continued interest in military/chivalric themes. C. Nall, *Reading and War in Fifteenth-Century England: From Lydgate to Malory* (Cambridge, 2012). On the enduring significance of martial attitudes and chivalric culture in fifteenth-century Yorkshire, Cheshire and Norfolk, see Pollard, *North-Eastern England*, pp. 198–215; Bennett, *Community, Class and Careerism*, pp. 162–91; Caudrey, 'War and Society in Medieval Norfolk', pp. 210–42. Obviously, the intellectual and cultural currents of the day influenced gentry perceptions of the military-chivalric lifestyle. D. Wakelin, *Humanism, Reading and English Literature 1430–1530* (Oxford, 2007); Grummitt, *The Wars of the Roses*, pp. 133–81.

[20] NRO, Norwich Mayors' Court Book 1510–32, unfoliated. This author came upon the tale when writing his doctoral thesis: Caudrey, War and Society in Medieval Norfolk. The ensuing anecdote has previously been described in, Grummitt, 'Changing Perceptions of the Soldier', p. 189. Sir Philip's ancestor, Sir William Calthorpe, deposed on behalf of Sir Edward Hastings. *PCM*, I, p. 457.

[21] A manuscript copy of the book still survives. BL, Add. MS 29506.

or the Elsing Brass of Sir Hugh Hastings I, one imagines they would have elicited much the same reaction, motivated by an essentially similar sense of pride and admiration for Norfolk's local heroes. This surely encapsulates the enduring potency of regional chivalric culture, of the sort expressed before the Court of Chivalry.

Appendix 1

Deponents' Collective Military Records According to their Own Testimony

Campaign-Siege-Battle	Year	No. of Participants
Scotland (misc.)	1314–1384	46
Buironfosse	1339	6
Sluys	1340	22
Tournai	1340	15
Morlaix	1342	11
Auberoche	1345	1
Crécy-Calais	1346–7	98
Winchelsea	1350	32
Mauron	1352	2
Poitiers	1356	9
Rheims	1359–60	109
Najéra	1367	28
Gascony	1369	92
Northern France	1373	4
St. Malo	1378	8
Brittany	1380	13
Scotland	1385	135
Spain	1386–8	22
Scotland	1400	4
Wales	c. 1402–3	6
Crusade (misc.)	c.1340–c.1400	19

Appendix 2

Lancastrian Retainers: Scrope and Hastings Defendants

Name	Annuity/Year Granted	Defendant
Sir Richard Abberbury[1]	£50 (1381)	Scrope
Edmund Barry[2]	£10 (1396)	Hastings
John Bathe[3]	£4 11s. 6d. (1372)	Scrope
Edward Beauchamp[4]	£20 (1372)	Scrope
Sir Robert Berney[5]	£40 (1399)	Hastings
Sir Walter Blount[6]	£176 13s. 4d.	Scrope
John Bolton[7]	(?) (1382)	Scrope
Sir John Boseville[8]	£20 (1373)	Scrope
Thomas Bradley[9]	20 marks (1372)	Scrope
Sir John Bromwich[10]	(?) (1382)	Scrope
Robert Caunsfield[11]	£10 (1372)	Scrope
Geoffrey Chaucer[12]	£10 (1374)	Scrope
William Chetwynd[13]	£10 (1373)	Scrope
Hugh, Lord Dacre[14]	(?) (1372)	Scrope
Sir John Deincourt[15]	£10 (1382)	Scrope

[1] DL 43/15/3, m. 3; *JG Reg II*, no. *613*; *Scrope v. Grosvenor*, I, pp. 70–1. 166–7.
[2] NRO, NRS 15171, m. 2; *CPR, 1396–9*, p. 542; *PCM*, I, pp. 392–5.
[3] DL 29/341/5516, m. 2; *JG Reg I*, no. 389; *JG Reg II*, p. 10; *Scrope v. Grosvenor*, I, p. 58.
[4] *JG Reg I*, no. 815; DL 29/615/9838, m. 2; DL 29/738/12096, m. 8; *Scrope v. Grosvenor*, I, p. 57.
[5] DL 42/17, f. 26; Castor, *The King, the Crown, and the Duchy of Lancaster*, p. 63; *PCM*, I, pp. 474–6.
[6] *JG Reg I*, no. 1042; DL 29/738/12096, m. 6; *Scrope v. Grosvenor*, I, p. 58.
[7] *JG Reg II*, p. 13; *Scrope v. Grosvenor*, I, pp. 63–4.
[8] *JG Reg I*, no. 1221; *JG Reg II*, pp. 8, 277; *Scrope v. Grosvenor*, I, p. 107.
[9] *JG Reg I*, no. 796; *Scrope v. Grosvenor*, I, p. 68.
[10] *JG Reg II*, p. 9; DL 29/584/9239, m. 1; *Scrope v. Grosvenor*, I, pp. 205–6.
[11] *JG Reg I*, nos. 825, 827; *Scrope v. Grosvenor*, I, p. 53.
[12] *JG Reg I*, no. 608; *Scrope v. Grosvenor*, I, pp. 178–9.
[13] *JG Reg I*, no. 809; *Scrope v. Grosvenor*, I, pp. 57–8.
[14] *JG Reg I*, no, 934; *JG Reg II*, p. 7; *Scrope v. Grosvenor*, I, p. 179.
[15] DL 29/463/7539, m. 2; *JG Reg II*, p. 9; *Scrope v. Grosvenor*, I, p. 54.

APPENDIX 2: LANCASTRIAN RETAINERS

Thomas Driffield[16]	No Fee (1380)	Scrope
Sir Thomas Erpingham[17]	£40 (1380)	Scrope & Hastings
Sir Thomas Fichet[18]	£40 (1373)	Scrope
Robert Fitzrauf[19]	£20 (1373)	Scrope
John Geney[20]	(?) (1382)	Hastings
William Hall[21]	(?) (1382)	Scrope
Thomas Haselden[22]	£20 (1365)	Scrope
Sir Ralph Hastings[23]	40 marks (1361)	Scrope
Sir Richard Houghton[24]	40 marks (1382)	Scrope
Sir Ralph Ipres[25]	£25 (1372)	Scrope
Sir John Loudham I[26]	(?) (1382)	Scrope
Sir John Loudham II[27]	40 marks (1382)	Scrope
Sir William Lucy[28]	£20 (1381)	Scrope
Sir Andrew Lutterell[29]	40 marks (1365)	Scrope
Sir William Mauleverer[30]	10 marks (1376)	Scrope
Sir Thomas Morieux[31]	£100 (1381)	Scrope
John Mynyot[32]	£10 (1382)	Scrope
Adam Neusom[33]	10 marks (1372)	Scrope
Sir Robert Neville[34]	£20 (pre-1399)	Scrope

[16] *JG Reg II*, p. 11; *Scrope v. Grosvenor*, I, p. 59.
[17] DL 42/15, f. 22; *CCR, 1381–5*, p. 557; *Scrope v. Grosvenor*, I, p. 59; *PCM*, I, pp. 439–42.
[18] *JG Reg I*, no. 845; DL 29/738/12104, m. 2; *Scrope v. Grosvenor*, I, p. 62.
[19] *JG Reg I*, no. 844; NRO, NRS 3343, m. 1; *Scrope v. Grosvenor*, I, p. 52.
[20] *JG Reg II*, p. 12; *PCM*, I, p. 425.
[21] *JG Reg II*, p. 12; *Scrope v. Grosvenor*, I, p. 61.
[22] *JG Reg I*, no. 506; DL 42/1, f. 190; *Scrope v. Grosvenor*, I, pp. 52–3.
[23] Walker, *The Lancastrian Affinity*, p. 271; *Scrope v. Grosvenor*, I, pp. 103–4.
[24] DL 42/15, f. 7v; *JG Reg II*, pp. 9, 11; *Scrope v. Grosvenor*, I, pp. 234–5.
[25] *JG Reg I*, no. 808; DL 43/15/9, m. 3; *Scrope v. Grosvenor*, I, p. 52.
[26] *JG Reg II*, p. 7; *Scrope v. Grosvenor*, I, pp. 150–1.
[27] *JG Reg II*, p. 9; DL 29/728/11975, m. 2; *Scrope v. Grosvenor*, I, p. 53.
[28] DL 29/615/9840, m. 2; *Scrope v. Grosvenor*, I, p. 66.
[29] DL 29/262/4069, m. 2; DL 29/262/4070, m. 2; *Scrope v. Grosvenor*, I, p. 243.
[30] DL 28/3/1, m. 8; *JG Reg II*, p. 9; *Scrope v. Grosvenor*, I, p. 55.
[31] *JG Reg II*, no. 543; NRO, NRS 11072, m. 2; *Scrope v. Grosvenor*, I, p. 56.
[32] *JG Reg II*, p. 11; DL 29/262/4071, m. 3; *Scrope v. Grosvenor*, I, p. 70.
[33] *JG Reg I*, nos. 851, 916; *Scrope v. Grosvenor*, I, pp. 68–9.
[34] DL 42/15, f. 17v; *Scrope v. Grosvenor*, I, pp. 106–7.

Sir Thomas Percy[35]	£100 (1387)	Scrope
Sir Edmund Pierrepoint[36]	£40 (1368)	Scrope
Robert Pilkington[37]	20 marks (1372)	Scrope
Sir Robert Plumpton[38]	20 marks (pre-1399)	Scrope
William Plumstead[39]	10 marks (pre-1399)	Hastings
Sir John de la Pole[40]	(?) (1383)	Scrope
Stephen Pulham[41]	10 marks (1371)	Scrope
Sir Thomas Rempston[42]	40 marks (pre-1399)	Scrope
John Reymes[43]	£10 (1392)	Hastings
John Rither (?)[44]	£10 17s. 8d. (1361)	Scrope
Sir John Rocheford[45]	£20 (pre-1399)	Scrope
Peter Roos[46]	£10 (1382)	Scrope
Sir Robert Roos[47]	£20 (1366)	Scrope
Thomas, Lord Roos[48]	£40 (1370)	Scrope
Sir David Roucliffe[49]	£40 (1382)	Scrope
Sir Richard Roucliffe[50]	(?) (1379)	Scrope
Sir Thomas Routhe[51]	10 marks (1379)	Scrope
Sir John Saville[52]	£20 (1372)	Scrope
John Scargill[53]	(?) (1380)	Scrope
Sir John St. Clere[54]	(?) (1372)	Scrope

[35] *CPR, 1399–1401*, p. 110; *Scrope v. Grosvenor*, I, pp. 50–1.
[36] DL 29/262/4069, m. 2; *Scrope v. Grosvenor*, I, pp. 153–4.
[37] *JG Reg I*, no, 794; *JG Reg II*, p. 10; *Scrope v. Grosvenor*, I, p. 63.
[38] DL 42/16, f. 202v; *Scrope v. Grosvenor*, I, pp. 118–19.
[39] DL 42/15, f. 125v; *PCM*, I, pp. 478–80.
[40] DL 29/402/6448, m. 2; *Scrope v. Grosvenor*, I, p. 83.
[41] *JG Reg I*, no. 777; *Scrope v. Grosvenor*, I, pp. 55–6.
[42] DL 42/16, f. 183; *Scrope v. Grosvenor*, I, p. 60.
[43] NRO, NRS 3344, m. 2; *PCM*, I, pp. 444–5.
[44] *JG Reg II*, no. 999; *Scrope v. Grosvenor*, I, pp. 144–50.
[45] DL 29/262/4071, m. 3; *Scrope v. Grosvenor*, I, pp. 241–2.
[46] *JG Reg II*, no. 47; *Scrope v. Grosvenor*, I, p. 72.
[47] DL 29/262/4069, m. 2; *JG Reg I*, no. 1261; *Scrope v. Grosvenor*, I, p. 105.
[48] *JG Reg I*, no. 945; *JG Reg II*, p. 7; *Scrope v. Grosvenor*, I, pp. 132–34.
[49] *JG Reg II*, p. 9; DL 29/738/12096, m. 5; *Scrope v. Grosvenor*, I, p. 65.
[50] *JG Reg II*, p. 7; *Scrope v. Grosvenor*, I, pp. 143–4.
[51] DL 29/738/12096, m. 5; *Scrope v. Grosvenor*, I, p. 64.
[52] *JG Reg I*, no. 1037; *Scrope v. Grosvenor*, I, p. 112.
[53] *JG Reg II*, p. 10; *Scrope v. Grosvenor*, I, p. 65.
[54] *JG Reg I*, no. 487; *JG Reg II*, p. 9; *Scrope v. Grosvenor*, I, p. 54.

APPENDIX 2: LANCASTRIAN RETAINERS 193

Sir John Seton[55]	20 marks (1377)	Scrope
William Sudbury[56]	No Fee (1373)	Scrope
Sir Robert Swillington[57]	£70 (1362)	Scrope
Sir Gilbert Talbot[58]	20 marks (1383)	Scrope
Sir Walter Urswick[59]	£123 6s. 8d. (1361)	Scrope
Hugh Waterton[60]	40 marks (1377)	Scrope
Sir John White[61]	£20 (1382)	Scrope

[55] DL 29/212/3247, m. 2; *Scrope v. Grosvenor*, I, pp. 56–7.
[56] *JG Reg I*, no. 856; *JG Reg II*, p. 11; *Scrope v. Grosvenor*, I, pp. 66–7.
[57] *CPR, 1361–4*, p. 397; *Scrope v. Grosvenor*, I, pp. 203–4.
[58] DL 29/738/12104, m. 1; *Scrope v. Grosvenor*, I, pp. 174–5.
[59] *CPR, 1367–70*, p. 77; *Scrope v. Grosvenor*, I, p. 51.
[60] DL 28/3/1, m. 7; *Scrope v. Grosvenor*, I, p. 58.
[61] *JG Reg II*, p. 12; NRO, NRS 15171, m. 2; *Scrope v. Grosvenor*, I, p. 59.

Appendix 3

Plaintiffs' and Defendants' Biographies

Richard, Lord Scrope of Bolton, Yorkshire (*c.* 1327–1403)[62]

The third son of Sir Henry Scrope (*c.* 1268–1336), a royal justice from the North Riding of Yorkshire, and, alongside his brother, Sir Geoffrey of Masham (d. 1340), co-founder of the Scrope family's fortunes. Richard made his early reputation as a soldier, fighting at the successive battles of Crécy (Aug. 1346) and Neville's Cross (Oct. 1346), receiving a knighthood in the aftermath of the latter victory. By 1359, he had entered the employ of the young John of Gaunt and would continue forging his career in Lancastrian service over the next 20 years. Between 1365 and 1385, he campaigned beneath Gaunt's banner on five separate occasions. In 1371, having begun to take an active role in Yorkshire politics, he was raised to the peerage and appointed treasurer of England. Scrope's honourable conduct amidst the crisis of the Good Parliament in 1376 earned him widespread respect, and two years later he was called upon once again to serve the Crown as steward of the royal household during the minority of the young Richard II. Scrope's armorial controversy with Sir Robert Grosvenor (1385–90) coincided with his growing disaffection with the actions of his sovereign, resulting in his support of the Lords Appellant in 1387–8. By 1391, the year his victory over Grosvenor was confirmed, Scrope was in semi-retirement. His personal standing and long years of Lancastrian service saw him survive the Revolution of 1399, despite the execution of his eldest son, William. He died on 30 May 1403 and was buried in Easby Abbey.

Sir Robert Grosvenor of Hulme, Cheshire (*d.* 1396)[63]

Sir Robert Grosvenor was probably the least-connected of the six protagonists across our three surviving armorial cases and little is known

---

[62] *Scrope v. Grosvenor*, II, pp. 1–39; Vale, 'The Scropes'; B. Vale, 'Richard Scrope, first Baron Scrope of Bolton (*c.* 1327-1403), in *ODNB*: www.oxforddnb.com

[63] Stewart-Browne, 'The Scrope and Grosvenor Controversy', pp. 1–22; Morgan, 'Sir Robert Grosvenor', pp. 75–94; P. Morgan, 'Sir Robert Grosvenor (*d.* 1396)', in *ODNB*: www.oxforddnb.com.

of his career beyond those facts explicated in *Scrope v. Grosvenor*. He served as a young man on the Gascony campaign of 1369 in the retinue of Sir James Audley, participating in the capture of La-Roche-sur-Yon and the sack of Limoges. He mustered for Edward III's abortive French expedition in 1372 and was next in arms in Scotland in 1385, during which campaign his arms were challenged by Lord Scrope. On the domestic scene, Grosvenor's landed wealth was located entirely in east Cheshire. At the time of his death, he possessed two manors, at Hulme and Allostock, held from his respective Court of Chivalry witnesses, John Holford and the Abbot of Vale Royal. He was in every sense a man of Cheshire, whose calculated wealth 'would have placed him at the lower margin of the second rank of gentle families'. He stood, in other words, not at the very apex of Cheshire gentry society, but was of sufficiently high status that he was an accepted member of the second tier of the shire's élite. The fact that he acted as a commissioner of the peace and twice held the office of sheriff underscores his standing in the region. Moreover, that a set of myths could have developed, tracing his family's lineage back to Sir Gilbert Grosvenor, kinsman of the eleventh-century Earl Hugh of Chester, reinforces just how distinguished his family had become in their native locality by the late fourteenth century. Sir Robert Grosvenor died in 1396. The Grosvenors of Hulme collapsed in the direct male line in 1465, upon the death of Sir Robert's eponymous grandson, who left only six daughters, amongst whom the Grosvenor lands were dispersed.

John, Lord Lovel of Oxfordshire and Wiltshire (*c.* 1342–1408)[64]

One of the wealthiest (and most litigious) barons of his day, John, Lord Lovel forged a stellar career for himself in war and politics over a period of more than 40 years. After gaining his initial military experience in Brittany in 1364, he accompanied Lionel, Duke of Clarence, to Milan in 1368, and, probably in 1371, crusaded on his own account in Prussia and the eastern Mediterranean. Shortly thereafter, Lovel acquired the good graces of Edmund Mortimer, Earl of March, campaigning in Mortimer's retinue in Brittany in 1375 and Ireland in 1380 and receiving an array of gifts and grants for his

---

[64] *Scrope v. Grosvenor*, I, pp. 190–1; II, pp. 450–2; *CP*, VIII, pp. 219–21; S. K. Walker, 'John, Lovell [Lovel], fifth Baron Lovell (*c.* 1342–1408)', in *ODNB*: www.oxforddnb.com.

services. Although this avenue of patronage was closed by Mortimer's untimely death in 1381, it made little difference to Lovel, who had already begun developing a new career for himself in the service of the royal household. He was appointed 'master of the king's hounds' in 1377 and was a 'king's knight' by 1383. Despite his close Ricardian ties, he successfully navigated the appellant crisis and re-emerged in 1389 as an active member of the royal council, a trier of parliamentary petitions, a witness to royal charters, and a participant on both of the royally-led Irish expeditions of the 1390s. He was formally retained by King Richard in 1395, yet weathered his master's fall with such deftness of political touch that by January 1400 he was appointed commander of Corfe Castle in Dorset at the behest of Henry IV, who declared his intention that the post should be held by a trustworthy subject. Lovel subsequently reinforced his newly-acquired Lancastrian credentials, accompanying King Henry to Scotland in 1400 and Wales in 1405, all the while remaining an incredibly active royal councilor, attending more council meetings than any other peer, until his retirement in 1406. He died two years later, leaving substantial estates across 13 counties, and a significant political and military legacy.

Thomas, Lord Morley of Hingham, Norfolk (*d.* 1416)[65]

Thomas, Lord Morley was heir to one of Norfolk's three dominant baronial families, his high standing underscored by his regular appointment as a commissioner of the peace and defender of the coast. The family's exalted status rested upon the martial exploits of Thomas' grandfather, Robert, during the wars of Edward III (upon which Thomas' deponents focused extensively in *Lovel v. Morley*) and it was as a soldier that Thomas, too, would make his own mark, albeit in a less militarily successful era. Having first borne arms in Brittany in 1375, it would be alongside King Edward's youngest son, Thomas of Woodstock, Duke of Gloucester, that Morley would find friendship and career advancement. He and Gloucester evidently became close companions, exchanging gifts, assisting each other in their private affairs, and campaigning together on a number of occasions. Morley accompanied Gloucester on the latter's Brittany expedition in 1380

---

[65] *PCM*, I, pp. 435–9; *CP*, IX, pp. 216–17; Richmond, 'Thomas Lord Morley', pp. 1–12; Morgan, 'Going to the Wars', pp. 289–92; Goodman, *The Loyal Conspiracy*, pp. 101, 124, 133.

and later joined him on his abandoned crusade to Prussia in 1391. Morley may, indeed, have fought in Gloucester's retinue amidst the appellant crisis at the battle of Radcot Bridge in 1387. At any rate, Morley survived Gloucester's execution a decade later and, after the Revolution of 1399, probably in equal measure to honour Gloucester's memory and to curry favour with the new regime, Morley accused the Earl of Salisbury of treason in the Parliament of 1399, claiming he had betrayed Gloucester's counsel to Richard II. A judicial duel was only avoided by Salisbury's own subsequent death during the Revolt of the Earls. Morley, though, had proven himself to Henry IV, and remained committed to the new dynasty, ultimately attaining membership of the Order of the Garter in 1411. And it was, appropriately enough, as a soldier that Morley lost his life, passing away from dysentery at Calais in July 1416, shortly after playing a much-acclaimed role in the relief of Harfleur. Lord Thomas was succeeded by his eponymous grandson, who would himself actively participate in the campaigns of the 1420s.

Reginald, Lord Grey of Ruthin (*c*. 1362–1440)[66]

One of the longest-lived magnates of his generation, Reginald, Lord Grey possessed extensive estates centered in Bedfordshire and Buckinghamshire, whilst enjoying a high degree of independent authority as Lord of Ruthin, the great marcher lordship in north Wales. His subsequent accession to the bulk of the estates of his recently extinct cousins, the Hastings earls of Pembroke, made him one of the greatest landowners in the realm, with further property in East Anglia, Kent, Leicester and Lincoln. Grey served successive royal governments in Parliament over a long and distinguished administrative career, whilst simultaneously becoming the dominant force in his resident shire of Bedfordshire, where he launched an aggressive retaining policy and developed a powerful network of clients. After the Revolution of 1399, Grey became a staunch ally of the new Lancastrian dynasty, sitting on the royal council and supporting his sovereign's policies in Parliament. Although he had borne arms occasionally, the outbreak of the Glyn Dwr Revolt in September 1400 thrust Grey into the military spotlight. Glyn Dwr attacked Ruthin two days after declaring himself Prince of Wales and by 1402 Grey was preparing an army to suppress the rebellion. Yet,

[66] Jack, 'Entail and Descent', pp. 1–19; Jack, 'The Greys of Ruthin'; *CP*, IV, pp. 105–6; *PCM*, 2 vols.; *Scrope v. Grosvenor*, I, pp. 207–8.

he was soon captured and forced to pay a hefty ransom, soon returning to his strong suit in administration. Under Henry V, he played no role in his sovereign's wars, instead serving as a prominent member of the ruling council in England. By Henry's death, Grey entered into a lengthy retirement, spending the remaining 18 years of his life pursuing his private interests. He died in 1440 and was succeeded by his equally long-lived grandson, Edmund, who consolidated his family's high standing, ultimately being elevated to the Earldom of Kent in 1465.

Sir Edward Hastings of Elsing, Norfolk (*d.* 1438)[67]

The Hastings of Elsing were a Norfolk-based cadet branch of the Hastings earls of Pembroke. Sir Edward Hastings was heir to three consecutive generations of Lancastrian bannerets. His great-grandfather, Sir Hugh Hastings I, had been a leading commander during the first phase of the Hundred Years War; his grandfather, Sir Hugh II, had campaigned extensively throughout the 1350s and 1360s; and his father, Sir Hugh III, had borne arms beneath the Lancastrian banner five times during the 1370s and 1380s. All three Sir Hugh Hastings had died on campaign, leaving Sir Edward, a younger son, who only inherited the family's estates upon the death of his elder brother, with a significant military legacy to maintain. He enjoyed an early measure of success, becoming a 'king's knight' to Henry IV and accompanying his sovereign to Scotland in 1400. It was there, however, that his arms were challenged by his cousin, Reginald, Lord Grey of Ruthin. Whilst the other five protagonists across *Scrope v. Grosvenor*, *Lovel v. Morley* and *Grey v. Hastings* were able to move on with their lives – win or lose – in the wake of the judges' final verdict, Hastings appeared never to recover emotionally from his loss of the Pembroke arms, which he remained convinced were rightfully his, as confirmed by his father having borne them in full, with the Countess of Pembroke's permission, when the last Earl was a child. Hastings consequently refused to pay the £987 he owed Grey in costs and damages, and, after an unsuccessful bid to re-open the case, found himself in debtors' prison in 1416, where he languished, in increasingly ill health, for the next 20 years. Only in 1436 was the dispute finally settled and Hastings released. He died two years later, emotionally rent and financially ruined.

[67] Jack, 'Entail and Descent', pp. 1–19; Caudrey, 'War and Society in Medieval Norfolk', pp. 267–8.

Bibliography

Manuscript Sources

Archives départementales de la Seine Maritime, Rouen
100J

Archives Nationales, Paris
Série K

Bibliothéque Nationale, Paris
Manuscrits français
Nouvelles acquisitions françaises

Bury St. Edmunds, Suffolk Record Office
MS IC/500/2/1: Registered Probate Wills

Chester, Eaton Hall
Grosvenor Estate Archives

Kew, The National Archives (TNA)
C 47 Chancery: Chancery Miscellanea
C 61 Chancery: Gascon Rolls
C 71 Chancery: Scotch Rolls
C 76 Chancery: Treaty Rolls
C 81 Chancery: Warrants
C 136 Chancery: Inquisitions Post Mortem, Series 1, Richard II
C 139 Chancery: Inquisitions Post Mortem, Series 1, Henry VI
CP 25 Chancery: Court of Common Pleas, Feet of Fines
DL 29 Duchy of Lancaster: Ministers' Accounts
DL 37 Duchy of Lancaster: Chancery Rolls
DL 42 Duchy of Lancaster: Miscellaneous Books
DL 43 Duchy of Lancaster: Rentals and Surveys
E 101 Exchequer: King's Remembrancer: Various Accounts
E 210 Exchequer: Ancient Deeds, Series D
E 326 Exchequer: Ancient Deeds, Series B
JUST 1 Justices: Justices in Eyre, of Assize, of Oyer and Terminer, and of the Peace
PRO 30/26: Documents Acquired by Gift, Deposit or Purchase: Miscellaneous

London, British Library
Additional Charters
Additional Manuscripts
Cotton Manuscripts
Harley Manuscripts
Lansdowne Manuscripts

London, College of Arms
Philipot Manuscripts
Processus in Curia Marescalli, 2 vols.

London, Lambeth Palace Library
Reg. Sudbury

Norwich, Norfolk Record Office
Le Strange: Le Strange MSS
NCC: Norwich Consistory Court, Register of Wills
Norwich Mayors' Court Book 1510–32
NRS: Norfolk Record Society MSS
Phi: Phillips MSS

Oxford, Magdalen College
Guton Deeds
Hickling MSS

Printed Primary Sources

The Anonimalle Chronicle 1333 to 1381, ed. V. H. Galbraith (Manchester, 1927).
Bishop Percy's Folio Manuscript, ed. J. W. Hales and F. J. Furnivall (London, 1868).
Calendar of Ancient Deeds, 6 vols. (London, 1890–1915).
Calendar of Close Rolls, 61 vols. (London, 1892–1963).
Calendar of Documents Relating to Scotland, 5 vols. (London, 1826–1911).
Calendar of the Fine Rolls, 22 vols. (London, 1911–62).
Calendar of Inquisitions Post Mortem, Vols. 7–26 (London, 1909–2009).
Calendar of Patent Rolls, 55 vols. (London, 1891–1916).
Chandos Herald, *The Life of the Black Prince*, ed. and trans. E. Lodge and M. K. Pope (Oxford, 1910).
Chandos Herald, *La Vie du Prince Noir*, ed. D. B. Tyson (Tübingen, 1975).
Charny, Geoffroi de, *The Book of Chivalry of Geoffroi de Charny: Text, Context, and Translation*, ed. R. W. Kaeuper and E. Kennedy (Philadelphia, 1996).

Chaucer, Geoffrey, *The Canterbury Tales*, ed. and trans. D. Wright (Oxford, 1998).

Chronicon Henrici Knighton, ed. J. R. Lumby, 2 vols. (RS, London, 1895).

The Controversy between Sir Richard Scrope and Sir Robert Grosvenor in the Court of Chivalry c.1385–1390, ed. Sir N. H. Nicolas, 2 vols. (London, 1832).

Crecy and Calais from the Original Records in the Public Record Office, ed. G. Wrottesley (London, 1898).

Early Lincoln Wills, ed. A. Gibbons (Lincoln, 1888).

Feet of Fines for Essex: Volume 3: A.D. 1327–A.D. 1422, ed. R. C. Fowler and S. C. Ratcliff (Essex Archaeological Society, 1929–49).

Foedera, Conventiones etc., ed. T. Rymer, 20 vols. (London, 1704–35).

Froissart, Jean, *Sir John Froissart's Chronicles of England, France, Spain, and the Adjoining Countries, from the Latter Part of the Reign of Edward II to the Coronation of Henry IV*, ed. and trans. T. Johnes, 5 vols. (London, 1803–10).

Froissart, Jean, *Oeuvres de Froissart publieés avec les variants des divers manuscrits par M. le Baron Kervyn de Lettenhove*, 25 vols. (Brussels, 1867–77).

Froissart, Jean, *Chroniques*, ed. S. Luce et al., 15 vols. (Paris, 1869–1975).

Gower, John, *The Major Latin Works of John Gower*, ed. E. W. Stockton (Seattle, 1962).

Historic Manuscripts Commission. Report on the Manuscripts of the late Reginald Rawdon Hastings, ed. F. Bickley, et al., 4 vols. (London, 1928–47).

John of Gaunt's Register 1372–1376, ed. S. Armitage-Smith (London, CS, 3rd Series, xx–xxi, 1911).

John of Gaunt's Register 1379–1383, ed. E. C. Lodge and R. Somerville, 2 vols. (London, CS, 3rd Series, lvi–lvii, 1937).

Le Bel, Jean, *Chronique*, ed. J. Viard and E. Deprez, 2 vols. (Paris, 1904–5).

Le Bel, Jean, *The True Chronicles of Jean Le Bel, 1290–1360*, trans. N. Bryant (Woodbridge, 2011).

L'Histoire de Guillaume le Maréchal, ed. P. Meyers, 2 vols. (Paris, 1891).

List of Sheriffs for England and Wales (London, PRO Lists and Indexes, 9, 1898).

'Morley v. Montagu', *Camden Miscellany XXXIV*, ed. M. Warner and M. H. Keen (CS, 5th Series, 10, 1997).

The Online Froissart, ed. P. Ainsworth and G. Croenen (Sheffield, 2013).

Parliamentary Writs, ed. F. Palgrave, 2 vols. (London, 1827–34).

Paston Letters and Papers of the Fifteenth Century, ed. N. Davis, 2 vols. (Oxford, 1971–6).

Plumpton Correspondence: A Series of Letters, Chiefly Domestick, Written in the Reigns of Edward IV, Richard III, Henry VII and Henry VIII, ed. T. Stapleton (CS, London, 1839).

Political Poems and Songs Relating to English History Composed during the Period from the Accession of Edward III to that of Richard II, ed. T. Wright, 2 vols. (London, 1859).

Proceedings and Ordinances of the Privy Council of England, 1386–1542, ed. Sir N. H. Nicolas, 7 vols. (London, 1834–7).
Register of Edward, the Black Prince, ed. M. C. B. Dawes, 4 vols. (London, 1929–33).
The Register of Henry Chichele, Archbishop of Canterbury, 1414–1443, ed. E. F. Jacob, 4 vols. (Oxford, Canterbury and York Society, 1938–47).
Reg. Wykeham: Wykeham Register, ed. T. F. Kirby, 2 vols. (Hampshire Record Society, 1896–9).
The Roll of Caerlaverock, ed. and trans. T. Wright (RS, London, 1864).
Rotuli Parliamentorum, ed. J. Strachey et al., 7 vols. (RS, London, 1810–28).
Statutes of the Realm, ed. A. Luders, T. E. Tomlins et al., 11 vols. (RS, London, 1810–28).
Testamenta Vetusta, ed. Sir N. H. Nicolas, 2 vols. (London, 1826).
Treaty Rolls Preserved in the Public Record Office. Volume 2: 1337–39, ed. J. Ferguson (London, 1972).
Walsingham, Thomas, *Historia Anglicana*, ed. H. T. Riley (RS, London, 1863–4).
Walsingham, Thomas, *The Chronica Maiora of Thomas Walsingham*, trans. D. Preest and ed. J. G. Clark (Woodbridge, 2005).
Worcester, William, *Itineraries*, ed. J. H. Harvey (Oxford, 1969).
The Yorkshire Archaeological Society Records Series, ed. M. J. Stanley-Price (York, 1955).

Secondary Texts

Acheson, E., *A Gentry Community: Leicestershire in the Fifteenth Century, c.1422–c.1485* (Cambridge, 1992).
Ailes, A., 'The Knight, Heraldry and Armour: The Role of Recognition and the Origins of Heraldry', in *Medieval Knighthood IV: Papers from the Fifth Strawberry Hill Conference, 1990*, ed. C. Harper-Bill and R. Harvey (Woodbridge, 1992), pp. 1–21.
Alban, J. R., 'English Coastal Defence: Some Fourteenth-Century Modifications within the System', in *Patronage, the Crown and the Provinces in Later Medieval England*, ed. R. A. Griffiths (Gloucester, 1981), pp. 57–78.
Armstrong, C. A. J., 'Politics and the Battle of St. Albans', *BIHR*, 33 (1960), pp. 1–72.
Ayton, A., 'William de Thweyt, Esquire: Deputy Constable of Corfe Castle in the 1340s', *Somerset and Dorset Notes and Queries*, 32 (1989), pp. 731–8.
_____ 'War and the English Gentry under Edward III', *History Today*, 42 (1992), pp. 34–40.
_____ *Knights and Warhorses. Military Service and the English Aristocracy under Edward III* (Woodbridge, 1994).
_____ 'Edward III and the English Aristocracy at the Beginning of the Hundred Years War', in *Armies, Chivalry and Warfare in Medieval Britain and France. Proceedings of the 1995 Harlaxton Symposium*, ed. M. Strickland (Stamford, 1998), pp. 173–206.

_____ 'Knights, Esquires and Military Service: The Evidence of the Armorial Cases before the Court of Chivalry', in *The Medieval Military Revolution: State, Society and Military Change in Medieval and Early Modern Europe*, ed. A. Ayton and J. L. Price (London, 1998), pp. 81–104.

_____ 'English Armies in the Fourteenth Century', in *The Wars of Edward III: Sources and Interpretations*, ed. C. J. Rogers (Woodbridge, 1999), pp. 303–19.

_____ 'Sir Thomas Ughtred and the Edwardian Military Revolution', in *The Age of Edward III*, ed. J. S. Bothwell (York, 2001), pp. 107–32.

_____ 'Robert, second Lord Morley (c. 1295–1360)', in *Oxford Dictionary of National Biography: From the Earliest Time to the Year 2000*, ed. H. C. G. Matthews and B. H. Harrison, 61 vols. (Oxford, 2004), XXXIX, pp. 236–7.

_____ 'The Crécy Campaign', in *The Battle of Crécy, 1346*, ed. A. Ayton and P. Preston (Woodbridge, 2005), pp. 35–107.

_____ 'The English Army at Crécy', in *The Battle of Crécy, 1346*, ed. A. Ayton and P. Preston (Woodbridge, 2005), pp. 159–251.

_____ 'Armies and Military Communities in Fourteenth-Century England', in *Soldiers, Nobles and Gentlemen: Essays in Honour of Maurice Keen*, ed. P. Coss and C. Tyerman (Woodbridge, 2009), pp. 215–39.

_____ 'Military Service and the Dynamics of Recruitment in Fourteenth-Century England', in *The Soldier Experience in the Fourteenth Century*, ed. A. R. Bell and A. Curry with A. Chapman, A. King and D. Simpkin (Woodbridge, 2011), pp. 9–59.

_____ 'The Military Careerist in Fourteenth-Century England', *Journal of Medieval History*, 43 (2017), pp. 4–23.

_____ 'From Brittany to the Black Sea: Nicholas Sabraham and English Military Experience in the Fourteenth Century', in *Courts of Chivalry and Admiralty in Late Medieval Europe*, ed. A. Musson and N. Ramsay (Woodbridge, 2018), pp. 95–120.

Barber, R., *The Black Prince* (London, 1978).

_____ *The Life and Campaigns of the Black Prince from Contemporary Letters, Diaries and Chronicles, including Chandos Herald's Life of the Black Prince* (Woodbridge, 1979).

_____ *Edward III and the Triumph of England: The Battle of Crécy and the Company of the Garter* (London, 2013).

_____ 'Heralds and the Court of Chivalry: From Collective Memory to Formal Institutions', in *Courts of Chivalry and Admiralty in Late Medieval Europe*, ed. A. Musson and N. Ramsay (Woodbridge, 2018), pp. 15–27.

Bean, J. M. W., *From Lord to Patron. Lordship in Medieval England* (Manchester, 1989).

Beanlands, C., 'The Swillingtons of Swillington', Thoresby Society, *Miscellania*, 15 (1909), pp. 185–211.

Bell, A. R., *War and the Soldier in the Fourteenth Century* (Woodbridge, 2004).

_____ 'The Fourteenth-Century Soldier: More Chaucer's Knight or Medieval Career Soldier?', in *Mercenaries and Paid Men. The Mercenary Identity in the Middle Ages*, ed. J. France (Leiden, 2008), pp. 301–15.

_____ 'The Soldier "hadde he ridden no man ferre"', in *The Soldier Experience in the Fourteenth Century*, ed. A. R. Bell and A. Curry with A. Chapman, A. King and D. Simpkin (Woodbridge, 2011), pp. 209–18.

Bell, A. R., A. Curry, A. King and D. Simpkin, *The Soldier in Later Medieval England* (Oxford, 2013).

Bellamy, J. G., 'Sir John de Annesley and the Chandos Inheritance', *Nottingham Medieval Studies*, 10 (1966), pp. 94–105.

Bennett, M. J., *Community, Class and Careerism: Cheshire and Lancashire Society in the Age of Sir Gawain and the Green Knight* (Cambridge, 1983).

_____ *Richard II and the Revolution of 1399* (Gloucester, 1999).

Biggs, D., *Three Armies in Britain. The Irish Campaign of Richard II and the Usurpation of Henry IV, 1397–1399* (Leiden, 2006).

Blomefield, F., *An Essay Towards a Topographical History of the County of Norfolk*, 11 vols. (London, 1805–10).

Bothwell, J. S., 'Edward III and the 'New Nobility': Largesse and Limitation in Fourteenth-Century England', *EHR*, 112 (1997), pp. 1111–40.

Bridge, J. C., 'Two Cheshire Soldiers of Fortune: Sir Hugh Calveley and Sir Robert Knolles', *JCAS*, 14 (1908), pp. 112–231.

Caffero, W., *John Hawkwood: An English Mercenary in Fourteenth-Century Italy* (Baltimore, 2006).

Carpenter, C., *Locality and Polity: A Study of Warwickshire Landed Society, 1401–1499* (Cambridge, 1992).

_____ 'Gentry and Community in Medieval England', *Journal of British Studies*, 33 (1994), pp. 340–80.

Carruthers, M. J., *The Book of Memory: A Study of Memory in Medieval Culture* (Cambridge, 1990).

Castor, H., *The King, the Crown, and the Duchy of Lancaster: Public Authority and Private Power, 1399–1461* (Oxford, 2000).

Caudrey, P. J., 'War, Chivalry and Regional Society: East Anglia's Warrior Gentry Before the Court of Chivalry', in *Fourteenth Century England VIII*, ed. J. S. Hamilton (Woodbridge, 2014), pp. 119–45.

Chapman, A., *Welsh Soldiers in the Later Middle Ages 1282–1422* (Woodbridge, 2015).

Cherry, M., 'The Courtenay Earls of Devon: Formation and Disintegration of a Late Medieval Aristocratic Affinity', *Southern History*, 1 (1979), pp. 71–99.

Clanchy, M. T., *From Memory to Written Record: England 1066–1307*, second edition (Oxford, 1993).

Cockayne, G. E., *The Complete Peerage of England, Scotland, Ireland, Great Britain and the United Kingdom*, ed. H. V. Gibbs et al., 13 vols. (London, 1910–59).

Collins, H. E. L., *The Order of the Garter 1348–1461: Chivalry and Politics in Late Medieval England* (Oxford, 2000).

_____ 'Sir John Fastolf, John Lord Talbot and the Dispute over Patay: Ambition and Chivalry in the Fifteenth Century', in *War and Society in Medieval and Early Modern Britain*, ed. D. Dunn (Liverpool, 2000), pp. 114–40.

Cooper, S., *Sir John Hawkwood: Chivalry and the Art of War* (Barnsley, 2008).

Crouch, D., *William Marshal: Court, Career and Chivalry in the Angevin Empire 1147–1219* (Harlow, 1990).

_____ *The Image of Aristocracy in Britain 1000–1300* (London, 1992).

Curry, A., 'English Armies in the Fifteenth Century', in *Arms, Armies and Fortifications in the Hundred Years War*, ed. A. Curry and M. Hughes (Woodbridge, 1994), pp. 39–68.

_____ 'Sir Thomas Erpingham', in *Agincourt 1415: Henry V, Sir Thomas Erpingham and the Triumph of the English Archers*, ed. A. Curry (Gloucester, 2000), pp. 53–77.

_____ *Agincourt: A New History* (Gloucester, 2005).

_____ 'The Military Ordinances of Henry V: Texts and Contexts', in *War, Government and Aristocracy in the British Isles, c. 1150–1500. Essays in Honour of Michael Prestwich*, ed. C. Given-Wilson, A. Kettle and L. Scales (Woodbridge, 2008), pp. 214–49.

Curry, A., A. R. Bell, A. King and D. Simpkin, 'New Regime, New Army? Henry IV's Scottish Expedition of 1400', *EHR*, 125 (2010), pp. 1382–413.

Davies, R. R., *The Revolt of Owain Glyn Dwr* (Oxford, 1995).

Dennison L., and N. Rogers, 'The Elsing Brass and its East Anglian Connections', in *Fourteenth Century England I*, ed. N. Saul (Woodbridge, 2000), pp. 167–93.

Dockray, K. R., 'The Yorkshire Rebellion of 1469', *The Ricardian*, 83 (1983), pp. 246–57.

Ellis, A. S., 'On the Arms of de Aton', *Yorkshire Archaeological Journal*, 12 (1893), pp. 263–6.

Farrer. W., and J. Brownhill, *The Victoria History of the County of Lancaster*, 8 vols. (London, 1906–14).

Fowler, K., *Medieval Mercenaries I: The Great Companies* (Oxford, 2001).

Given-Wilson, C., *The Royal Household and the King's Affinity: Service, Politics and Finance in England, 1360–1413* (New Haven, 1986).

_____ *Henry IV* (New Haven, 2016).

Goodman, A., *The Loyal Conspiracy* (London, 1971).

_____ 'The Military Subcontracts of Sir Hugh Hastings, 1380', *EHR*, 95 (1980), pp. 114–20.

_____ *John of Gaunt: The Exercise of Princely Power in Fourteenth-Century Europe* (London, 1992).

_____ 'Introduction', in *War and Border Societies in the Middle Ages*, ed. A. Goodman and J. A. Tuck (London, 1992), pp. 1–29.

Gorski, R., *The Fourteenth-Century Sheriff: English Local Administration in the Late Middle Ages* (Woodbridge, 2003).
Green, D. S., 'Edward the Black Prince and East Anglia: An Unlikely Association?', in *Fourteenth Century England III*, ed. W. M. Ormrod (Woodbridge, 2004), pp. 83–98.
Griffiths, R. A., 'Local Rivalries and National Politics: The Percies, the Nevilles and the Duke of Exeter, 1452–1455', *Speculum*, 43 (1968), pp. 589–632.
Grummitt, D., *The Calais Garrison: War and Military Service in England, 1436–1558* (Woodbridge, 2008).
_____ 'Changing Perceptions of the Soldier in Late Medieval England', in *The Fifteenth Century X: Parliament, Personalities and Power. Papers Presented to Linda S. Clark*, ed. H. Kleineke (Woodbridge, 2011), pp. 189–202.
_____ *A Short History of the Wars of the Roses* (London, 2013).
Guard, T., *Chivalry, Kingship and Crusade: The English Experience in the Fourteenth Century* (Woodbridge, 2013).
Gunn, S. J., *The English People at War in the Reign of Henry VIII* (Oxford, 2018).
Gunn, S. J., D. Grummitt and H. Cools, *War, State and Society in England and the Netherlands, 1477–1559* (Oxford, 2007).
Hablot, L., 'French Armorial Disputes and Controls', in *Courts of Chivalry and Admiralty in Late Medieval Europe*, ed. A. Musson and N. Ramsay (Woodbridge, 2018), pp. 29–45.
Harriss, G. L., 'Introduction', in *England in the Fifteenth Century: Collected Essays of K. B. McFarlane* (London, 1981), pp. ix–xxvii.
_____ *Shaping the Nation: England 1360–1461* (Oxford, 2005).
Heebøll-Holm, K., 'The Origins and Jurisdiction of the English Court of Admiralty in the Fourteenth Century', in *Courts of Chivalry and Admiralty in Late Medieval Europe*, ed. A. Musson and N. Ramsay (Woodbridge, 2018), pp. 149–70.
Hewitt, H. J., *The Black Prince's Expedition, 1355–1357* (Manchester, 1958).
Hicks, M. A., *Bastard Feudalism* (London, 1995).
_____ *The Wars of the Roses* (New Haven, 2010).
Holmes, G. A., *The Estates of the Higher Nobility in Fourteenth-Century England* (Cambridge, 1957).
Horrox, R. E., 'Service', in *Fifteenth-Century Attitudes: Perceptions of Society in Late Medieval England*, ed. R. Horrox (Cambridge, 1994), pp. 61–78.
Hughes, J., 'Stephen Scrope and the Circle of Sir John Fastolf: Moral and Intellectual Outlooks', in *Medieval Knighthood IV: Papers from the fifth Strawberry Hill Conference, 1990*, ed. C. Harper-Hill and R. Harvey (Woodbridge, 1992), pp. 109–46.
Jack, R. I., 'Entail and Descent: The Hastings Inheritance, 1370–1436', *BIHR*, 38 (1965), pp. 1–19.

Jones, M. C., 'Roches contre Hawley: la cour anglaise de chevalerie et un cas de piraterie à Brest 1386–1402', *Mémoires de la Société d'Histoire et d'Archéologie de Bretagne*, 64 (1987), pp. 53–64.
Jones, R. W., *Bloodied Banners: Martial Display on the Medieval Battlefield* (Woodbridge, 2010).
Keegan, J., *The Face of Battle* (London, 1976).
Keen, M. H., *The Laws of War in the Late Middle Ages* (London, 1965).
_____ 'Chivalrous Culture in Fourteenth-Century England', *Historical Studies*, 10 (1976), pp. 1–22.
_____ *Chivalry* (London, 1984).
_____ 'Richard II's Ordinances of War of 1385', in *Rulers and Ruled in Late Medieval England. Essays Presented to Gerald Harriss*, ed. R. E. Archer and S. K. Walker (London, 1995), pp. 33–48.
_____ 'Chaucer's Knight, the English Aristocracy and the Crusade', in *Nobles, Knights and Men-At-Arms*, ed. M. H. Keen (London, 1996), pp. 101–19.
_____ 'The Jurisdiction and Origins of the Constable's Court', in *Nobles, Knights and Men-At-Arms*, ed. M. H. Keen (London, 1996), pp. 135–48.
_____ 'Treason Trials under the Law of Arms', in *Nobles, Knights and Men-At-Arms*, ed. M. H. Keen (London, 1996), pp. 149–66.
_____ 'English Military Experience and the Court of Chivalry: The Case of Grey v. Hastings', in *Nobles, Knights and Men-At-Arms in the Middle Ages*, ed. M. H. Keen (London, 1996), pp. 167–85.
_____ *Origins of the English Gentleman: Heraldry, Chivalry and Gentility in Medieval England, c.1300–c.1500* (Gloucester, 2002).
King, A., 'Best of Enemies: Were the Fourteenth-Century Anglo-Scottish Marches a "Frontier Society"?', in *England and Scotland in the Fourteenth Century: New Perspectives*, ed. A. King and M. Penman (Woodbridge, 2007), pp. 116–35.
_____ 'The English Gentry and Military Service, 1300–1450', *History Compass*, 12 (2014), pp. 759–69.
King, A. and D. Simpkin (ed.), *England and Scotland at War, c.1296–c.1513* (Leiden, 2012).
Lambert, C. L., *Shipping the Medieval Military: English Maritime Logistics in the Fourteenth Century* (Woodbridge, 2011).
Lee-Warner, J., 'The Stapeltons of Ingham', *Norfolk Archaeology*, 8 (1879), pp. 183–223.
Le Strange, H., *Norfolk Official Lists* (Norwich, 1890).
Luxford, J., 'Art, Objects and Ideas in the Records of the Medieval Court of Chivalry', in *Courts of Chivalry and Admiralty in Late Medieval Europe*, ed. A. Musson and N. Ramsay (Woodbridge, 2018), pp. 47–74.
Maddern, P. C., '"Best Trusted Friends": Concepts and Practices of Friendship among Fifteenth-Century Norfolk Gentry', in *England in the Fifteenth Century: Proceedings of the 1992 Harlaxton Symposium*, ed. N. Rogers (Stamford, 1994), pp. 100–17.

Magee, J., 'Sir William Elmham and the Recruitment for Henry Despenser's Crusade of 1383', *Medieval Prosopography*, 20 (1999), pp. 181–90.

Marshall, A., 'An Early Fourteenth-Century Affinity: The Earl of Norfolk and His Followers', in *Fourteenth Century England V*, ed. N. Saul (Woodbridge, 2008), pp. 1–12.

McFarlane, K. B., 'Parliament and Bastard Feudalism', *TRHS*, 4th Series, 26 (1944), pp. 53–79.

_____ 'Bastard Feudalism', *BIHR*, 20 (1945) pp. 161–80.

Mercer, M., *The Medieval Gentry: Power, Leadership and Choice during the Wars of the Roses* (London, 2010).

Milner, J. D., 'Sir Simon Felbrigg, KG: The Lancastrian Revolution and Personal Fortune', *Norfolk Archaeology*, 37 (1978), pp. 84–91.

_____ 'The English Enterprise in France, 1412–13', in *Trade, Devotion and Governance: Papers in Later Medieval History*, ed. D. J. Clayton, R. G. Davies and P. McNiven (Gloucester, 1994), pp. 80–101.

Moreton, C. E., 'A Social Gulf? The Upper and Lesser Gentry of Later Medieval England', *Journal of Medieval History*, 17 (1991), pp. 255–62.

_____ *The Townshends and their World: Gentry, Law and Land in Norfolk, c.1450–1551* (Oxford, 1992).

Morgan, P., *War and Society in Medieval Cheshire, 1277–1403* (Chetham Society, 3rd Series, 34, Manchester, 1987).

_____ 'Sir Thomas Felton (d. 1381)', *Oxford Dictionary of National Biography: From the Earliest Time to the Year 2000*, ed. H. C. G. Matthews and B. H. Harrison, 61 vols. (Oxford, 2004), XIX, pp. 286–7.

_____ 'Going to the Wars: Thomas, Lord Morley in France, 1416', in *The Hundred Years War (Part III): Further Considerations*, ed. L. J. A. Villalon and D. J. Kagay (Leiden, 2013), pp. 285–314.

_____ 'Sir Robert Grosvenor and the Scrope-Grosvenor Controversy', in *Courts of Chivalry and Admiralty in Late Medieval Europe*, ed. A. Musson and N. Ramsay (Woodbridge, 2018), pp. 75–94.

Musson, A. and W. M. Ormrod, *The Evolution of English Justice: Law, Politics and Society in the Fourteenth Century* (London, 1998).

Musson, A. and N. Ramsay, 'Introduction', in *Courts of Chivalry and Admiralty in Late Medieval Europe*, ed. A. Musson and N. Ramsay (Woodbridge, 2018), pp. 1–13.

Nall, C., *Reading and War in Fifteenth-Century England: From Lydgate to Malory* (Cambridge, 2012).

Nichols, J. G., 'The Scrope and Grosvenor Controversy', *Herald and Genealogist*, 1 (1863), pp. 385–400.

Ormrod, W. M., 'Knights of Venus', *Medium Aevum*, 73 (2004), pp. 290–305.

_____ *Edward III* (New Haven, 2011).

Palmer, J. J. N., *England, France and Christendom, 1377–99* (London, 1972).

Pamela-Graves, C., *The Form and Fabric of Belief: An Archaeology of the Lay Experience of Religion in Medieval Norfolk and Devon* (British Archaeological Reports 311, Oxford, 2000).

Parsons, W. L. E., *Salle: The Story of a Norfolk Parish: Its Churches, Manors and People* (Norwich, 1937).

Payling, S., *Political Society in Lancastrian England: The Greater Gentry in Nottinghamshire* (Oxford, 1991).

_____ 'War and Peace: Military and Administrative Service amongst the English Gentry in the Reign of Henry VI', in *Soldiers, Nobles and Gentlemen: Essays in Honour of Maurice Keen*, ed. P. Coss and C. Tyerman (Woodbridge, 2009), pp. 240–58.

Pollard, A. J., 'The Richmondshire Community of Gentry during the Wars of the Roses', in *Patronage, Pedigree and Power in Late Medieval England*, ed. C. D. Ross (Gloucester, 1979), pp. 37–59.

_____ *North-Eastern England During the Wars of the Roses: Lay Society, War and Politics 1450–1500* (Oxford, 1990).

Prestwich, J. O., 'The Military Household of the Norman Kings', *EHR*, 96 (1981), pp. 1–35.

Prestwich, M., *Armies and Warfare in the Middle Ages: The English Experience* (London, 1996).

Reynolds, D., *The Long Shadow: The Great War and the Twentieth Century* (London, 2013).

Richmond, C., *John Hopton: A Fifteenth-Century Suffolk Gentleman* (Cambridge, 1981).

_____ 'Thomas Lord Morley (d. 1416) and the Morleys of Hingham', *Norfolk Archaeology*, 39 pt. 1 (1984), pp. 1–12.

_____ '1485 and All That, or what was going on at the Battle of Bosworth', in *Richard III: Lordship, Loyalty and Law*, ed. P. W. Hammond (Gloucester, 1986), pp. 199–236.

_____ *The Paston Family in the Fifteenth Century: The First Phase* (Cambridge, 1990).

_____ *The Paston Family in the Fifteenth Century: Fastolf's Will* (Cambridge, 1996).

_____ *The Paston Family in the Fifteenth Century: Endings* (Manchester, 2000).

Rickard, J., *The Castle Community: The Personnel of English and Welsh Castles, 1272–1422* (Woodbridge, 2002).

Rogers, A., 'Hoton v. Shakell: A Ransom Case in the Court of Chivalry, 1390–5', *Nottingham Medieval Studies*, 7 (1962), pp. 74–108.

_____ 'Hoton v. Shakell: A Ransom Case in the Court of Chivalry, 1390–5', *Nottingham Medieval Studies*, 7 (1963), pp. 53–78.

Rosenthal, J. T., *Telling Tales: Sources and Narration in Late Medieval England* (Philadelphia, 2003).

Roskell, J. S., 'Sir Richard Waldegrave', *Proceedings of the Suffolk Institute of Archaeology*, 27 (1957), pp. 154–75.

_____ 'Sir William Oldhall. Speaker in the Parliament of 1450–1', *Nottingham Medieval Studies*, 5 (1961), pp. 87–112.

_____ *The Commons and their Speakers in English Parliaments 1376–1523* (Manchester, 1965).

Roskell, J. S., L. Clark and C. Rawcliffe (ed.), *The History of Parliament. The House of Commons, 1386–1421*, 4 vols. (Gloucester, 1992).

Ross, C. D., *The Yorkshire Baronage, 1399–1435* (Oxford, 1950).

_____ *Richard III* (London, 1981).

Rubin, M., 'Small Groups: Identity and Solidarity in the Late Middle Ages', in *Enterprise and Individuals in Fifteenth-Century England*, ed. J. Kermode (Gloucester, 1991), pp. 132–50.

Russell, P. E., *The English Intervention in Spain and Portugal in the Time of Edward II and Richard II* (Oxford, 1955).

Saul, N., *Knights and Esquires: The Gloucestershire Gentry in the Fourteenth Century* (Oxford, 1981).

_____ *Scenes from Provincial Life: Knightly Families in Sussex 1280–1400* (Oxford, 1986).

_____ 'A Farewell to Arms? Criticism of Warfare in Late Fourteenth-Century England', in *Fourteenth Century England II*, ed. C. Given-Wilson (Woodbridge, 2002), pp. 131–46.

_____ *Chivalry in Medieval England* (Cambridge, Mass., 2011).

Scattergood, V. J., 'Chaucer and the French War: Sir Thopas and Melibeé', in *Court and Poet: Select Proceedings of the Third Congress of the International Courtly Literature Society*, ed. G. S. Burgess (Liverpool, 1981), pp. 287–96.

Schnerb, B., 'The Jurisdiction of the Constable and Marshals of France in the Later Middle Ages', in *Courts of Chivalry and Admiralty in Late Medieval Europe*, ed. A. Musson and N. Ramsay (Woodbridge, 2018), pp. 135–47.

Sherborne, J., 'Indentured Retinues and the English Expeditions to France, 1369–80', *EHR*, 79 (1964), pp. 718–46.

Simpkin, D., *The English Aristocracy at War, from the Welsh Wars of Edward I to the Battle of Bannockburn* (Woodbridge, 2008).

Somerville, R., *History of the Duchy of Lancaster*, 2 vols. (London, 1953–70).

Squibb, G. D., *The High Court of Chivalry* (Oxford, 1959).

Stewart-Brown, R., 'The Scrope and Grosvenor Controversy, 1385–1391', *LCHS*, 89 (1938 for 1937), pp. 1–22.

Sumption, J., *Trial by Fire: The Hundred Years War II* (London, 2001).

_____ *Divided Houses: The Hundred Years War III* (London, 2009).

Tanzini, L., 'The *Consulate of the Sea* and its Fortunes in Late Medieval Mediterranean Countries', in *Courts of Chivalry and Admiralty in Late Medieval Europe*, ed. A. Musson and N. Ramsay (Woodbridge, 2018), pp. 171–85.

Trim, D. J. B., 'Introduction', in *The Chivalric Ethos and the Development of Military Professionalism*, ed. D. J. B. Trim (Boston, 2003), pp. 1–38.

Tuck, J. A., 'Why Men Fought the Hundred Years War', *History Today*, 33 (1983), pp. 35–40.

_____ 'War and Society in the Medieval North', *Northern History*, 21 (1985), pp. 33–52.

Vale, J., *Edward III and Chivalry: Chivalric Society and its Context 1270–1350* (Woodbridge, 1983).

Virgoe, R., 'The Government and Society of Suffolk in the Later Middle Ages', *Lowestoft Archaeological and Local History Society* (1967–8), pp. 28–32.

_____ 'The Crown and Local Government: East Anglia under Richard II', in *The Reign of Richard II*, ed. F. R. H. du Boulay and C. M. Barron (London, 1971), pp. 218–41.

_____ 'The Murder of Edmund Clippesby', *Norfolk Archaeology*, 35 (1972), pp. 302–7.

_____ 'Aspects of the County Community in the Fifteenth Century', in *Profit, Piety and the Professions in Later Medieval England*, ed. M. A. Hicks (Gloucester, 1990), pp. 1–13.

Wakelin, D., *Humanism, Reading and English Literature 1430–1530* (Oxford, 2007).

Walker, S. K., 'Profit and Loss in the Hundred Years War: The Subcontract of Sir John Strother, 1374', *BIHR*, 58 (1985), pp. 100–6.

_____ *The Lancastrian Affinity, 1361–1399* (Oxford, 1990).

_____ 'Janico Dartasso: Chivalry, Nationality and the Man-At-Arms', *History*, 84 (1999), pp. 31–51.

Winter, J. M., *The Great War and the British People* (London, 1985).

Wright, N., *Knights and Peasants: The Hundred Years War in the French Countryside* (Woodbridge, 1998).

Wright, S. M., *The Derbyshire Gentry in the Fifteenth Century* (Chesterfield, Derbyshire Record Society, 8, 1983).

Yeager, R. F., '*Pax poetica*: On the Pacifism of Chaucer and Gower', *Studies in the Age of Chaucer*, 9 (1987), pp. 97–121.

Young, C. G., *An Account of the Controversy between Reginald Lord Grey of Ruthyn and Sir Edward Hastings in the Court of Chivalry* (London, 1841).

Unpublished Theses

Baker, G. P., 'The English Way of War, 1360–99' (PhD, University of Hull, 2011).

Caudrey, P. J., 'War and Society in Medieval Norfolk: The Warrior Gentry, c. 1350–c. 1430' (PhD, University of Tasmania, 2010).

Cornell, D. J., 'Northern Castles and Garrisons in the Later Middle Ages' (PhD, Durham University, 2006).

Curry, A., 'Military Organization in Lancastrian Normandy 1422–1450', 2 vols. (PhD, CNAA, Teeside Polytechnic, 1985).

Green, D. S., 'The Household and Military Retinue of Edward the Black Prince' (D.Phil, University of Nottingham, 1999).
Jack, R. I., 'The Greys of Ruthin, 1325 to 1490' (PhD, University of London, 1961).
Vale, B., 'The Scropes of Bolton and Masham, c. 1300–c. 1450: A Study of a Northern Noble Family with a Calendar of the Scrope of Bolton Cartulary', 2 vols. (D. Phil, University of York, 1987).
Walker, S. K., 'John of Gaunt and his Retainers, 1361–99' (D.Phil, University of Oxford, 1986).

Electronic Resources

www.agincourt600.com
www.dhi.ac.uk/onlinefroissart/
www.historyofparliamentonline.org
www.medievalsoldier.org
www.soldier-lews1.rdg.ac.uk
Oxford Dictionary of National Biography: www.oxforddnb.com

Index

Abberbury, Sir Richard, 69
Abbotsbury, Abbey of (Dor.), 113
Agincourt, battle of (1415), 40, 41, 41n., 42, 43–5, 129, 181
Archer, John, 94
Arms, Law of, 11, 12, 13
Aske, Conan, 74–5, 101
Assheton, Sir John, 30n., 31n., 40n.
Aton, Sir William, 112, 139, 140
Atte Lee, Sir Walter, 159
Attysley, Adelston, 187
Auberoche, battle of (1345), 23, 56
Audley, Sir James, 27
Ayton, Andrew, 16–17, 145n., 183

Baa, Robert, 169n.
Bannockburn, battle of (1314), 23, 174
Barre, Hildebrand, 173
Barry, Edmund, 29n., 30n., 36n., 77n., 81, 127n., 129
Bastard Feudalism, 65–7, 91, 96n., 96–7
Beauchamp, Edward, 69
Beauchamp, Thomas, Earl of Warwick (d. 1369), 83, 108, 163
Beauchamp, Sir Thomas, 6, 139, 145n.
Beaulieu, Richard, 162
Beche, John, 93
Bedfordshire, 105
Bell, Adrian, 16–17
Belle Perche, siege of (1369), 28
Berdewell Church (Suff.), 52
Berdewell, Robert, 52
Berdewell, Sir William, 29n., 30n., 31n., 33n., 51–3, 54, 61, 80, 81, 145n., 177n.
Bere, John, 30n., 153n., 177
Berney, John, 126,
Berney, Sir Robert, 29n., 33n., 36n., 77n., 80, 128, 175
Berwick, siege of (1355–6), 102, 135
Bingham, Sir Richard, 111n., 167
Biset, William, 58n., 85, 85n., 108
Blomefield, Rev. Francis, 15–16, 23n.
Blount, Sir Thomas, 172–3
Blount, Sir Walter, 69, 104
Bocking, Sir Ralph, 121
Bohun Family
  Affinity, 58n., 83–6, 88–90, 110, 116, 181
  Humphrey, earl of Hereford (d. 1373) 58n., 85–6, 88, 106, 107
  Joan, countess of Hereford (d. 1419), 89
  William, earl of Northampton (d. 1360), 9, 58n., 83–5, 88, 107–8, 137, 145
Boidell, Geoffrey, 30n., 39n.
Bolde, Sir Richard, 30n.
Bolyngton, Sir Thomas, 141
Bonville, Sir William, 113
Bosville, Sir John, 160
Boynton, Sir Thomas, 99, 139, 144n.
Boys, Sir Miles, 109n.
Braybrooke, Sir Gerard, 105
Braynton, Nicholas, 29n, 153
Brereton, Sir William, 30n., 31n., 111n., 165, 168
Bressingham, William, 45
Brétigny, Treaty of (1360), 37, 149, 153
Breton, Esmond, 88

Brewes, Sir John, 87, 107, 109, 109n., 110n., 121, 125, 129n., 141, 145, 145n., 146, 166, 172
Brian, Guy, Lord, 48–9, 49n., 58, 61, 89, 104, 113
Brotherton, Margaret, Countess of Norfolk (d. 1399), 6, 174, 175, 176
Browe, Sir Hugh, 30n., 31n., 34, 35, 35n., 37, 39, 40n., 59, 61, 111n., 164, 167
Broyn, John, 173
Brux, siege of (1369), 27–8
Bryston, John, 29n., 176
Burgh, Sir John, 86, 89, 116
Burgh, Simon, 29n., 30n., 79
Buironfosse, battle of (1339), 23 53, 135
Burley, Sir Simon, 105
Burlingham, John, 175
Burnell, Hugh Lord, 107

Calais, siege of (1347), 9, 10, 48, 55n., 85, 134, 135, 141, 146, 152, 172
Calthorpe, Sir John, 45n.
Calthorpe, Sir Philip, 187
Calthorpe, Sir William, 30n., 45, 81, 175, 187n.
Calveley, Hugh, 170
Campaigns
  Aborted Campaign (1372), 27, 48
  Aquitaine (1345), 56
  Brittany (1342–3), 55n., 85
  Brittany (1345), 134
  Brittany (1374–5), 31, 48
  Brittany (1380), 30, 31, 42, 77–8, 92, 152
  Crécy-Calais (1346–7), 9, 23, 56, 153
  Flanders (1339), 48
  Flanders (1346), 76, 152
  Gascony (1355–7), 50, 84, 108, 110
  Gascony (1369), 23, 27, 29, 30, 34, 40, 48, 50, 53, 55n., 77, 78, 106, 107, 135, 152, 175
  Gascony (1370), 29, 31, 77
  Ireland (1380), 31, 48–9, 51
  Ireland (1394), 38, 39
  Ireland (1399), 38, 39
  Naval Disaster (Arundel Fleet) (1379), 29–30, 51, 77, 92, 152, 153, 155
  Naval Service (1387 and 1388), 38, 52
  Naval Service (other), 30, 31, 48, 78
  Northern France (1373), 29, 31, 68, 71, 77, 78, 106, 107, 121, 152, 153, 155
  Rheims (1359–60), 23, 27, 34, 48, 50, 58, 67–8, 77, 91, 105, 106, 121, 122, 134, 136, 138, 139, 141, 145–6, 163, 167, 169, 170, 173
  Scotland (1385), 2, 23, 27, 29, 30, 33, 42, 51, 58, 68, 71, 78, 152
  Scotland (1400), 38, 39, 93, 152
  Scotland (other), 23, 38, 48, 54, 58, 68, 134, 163
  Spain (1366–7), 23, 37, 50, 68, 71, 77, 108, 110
  Spain (1386–8), 23, 29, 31, 38, 51–2, 70–5, 72n., 77, 78, 88, 152, 153, 155, 175
  Wales (1402–3), 23, 38, 93
Carminowe, Thomas, 27, 68, 68n., 169
Carrington, Sir Charles, 148n.
Chandos Herald, 137
Charnels, John, 154
Chaucer, Geoffrey, 105, 149, 170–1, 183

Chauncy, Sir William, 100
Cheney, Sir Ralph, 113, 166
Cheshire, 3, 27, 34, 35–7, 40, 41, 52n., 86–7, 96, 104, 163–71, 182
Chester, 2, 111, 167–8
  Abbey, 170
  Abbot of, 164,
  Church of Friars Minor, 165
Chisnale, William, 30n., 31n.
Chivalry, Court of,
  Descendants of Testators, 185n., 186n.
  Historiography, 1, 16, 17, 18, 19, 20, 24–5, 59, 82–3, 96, 132, 180
  Origins, 8, 9, 10, 11, 169
  Other Cases, 11, 12, 13, 14, 14n.
  Testimony (overview), 31, 32–3, 73n., 82–3, 111n., 116, 133–4
  see also Grey v. Hastings; Lovel v. Morley; Scrope v. Grosvenor
Chuddleigh, Sir James, 113
Chydioke, Sir John, 113
Chyrche, Richard, 29n.,
Clanvowe, Sir John, 85–6, 105
Claxton, Hamo, 29n., 40n., 175
Clifford, Sir Lewis, 105
Clifford, Thomas, 29n., 30n., 33n., 105
Clifton, Sir Gerveys, 139–40
Clifton, John, Lord, 51
Clippesby, Edmund, 123–4
Constable, Sir Robert, 71, 101, 102
Conyers, John, 100
Conyers, Sir Robert, 159
Corfe Castle (Dor.), 55, 58
Cosyn, Sir Richard, 122
Cotton, Hugh, 30n., 36n., 39n., 164
Courtenay, Edward, Earl of Devon (d. 1419), 112n.
Coverham, Abbot of (Yorks.), 161

Crécy, battle of (1346), 1, 42, 53, 55n., 56, 77, 78, 85, 102, 126, 134, 135, 138, 143, 147–8
Culwyn, Roger, 85, 85n.
Curson, Hugh, 56–7, 61, 90, 118
Curson, John, 129
Curson, Sir John, 56–7, 118, 125, 129
Curson, William, 56, 118

Dacre, Hugh, Lord, 107, 162
Dalyngridge, Sir Edward, 105
Danyell, Emond, 41n.
Danyell, John, 41n., 169
Danyell, Robert, 30n., 31n., 111n.
Danyell, William, 41n., 165
Davenham Church (Ches.), 165
Davenport, Arthur, 30n., 36n., 39n., 40n.
Davenport, Thomas, 30n., 40n., 165
De Bruyn, Sir Maurice, 145n., 173
De Charny, Sir Geoffroi, 138n.
Deincourt, Sir John, 104
De La Pole, Sir John, 69
De La Pole, Michael, Earl of Suffolk (d. 1415), 52
De La Zouche, Sir Richard, 85n.
Denton, Alexander, 152n., 153, 175
Derbyshire, 104
Despenser, Henry, Bishop of Norwich (d. 1406), 30, 36n., 51, 78, 124, 175, 176
Devonshire, 104, 105, 112–13
Dorset, 4, 104, 112–13, 166
Duncalf, Thomas, 30n.
Dutton, John, 41n.
Dutton, Sir Laurence, 111n., 164, 165, 168
Dutton, Nicholas, 41n.,
Dutton, Sir Thomas, 165
Dutton, William, 41n.

East Anglia, 2, 4, 21, 27, 34, 35, 52, 87, 110, 112, 114, 117, 118, 121, 122, 125, 126, 130, 131, 172, 173, 179, 181, 187
Edmund of Langley, Duke of York (d. 1402), 90, 175
Edward III (d. 1377), 37–8, 48–9, 49n., 63, 147–8, 150, 173, 177
Edward of Woodstock, the Black Prince (d. 1376), 50–1, 63, 78, 83–4, 86–7, 89, 90, 108, 110, 125–6, 141, 143, 147n., 166
Elmham, Sir William, 124, 129n.
Elsing Brass, 76, 188
Elsing Church (Norf.), 188
Enderby, John, 169n.
England, Constable of, 9, 11–12
England, Marshal of, 11–12
Erpingham, Sir Thomas, 29n., 33n., 36n., 40–1, 43–5, 76–7, 77n., 78, 79, 80, 81, 109n., 110, 126–7, 127n., 128, 128n., 129, 145n., 153, 156n.
Essex, 108, 115, 116, 118, 144n.
Eton, John, 164
Eyrdale, Waryn, 160

Falmouth Church (Cnl.), 153, 155
Faxwist, Vivian, 30n.
Felbrigg, Sir Simon, 39n., 40, 43–5, 80, 81, 127n., 128, 129, 156n.
Felton, Sir Thomas, 78, 119n., 125, 126
Feltons of Litcham, 57, 90n., 119n., 125, 126
Ferrers, Sir Henry, 108, 139, 141, 144n.
Ferrers, Sir Ralph, 111, 139, 140
Fishlake, Robert, 29n., 30n., 31n., 81, 92–3, 152n., 153
Fitzalan, Richard, Earl of Arundel (d. 1397), 155–6
Fitz Alan, Brian, 9

Fitz Henry, Sir Thomas, 139, 144n.
Fitz Hugh, Henry, Lord, 106
Fitz Payne, Sir Robert, 113
Fitzralph, Robert, 88, 109n.
Fitzwalter, Walter, Lord, 78, 153
Flamville, Sir William, 85n.
Frodesham, John, 30n., 31n.
Froissart, Jean, 136–7, 155n.

Garter, Order of the, 40, 49, 147
Gaunt, John of, Duke of Lancaster (d. 1399)
    Deposition, Court of Chivalry, 3, 68, 106, 158
    Hastings of Elsing, Relationship with, 28, 29, 33, 36, 64, 75–6, 81, 176, 177
    Income, 67–8
    Lancastrian Affinity, 19, 33, 36, 43, 63, 64, 67–82, 77n., 88, 90, 126–7, 170, 181
    Military Retinue, 33, 43, 63, 64, 67, 70, 72–5, 79, 80, 81
    Political Ambitions, 63, 80, 155
    Recruitment, East Anglia, 33, 43, 78–80, 107, 109
    Recruitment, Yorkshire, 73–5, 99–100, 104, 106–7
    Richard, Lord Scrope, Relationship with, 2, 64, 67–8, 99, 104, 108, 181
    Rewards, 67–8, 69–70, 71, 76, 77n., 88
    Spanish Campaign (1386–8), 63, 64, 70–5, 72n., 73n., 80, 87, 109
    'Well Willers', 66, 78, 79–80
Geney, Sir John, 29n., 33n., 45, 77n., 81, 127n., 177
Geney, Sir Thomas, 45n., 109n., 145n.
Gerbergh, Sir Thomas, 29n., 30n., 81, 90, 118, 124, 127n., 129, 129n., 145n., 152n., 175

Gildesburgh, Sir John, 88
Gloucestershire, 48, 104
Glyn Dwr, Owain, 30n., 35n., 38, 40n., 164
Godard, Sir John, 71
Goldingham, Sir Alexander, 44, 108, 144n.
Goushill, Sir Nicholas, 116
Gower, John, 149
Great Hallingbury (Esx.), 115
Grey, Sir Nicholas, 154n.
Grey, Reginald, Lord (of Ruthin) (d. 1440), 5, 6, 7, 14n., 23, 93–4, 168–9, 171–2
Grey v. Hastings
  Case, Details of, 5, 6, 7, 7n, 16, 27, 31, 171–2
  Costs and Damages, 7, 7n.
  Documentary/Iconographic Evidence, 132, 175, 176, 177, 187
  Historiography, 17, 26, 151–7, 178
  Lancastrian Ties, 28, 29, 33, 36, 64, 75–82, 182
  Memory and Memorialisation, 132, 151–7, 158, 172, 174–7
  Military Traditions, Family, 37, 40, 41, 42, 44–5
  Regionalism, 27, 36, 40, 41, 45, 64, 92–3, 127–9, 158, 172, 174–7, 179, 184–5
  Testimony, Chivalric 132, 151–7, 175, 176, 177, 178
  Testimony, Military, 28, 29, 30, 31, 32, 33, 34, 35, 92, 93, 151–7, 175–7
  Witnesses, Age of, 28, 40, 152–3
  Witnesses, Numbers of, 16, 23n, 24, 28–30, 41–2
Grosmont, Henry of, earl of Derby and duke of Lancaster (d. 1361), 56, 172

Grosvenor, Sir Robert (d. 1349), 165
Grosvenor, Sir Robert (d. 1396), 1, 2, 3, 4, 7, 26, 27, 34n., 62, 96, 98, 104, 114, 163, 164–71, 182
Guisborough, Prior of, 160
Gybbethorpe, Sir John, 166

Hales, Sir Stephen, 49–51, 61, 87, 109n., 110, 140, 145n., 166
Halghton, Thomas, 30n., 35n.
Halidon Hill, battle of (1333), 55n., 102, 116, 138, 143, 144, 148, 183
Hampton, Richard, 162
Hanmere, John, 30n., 40n.
Harrington, Sir Nicholas, 101
Harsyk, Sir John, 129n.
Harvey, John, 94
Hasethorpe, Sir John, 168n.
Hastings of Elsing, Family
  Affinity, 81, 92–3
  Sir Edward (d. 1438), 5, 6, 7, 26, 27, 39, 39n., 62, 64, 75–6, 77, 82, 117, 127, 128, 152, 172, 174, 177, 178, 179, 184, 187n.
  Sir Hugh I (d. 1347), 76, 152, 153, 177, 188
  Sir Hugh II (d. 1369), 76, 77, 78, 92, 152, 153, 175, 176
  Sir Hugh III (d. 1388), 6, 28, 68, 73n., 76, 77, 78, 81, 92, 109, 109n., 127, 143, 151, 152, 153, 155, 156, 171, 172, 174, 175, 176
  Sir Hugh IV (d. 1396), 176, 177
Hastings, Anne, countess of Pembroke (d. 1384), 6, 6n., 174, 175, 176
Hastings, John, earl of Pembroke (d. 1375), 6, 6n.
Hastings, John, earl of Pembroke (d. 1389), 5, 171–2, 174

Hastings, Sir Ralph, 74–5, 101, 147n.
Hawkwood, Sir John, 135
Hemenhale, David, 29n., 30n., 42, 153, 175, 176
Hemenhale, Sir John, 42
Hemenhale, Sir Ralph, 42
Hemenhale, Sir Robert, 42
Hengrave, Sir Thomas, 29n., 40n., 81
Henry IV (d. 1413), 36, 38, 39, 43, 64, 88, 100, 127, 152
Henry V (d. 1422), 28, 40, 41, 42, 44, 45, 106, 179, 180, 185
Henry VIII (d. 1547), 186
Henry, John, 169n.
Heraldic Identity, 7, 8, 9, 10, 46, 139, 141–2, 150, 158–63, 164–5, 168–9
Hereford, 105
Hesilrige, William, 85, 85n., 108, 139, 145n.
Heton, Sir Alan, 116
Hilton, Sir Richard, 168n.
Hilton, William, 30n., 31n., 35n., 36, 36n.
Holand, John, 31n.
Holcroft, John, 165
Holme, William, 161
Hoo, Henry, 172, 173
Houghton, Sir Richard, 101, 105
Howard, Henry, 93
Hulme, William, 30n.

Ipres, Sir Ralph, 100–1, 154n.

Jervaulx, Abbot of, 103, 161

Keegan, John, 133n., 134n.
Keen, Maurice, 13, 16–17, 26, 89n., 132, 145n., 151, 183
Kerdiston Family
    Sir Leonard (d. 1421), 29n., 30n., 118, 123–4, 125, 127n., 129n., 145n.
    Sir Roger (d. 1337), 123
    Sir Thomas (d. 1446), 124, 129
    Sir William II (d. 1361), 83, 120, 123, 125, 126
    William III (d. 1391), 123
Kirkstead, John, 29n.
Knolles, Sir Robert, 36
Königsberg Cathedral, 138, 139, 144
Kyng, William, 172

Lakyngheth, Sir John, 121, 145, 145n.
Lampete, Thomas, 88, 88n.
Lancashire, 3, 27, 34, 101, 104, 105, 114, 163, 165, 166, 170
Lanercost, Prior of, 159–60, 161, 162
Langon, siege of (1346), 56
La Reole, siege of (1346), 56
La Rochelle, battle of (1372), 77, 152
La Roche-sur-Yon, siege of (1369), 28
Laton, Sir Robert, 99, 101, 143
Le Bel, Jean, 136–7, 155n.
Lee, John, 169n.
Legh, Thomas, 30n., 31n.
Legh, William, 30n., 31n.
Legh, Sir William, 30n., 31n., 36n., 39n., 41n.
Leicestershire, 108
Leulinghem, Truce of (1389), 38, 40, 62
Leycestre, John, 31n., 111n., 167
Limoges, siege of (1369), 28
Lincolnshire, 104
London, 2, 5, 104, 108, 111–12, 115, 171
Loudham, Sir John I, 109n., 121n.
Loudham, Sir John II, 109n., 121, 121n., 154n.
Lound, Sir Gerard, 99

INDEX

Lound, Thomas, 94
Lovel, John, Lord (d. 1408), 4, 5, 117, 171–2, 174, 177
Lovel v. Morley
   Burnell v. Morley, 9, 146, 171, 172–4, 177, 179, 184
   Case, Details of, 4, 5, 23, 171
   Documentary/Iconographic Evidence, 132, 141, 154, 173–4
   Historiography, 17, 18, 26
   Memory and Memorialisation, 132, 145–7, 148, 154–5, 158, 172–4
   Testimony, Chivalric, 132, 138–9, 140, 141, 144, 153–4, 172–4
   Testimony, Ecclesiastical, 115–16, 140
   Testimony, Military, 58, 83, 90, 91, 92, 116, 141, 142–3, 144, 145–6
   Regionalism, 42, 90–2, 115–29, 158, 172–4, 179, 182, 184–5
   Witnesses, Age of, 91, 153–4
   Witnesses, Numbers of, 4, 5, 15, 23n, 24, 42, 87, 91, 115–16, 117, 122, 138, 139, 140, 144, 172
Lucas, Thomas, 29n., 153, 176
Lucy, Sir William, 85, 88, 108, 113
Lutterell, Sir Andrew, 74–5, 101
Lye, Sir William, 111n.
Lymworth, Robert, 29n., 30n., 31n., 92, 153, 175

Mandeville, Sir Thomas, 86, 88, 89, 116
Marian, Robert, 29n.
Marienburg Cathedral (Prussia), 153
Marney, Sir Robert, 85n., 108, 144n., 145n.
Marshalsea Prison, 7

Mauleverer, Sir John, 143, 159
Massy, John, 30n., 31n., 34, 35n., 39n., 41n.
Massy, Sir John of Puddington, 30n., 35n., 37, 39, 40n., 111n., 164
Massy, Sir John of Tatton, 111n., 168
Massy, Nicholas, 41n.
Massy, Richard, 31n., 35n., 36
Mauron, battle of (1352), 23, 145
Mauteby, Sir John, 118
Maynwaring, John, 30n., 36n., 39n., 40n.
Melton, Sir William, 101
Mendham, Oliver, 91–2
Mercer, Malcolm, 183
Military Service
   Army Discipline, Organisation and Structure, 10, 32n., 37, 41, 41n., 46–7, 63, 82–3
   Careerism, 24, 25, 37–8, 46–61, 80, 82–3, 102–3, 134–5, 139
   Crusading, 24, 30, 30n., 36n., 37, 51, 54, 77, 78, 85, 92, 106, 107–8, 134–5, 137–8, 139, 141, 144, 152, 153, 182–3
   Esquires, 24, 29, 32–3, 37, 50–1, 53–7, 90–4, 109, 129n., 134–5, 148, 150
   Garrison Service, 24, 35–6, 38–9, 47, 48, 49, 55, 58–60, 134
   Knighthood, Dubbing to, 45n., 53, 78, 102, 139–40, 143, 150, 153, 155, 176
   Mercenaries, 37, 134–5, 149
   Military Community, England, 53, 55–6, 59, 147–51, 157
   Military Traditions, Family, 25, 37, 46, 52–3, 156–7
   Professionalism, 24, 29, 34, 46–7, 47n., 50, 51–3, 54–6, 58–60, 79, 80, 134–5, 149

Recruitment, Dynamics of, 24, 43–5, 46, 50–1, 79–80, 82–3, 129n.
Sub–Contracting, 24, 43–5, 54, 54n.
Tournaments, 135, 137, 139–40
Mobberley Church (Ches.), 165
Mobberley, Sir Ralph, 45
Moigne, Sir William, 141
Molham, John, 9
Monceaux, Armand, 168n.
Monlegh, Richard, 30n.
Moreys, William, 172, 173
Morieux, Sir Thomas, 73n., 88, 104, 109, 109n., 158–9, 165–6
Morlaix, battle and siege of (1342), 23, 53, 85, 135, 145
Morley Family
  Affinity, 56–7, 90–2, 115–16, 117–18, 123
  Gentry Relations, 114–29
  Sir John (d. 1367), 90, 90n., 143
  Robert, second Lord, (d. 1360), 9, 57, 84, 90, 91, 92, 116, 120, 121, 123, 138, 139, 141, 142–3, 172, 173, 177
  Sir Robert (d. 1390), 29n., 30n., 33n., 87, 109n., 109–10, 123–4, 127n., 143, 145n.
  Thomas, fourth Lord, (d. 1416), 4, 5, 9, 29n., 30n., 39n., 57, 83, 90, 91, 96, 114–15, 118–19, 123, 127n., 128, 171–4, 176, 182
  Thomas, fifth Lord, (d. 1425), 124
  Sir Thomas, 125
  William, third Lord, (d. 1379), 56, 84, 123, 126, 141, 143, 173
Mortimer, Constantine, 29n., 127n.
Mortimer, Edmund, Earl of March (d. 1381), 83
Mortimer, John, 93

Nájera, battle of (1367), 1, 50, 54, 86, 135, 138, 143, 147n., 148, 152, 183
Nowell, Jankyn, 54n.
Neuland, John, 59–60, 61
Neusom, Adam, 170
Neville, John, Lord, 101, 106–7
Neville, Sir Robert, 73, 75, 100
Neville's Cross, battle of (1346), 102
Newburgh, Prior of, 160
Nicolas, Sir Harris, 1, 16, 54n., 132, 140, 183
Norfolk
  Economy, 57, 114–15
  Gentry Relations, 43–5, 56–7, 78, 80, 81, 101, 118, 125–9, 174–7
  Lordship, 33, 43, 50, 55, 56–7, 76, 78–9, 80, 81, 114–15, 125–9
  Memory and Memorialisation, 172–7
  Military Community, 33–4, 43–5, 55, 78–9, 80, 81, 104, 109–10, 114–15, 185, 186
  North-East, 43–5, 76, 78–9, 80, 81
  Political Society, 36, 50, 56–7, 76–7, 78–9, 80, 81, 114–15, 125–9, 174n.
Northumberland, 108
Norwich, 4–5, 115, 116
Norwich, Sir John, 56, 83, 120, 122, 125
Nottingham, 104, 111

Oldhall, Edmund, 129
Oxfordshire, 4–5, 173–4

Papeworth, Sir William, 116–17
Parker, John, 92, 153n.
Parker, William, 94
Parliament, 12, 50, 57, 71, 80, 89, 101, 106, 150
Payling, Simon, 25
Payn, John, 29n., 36n., 39n., 176

INDEX

Percy, Henry, Earl of
  Northumberland (d. 1408), 107
Percy, Sir Henry, 107
Percy, Sir Thomas, 107
Peter, King of Cyprus, 135, 137
Peteyvan, Sir Thomas, 141
Phelip, William, 122
Phelip, Sir William, 129
Pickering, Sir James, 101
Pickworth, Thomas, 30n., 92, 153
Pierrepoint, Sir Edmund, 69, 104
Pilkington, Robert, 30n., 31n., 35n.
Plays, Sir John, 78
Plumpton, Sir Robert, 100
Plumstead, William, 29n., 30n., 31n., 39n., 77n., 175, 176
Plymouth, 2, 70, 73n., 108 109, 111–12
Pointz, Hugh, 9
Poitiers, battle of (1356), 1, 23, 78, 122, 126, 138, 143, 147n., 148
Pole, Sir John, 111n., 167–8
Poley, Robert, 29n., 33n., 79
Praers, William, 30n., 164, 165
Pygot, Sir Randolf, 57–8, 61, 100, 159, 162

Quarranteau Castle (Fra.), 154
Queldrike, John, 161

Ragour, Reginald, 94
Raven, John, 33n.
Rennes, siege of (1356–7), 53, 77, 135
Reresby, Sir Thomas, 147n.
Reydon Church (Norf.), 141, 187
Reymes, John I, 29n., 33n., 36n., 39n., 77n., 80, 81, 128, 175
Reymes, John II, 44
Richard II
  Cheshire Bodyguard, 36, 39
  Chivalric Crisis, 148–51
  Revolution (1399), 118, 126, 128, 154–5

Royal Household, 43, 49, 50, 80, 87, 89, 104–6, 110, 150, 171
Rievelaux, Abbot of, 103, 159
Rither, John, 53–6, 61, 85n., 112, 134–8, 139, 144n., 145n.
Roger, John, 29n., 30n., 32
Rokeby, Sir Thomas, 99, 101
Roos, Sir Peter, 168
Roos, Sir Robert, 99
Roos, Thomas, Lord, 101
Roos, Sir Thomas, 101, 102, 106, 107, 140
Rose, Thomas, 92
Roucliffe, Sir David, 71, 154n.
Roucliffe, Sir Richard, 71, 112
Roxburgh Castle (Scots.), 71
Russell, Thibaud, 10

Sabraham, Nicholas, 85, 85n., 134–8
Salle Church (Norf.), 124
Saltmersshe, Thomas, 160, 162–3
Saville, Sir John, 101, 102
Scales, Roger, Lord, 107, 109n.
Scargill, Sir John, 74–5, 99, 101
Scropes of Bolton and Masham, Family
  Gentry Relations, 98–104
  Northern Peerage, 106–7
Scrope, Archbishop Richard of Masham (d. 1405), 100
Scrope, Sir Geoffrey of Masham (d. 1340), 48, 98, 99, 103, 105, 107, 135, 139–40, 142, 143, 168, 177
Scrope, Sir Geoffrey of Masham (d. 1362), 84, 107, 135, 139, 141, 144
Scrope, Sir Henry of Bolton (d. 1336), 98, 103, 107, 135, 139–40, 142, 162, 168
Scrope, Henry, Lord of Masham (d. 1391), 102, 105, 107–8, 134, 135, 163, 166, 168

Scrope, Richard, Lord of Bolton (d. 1403), 1, 2, 3, 4, 7, 54n., 57, 64, 67–8, 68n., 83, 84, 87, 96, 98, 100, 102, 103, 104, 105, 106–8, 109–10, 111, 134, 147n., 162–3, 165, 166, 167, 168, 168n., 169, 179, 181
Scrope, Sir Stephen of Masham (d. 1406), 134
Scrope, Sir William of Bolton (d. 1344), 84, 103, 107, 135, 139, 145
Scrope, Sir William of Masham (d. 1367), 84, 134, 141, 147n.
Scrope, William (d. c. 1302), 143, 168
Scrope v. Grosvenor
Case, Details of, 2, 3, 4, 7, 23, 27, 31, 34, 67–8
Documentary/Iconographic Evidence, 97, 103, 132, 154, 160, 161–4, 165, 170–1
Historiography, 17, 18, 64, 96–7, 132–5, 153–4, 180–4
Lancastrian Ties, 2, 64, 67–75, 99, 104
Memory and Memorialisation, 87, 132, 136–8, 142–3, 145–7, 148, 154–5, 158–62, 163–71
Testimony, Chivalric, 1, 17, 134–41, 143, 145–6, 151, 154
Testimony, Ecclesiastical, 97, 103n., 103–4, 159–60, 161, 162, 164, 165
Testimony, Military, 27–8, 30–1, 34–7, 39, 41, 48–9, 53–4, 58–9, 70–1, 72–4, 85–7, 102–3, 105–8, 109–10, 112–13, 134–6, 138–9, 141, 144–5, 154
Regionalism, 2–3, 27, 34, 35–7, 40, 41, 42, 45, 54n., 64, 73–5, 86–7, 99–114, 158–62, 163–71, 179, 181, 184–5

Witnesses, Age of, 28, 28n., 34, 40, 57, 70–1, 72, 85, 112, 134, 153–4
Witnesses, Number of, 3, 23n, 24, 30–1, 34, 41, 42, 57, 70, 72, 84–5, 86, 87, 98n., 109, 139, 140, 144, 167
Selby, Abbot of, 103, 159, 161
Shelton, Oliver, 44
Shelton, Sir Ralph I, 78
Shelton, Sir Ralph II, 29n., 30n., 32–3, 33n., 39n., 78–9, 81, 127n., 128, 156n., 177
Shrewsbury, battle of (1403), 37
Slene, William, 30n.
Sluys, battle of (1340), 23, 53, 55n., 58, 135, 138, 143
Sodyngton, William, 30n.
Somerset, 108
Somerton Church (Norf.), 141
Spekkesworth, John, 29n., 176
Stanhope Park, battle of (1327), 48, 102, 113
Stanton, Thomas, 29n., 30n., 39, 81, 176
Stapleton, Sir Brian, 99, 139
Stapleton, Sir Miles, 30n., 81, 129, 156n., 175
St. Agatha's, Abbot of, 103, 162
St. Briavel's Castle (Gloucs.), 48
St. Malo, siege of (1378), 29, 31, 33, 42, 51, 77, 78, 81, 122, 152, 153, 155–6
St. Pierre, Thomas, 30n.
St. Quintin Family, 85n., 100, 154n.
Strange, Sir Hamo, 45n.
Strange, Sir John, 45, 78, 90, 90n., 124–5, 126, 129n.
Stratfield Mortimer Church (Berks.), 174
Stratton, Sir Godfrey, 122
Strother, Sir John, 45
Styrecle, John, 169n.

Suffolk, 51, 52, 78, 101, 104, 109–10, 118, 119, 120, 122, 130, 141, 158–9, 175
Sully, Sir John, 105, 112, 113, 138–9, 147n.
Sutton, Sir John, 118n.
Sutton, Sir Richard, 89, 118n., 145n.
Sutton, William, 118n.
Sussex, 105
Swillington, Sir Robert, 69, 74–5, 99, 100
Swinborne, Thomas, 29n., 30n., 92

Tempest, Sir Richard, 71, 100–01
Thomas of Woodstock, Duke of Gloucester (d. 1397), 84, 88, 117n.
Thirlewalle, John, 143, 168
Thorpe, Sir Edmund, 129n.,
Thweyt, William, 55–6, 58, 61, 122
Toft, Robert, 30n., 36n., 39n.
Tournai, siege of (1340), 53, 135
Tranmer, William, 30n.
Tunstall, Roger, 94

Ufford Family
  Affinity, 55, 79, 83, 107, 109–10, 119–22, 125–6
Ufford, Edmund, 107
Ufford, John, 120
Ufford, Sir Ralph, 55
Ufford, Sir Robert, 121, 123, 124, 125, 129n.
Ufford, Robert, earl of Suffolk (d. 1369), 55, 79, 83, 107, 121–2, 125, 126, 141, 146
Ufford, William, earl of Suffolk (d. 1382), 79, 83, 107, 110n., 121, 122, 126,
Ughtred, Sir Thomas, 45
Urswick, Sir Walter, 69, 72, 139, 145n., 165

Vale Royal, Abbot of, 164, 165
Vannes, siege of (1342), 85, 135
Vernon, Sir Ralph, 30n., 31n., 40n., 111n.
Vernon, Richard, 30n., 31n., 34, 35n., 36n., 39n.

Waldegrave, Sir Richard, 85, 85n., 88–90, 89n., 105, 109n., 110, 144n., 159
Walkefare, Sir Richard, 126
Walker, Simon, 33
Walkern (Herts.), 115
Walsingham, Thomas, 151
Warbleton, John, 10
Warde, Sir John, 100
The Wars of the Roses (c. 1455–c. 1487), 183, 185–6
Watton Priory (Yorks.), 161
Waverton Church (Ches.), 165,
Weatherall Church (Ches.), 162,
Wellon, siege of (1362), 54, 135
Wensley Church (Yorks.), 100, 161–2
Wensley, Simon, 100
West, Sir Thomas, 173
Wheteley, William, 177
White, Sir John, 109, 109n., 125, 129n., 145n.
White, Robert, 44
Willoughby, Robert, Lord, 51
Wilton, Sir John, 29n., 30n., 33n., 109n.
Wiltshire, 4
Wiltshire, Sir John, 29n., 33n., 79, 153, 175
Winchelsea, battle of (1350), 23, 50, 85, 105, 122, 138, 143
Wingfield, Sir John, 126, 129n.
Wingfield, Sir William, 87, 109n., 110, 110n., 124, 129n., 145–6
Winter, William, 78
Wisham, Sir William, 29n., 30n.
Wollaston, William, 174

Yeversley, John, 161
Yorkshire
   East Riding, 98–9
   Ecclesiastical Community, 103–4, 159–62
   Gentry Relations, 54, 71, 73–5, 99–104, 111, 139–40, 143, 159–63
   Lancastrian Ties, 21, 69, 71, 74–5, 99, 181
   Memory and Memorialisation, 140, 143, 159–63, 178–9, 184–5
   Military Community, 54, 71, 73–5, 102–3, 111, 135, 138–41, 143, 185, 186
   North Riding, 74–5, 99–104, 106–7, 159–63, 169, 181, 184
   Peerage, 106–7
   Richmond, 99, 160, 162
   York, 2, 54n., 100, 104, 108, 111, 112
Young, Sir Charles, 16

Warfare in History

The Battle of Hastings: Sources and Interpretations, *edited and introduced by Stephen Morillo*

Infantry Warfare in the Early Fourteenth Century: Discipline, Tactics, and Technology, *Kelly DeVries*

The Art of Warfare in Western Europe during the Middle Ages, from the Eighth Century to 1340 (second edition), *J.F. Verbruggen*

Knights and Peasants: The Hundred Years War in the French Countryside, *Nicholas Wright*

Society at War: The Experience of England and France during the Hundred Years War, *edited by Christopher Allmand*

The Circle of War in the Middle Ages: Essays on Medieval Military and Naval History, *edited by Donald J. Kagay and L.J. Andrew Villalon*

The Anglo-Scots Wars, 1513–1550: A Military History, *Gervase Phillips*

The Norwegian Invasion of England in 1066, *Kelly DeVries*

The Wars of Edward III: Sources and Interpretations, *edited by Clifford J. Rogers*

The Battle of Agincourt: Sources and Interpretations, *Anne Curry*

War Cruel and Sharp: English Strategy under Edward III, 1327–1360, *Clifford J. Rogers*

The Normans and their Adversaries at War: Essays in Memory of C. Warren Hollister, *edited by Richard P. Abels and Bernard S. Bachrach*

The Battle of the Golden Spurs (Courtrai, 11 July 1302): A Contribution to the History of Flanders' War of Liberation, 1297–1305, *J.F. Verbruggen*

War at Sea in the Middle Ages and the Renaissance, *edited by John B. Hattendorf and Richard W. Unger*

Swein Forkbeard's Invasions and the Danish Conquest of England, 991–1017, *Ian Howard*

Religion and the Conduct of War, c.300–1215, *David S. Bachrach*

Warfare in Medieval Brabant, 1356–1406, *Sergio Boffa*

Renaissance Military Memoirs: War, History and Identity, 1450–1600, *Yuval Harari*

The Place of War in English History, 1066–1214, *J.O. Prestwich, edited by Michael Prestwich*

War and the Soldier in the Fourteenth Century, *Adrian R. Bell*

German War Planning, 1891–1914: Sources and Interpretations, *Terence Zuber*

The Battle of Crécy, 1346, *Andrew Ayton and Sir Philip Preston*

The Battle of Yorktown, 1781: A Reassessment, *John D. Grainger*

Special Operations in the Age of Chivalry, 1100–1550, *Yuval Noah Harari*

Women, Crusading and the Holy Land in Historical Narrative, *Natasha R. Hodgson*

The English Aristocracy at War: From the Welsh Wars of Edward I to the Battle of Bannockburn, *David Simpkin*

The Calais Garrison: War and Military Service in England, 1436–1558, *David Grummitt*

Renaissance France at War: Armies, Culture and Society, c. 1480–1560, *David Potter*

Bloodied Banners: Martial Display on the Medieval Battlefield, *Robert W. Jones*

Alfred's Wars: Sources and Interpretations of Anglo-Saxon Warfare in the Viking Age, *Ryan Lavelle*

The Dutch Army and the Military Revolutions, 1588–1688, *Olaf van Nimwegen*

In the Steps of the Black Prince: The Road to Poitiers, 1355–1356, *Peter Hoskins*

Norman Naval Operations in the Mediterranean, *Charles D. Stanton*

Shipping the Medieval Military: English Maritime Logistics in the Fourteenth Century, *Craig L. Lambert*

Edward III and the War at Sea: The English Navy, 1327–1377, *Graham Cushway*

The Soldier Experience in the Fourteenth Century, *edited by Adrian R. Bell and Anne Curry*

Warfare in Tenth-Century Germany, *David S. Bachrach*

Chivalry, Kingship and Crusade: The English Experience in the Fourteenth Century, *Timothy Guard*

The Norman Campaigns in the Balkans, 1081–1108, *Georgios Theotokis*

Welsh Soldiers in the Later Middle Ages, 1282–1422, *Adam Chapman*

Merchant Crusaders in the Aegean, 1291–1352, *Mike Carr*

Henry of Lancaster's Expedition to Aquitaine, 1345–1346: Military Service and Professionalism in the Hundred Years War, *Nicholas A. Gribit*

Scotland's Second War of Independence, 1332–1357, *Iain A. MacInnes*

Military Communities in Late Medieval England: Essays in Honour of Andrew Ayton, *edited by Gary P. Baker, Craig L. Lambert and David Simpkin*

The Black Prince and the *Grande Chevauchée* of 1355, *Mollie M. Madden*

Military Society and the Court of Chivalry in the Age of the Hundred Years War, *Philip J. Caudrey*

Warfare in the Norman Mediterranean, *Georgios Theotokis*

Chivalry and Violence in Late Medieval Castile, *Samuel A. Claussen*

The Household Knights of Edward III: Warfare, Politics and Kingship in Fourteenth-Century England, *Matthew Hefferan*

Elite Participation in the Third Crusade, *Stephen Bennett*

The Agincourt Campaign of 1415: The Retinues of the Dukes of Clarence and Gloucester, *Michael P. Warner*

Deception in Medieval Warfare: Trickery and Cunning in the Central Middle Ages, *James Titterton*

www.ingramcontent.com/pod-product-compliance
Lightning Source LLC
Chambersburg PA
CBHW070801230426
43665CB00017B/2446